COVERING GROUND

COVERING GROUND

Unexpected Ideas for Landscaping with
Colorful, Low-Maintenance Ground Covers

BARBARA W. ELLIS

Storey Publishing

The mission of Storey Publishing is to serve our customers by publishing practical information that encourages personal independence in harmony with the environment.

Edited by Carleen Madigan Perkins, Gwen Steege, and Nancy J. Ondra
Art direction by Cindy McFarland
Cover design by Jessica Armstrong
Text design and production by Jessica Armstrong

Front cover photography by © Marion Brenner: top; © Karen Bussolini:
    bottom: center and right; © Saxon Holt/PhotoBotanic: bottom: 2nd from
    right; © Jerry Pavia: bottom: left and 2nd from left
Back cover photography by © Saxon Holt/PhotoBotanic: top;
    © Charles Mann: bottom
Spine photography by © Jerry Pavia
Interior photography credits appear on page 211

Illustrations © by Dolores R. Santoliquido
Indexed by Susan Olason, Indexes & Knowledge Maps

Printed in China by Toppan
10 9 8 7 6 5 4 3 2 1

Library of Congress Cataloging-in-Publication Data

Ellis, Barbara W.
     Covering ground / Barbara W. Ellis.
         p. cm.
     Includes index.
     ISBN 13: 978-1-58017-665-1 (pbk. : alk. paper)
     ISBN 13: 978-1-58017-664-4 (hardcover jacketed : alk. paper)
     1. Ground cover plants. 2. Landscape gardening. I. Title.
SB432.E45 2007
635.9'64—dc22
                                                    2007000335

Acknowledgments

For my husband, Peter, who is happy with whatever I want to plant and wherever I want to plant it.

Special thanks go to Nancy Ondra for her helpful advice, quick answers to questions, and her eagle eyes, as well as to my editors at Storey, Gwen Steege and Carleen Perkins, for all their work on this project, as well as their endless enthusiasm. Finally, I'd also like to thank book designer Jessica Armstrong and art director Cindy McFarland for creating such a wonderful-looking book.

CONTENTS

3 PLANTING, GROWING & PROPAGATING................185

Getting Creative
with Ground Covers

My appreciation for ground covers increases with every growing season. Adaptable and utilitarian, they perform a multitude of landscape tasks. These low-maintenance garden plants can be used to smooth out the edges of flower beds, carpet pathways, smother weeds, and fill in under trees and shrubs. They receive far less respect than they deserve, though. Commonly relegated to waste areas and sites where not much else will grow, they are often viewed as little more than plants of last resort. Granted, the ability to grow where little else will is a valuable characteristic not to be taken lightly, but ground covers are handsome and immensely satisfying plants to grow. They are worthy of more creative uses.

GROUND COVERS APPEAL TO ME on many levels and for many reasons. Since all of my own gardens have started out as little more than large stretches of lawn, I especially appreciate their labor-saving features. I've used them to reduce overall mowing time, replace grass on hard-to-mow slopes, eliminate lawn on sites that require lots of fussy trimming, and create island beds by underplanting, and thus connecting, scattered trees and shrubs. I've also used ground covers to create naturalistic plantings that are more wildlife friendly than lawn grass.

Plantings of ground cover also appeal to me because they're more environmentally friendly than lawn, provided they don't include nonnative invasive selections that can escape and blanket natural areas. Since ground covers don't need regular mowing, they don't require fossil fuel for maintenance. Less mowing also means fewer fumes and less noise. Well-chosen ground covers — those selected to thrive in the conditions available — also require less water and need fewer pesticides, fertilizers, and other chemicals than lawn does to keep them healthy. Ground covers also help manage stormwater runoff, an environmental problem in many areas. They are permeable, meaning they allow stormwater to percolate down into the soil instead of causing it to run off into storm drains as asphalt and other hardscape surfaces do.

Since spreading is one of the things good ground covers do best, careful selection is the key to creating really successful ground cover plantings — ones that grow well, require minimal maintenance, and fill the spaces they've been allotted without getting out of hand. Many of the most commonly available ground covers are big-time travelers that will annex large chunks of real estate if given half a chance. The spreading tendencies of English ivy (*Hedera helix*) are apparent to anyone who has grown it for even a few seasons: its vining stems blanket and smother anything and also quickly scale trees, fences, and buildings. Common periwinkle (*Vinca minor*) seems more benign, but established plants can cover woodland sites so densely they crowd out native species. Plants also are surprisingly difficult to remove. See Aggressive & Invasive Ground Covers on page 50 for more on coping with problem plants and The Dirty Dozen starting on page 52 for a list of the major offenders.

I ADD MORE GROUND COVERS to my garden every year. About the time I started writing this book, my husband and I moved to Maryland, on the eastern shore of the Chesapeake Bay. I left behind a garden with all manner of ground cover plantings, and today, I'm digging beds and installing plants on a landscape that was managed solely by lawn mower and string trimmer for 30 years. Nonnative invasives — first planted as ground covers — are a major feature of what passes for landscaping at our current house. As I slowly eliminate lawn and carve out gardens, I chop away at blankets of English ivy and common periwinkle, to name only two of the worst offenders.

One day I'll have a moss garden decorated with patches of partridgeberry (*Mitchella repens*) and other choice plants, since the soil is quite acid. But at this stage in the process, I need more robust allies. To cover an impossible-to-mow slope, I'm combining dwarf forsythia (*Forsythia* 'Bronxensis') with 'Grow-low' fragrant sumac (*Rhus aromatica*), a native species. Meehan's mint (*Meehania cordata*), another native, now fills a shady drainage swale. Fortunately, I didn't leave my Pennsylvania garden empty-handed, and I have holding beds packed with various transplanted perennials including hostas, epimediums (*Epimedium* spp.), and native Allegheny pachysandra (*Pachysandra procumbens*). Before they find their permanent homes, all my transplants will undoubtedly be chopped up for propagation so they can cover more ground. I also have replaced lawn on a good-size sunny site with a wildflower meadow.

For the most part, I don't plant the large, single-species drifts so typical of commercially designed landscapes today. For one thing, I'm too much of a plant collector to devote a major portion of real estate to a single species. Since I'd rather grow six ground covers — or two dozen — instead of one, I'm much more likely to combine several species and let them mingle or form small adjacent drifts. Not only do these plantings satisfy my collector tendencies, beds of mixed ground covers also look very much like flower beds yet require far less maintenance. As a result, they add appeal without substantially adding to my gardening workload. (See Creating Combinations on page 42, for more on mixed plantings.)

THIS BOOK IS DESIGNED TO GUIDE YOU in creating handsome, healthy, and manageable ground cover plantings for every part of your own landscape. In part 1, Rolling Out the Carpet, you'll find information on identifying sites where ground covers would reduce maintenance and on selecting the best ground covers for those sites. You'll also find a wealth of ideas for creating plantings that look good, reduce maintenance, and cover the ground thickly and happily. Part 2 gets to the heart of the selection process. There, you'll find details on ground covers that will thrive in many different types of sites and soils, including on sunny slopes, in shady woodlands, between stepping stones, in sandy soil, and on boggy spots. Part 3 covers site preparation, planting, and after care. It also covers a subject near and dear to my heart — propagation. There's nothing like a large, unplanted site to get me to pull out my pots and potting medium to start making more plants!

Certainly saving time and solving maintenance problems will always be a major reason gardeners grow ground covers, but I hope this book inspires you to look for strictly ornamental uses for these plants as well. Try some new ground covers just for fun — because you want to grow some new variegated plants, need a collection of evergreens, or would like an easy-care bed full of perennials that sport both great foliage and flowers. Pay special attention to native ground covers, which are featured throughout this book. They are overlooked far too often and are especially suited to gardens in North America. Once you've grown just a few of the vibrant, handsome, hardworking ground covers you find here, they'll be among the first plants you turn to, not plants of last resort! Be aware that covering ground can become an obsession — albeit a satisfying one — that not only leaves your garden looking great, but also gives you more time to enjoy it.

WELL-USED GROUND COVERS are the team players of the horticultural world. They play nearly any position: replacing lawn, reducing maintenance, making mowing easier, accenting landscape features, fixing problem spots, crowding out weeds, controlling erosion, edging beds, filling in under shrubs or perennials, and more. They're not just problem-solvers, though. These hardworking plants have personality and character in their own right. They bring color, texture, and appeal to any garden regardless of style — without adding much maintenance. Ground covers also bring unseen benefits to the landscape. They contribute to the health of a garden by covering soil as a living mulch, thus keeping it cooler, helping to retain moisture, and also protecting it from compaction by raindrops and erosion by rain and wind.

full) a year. While mulching mowers and municipal composting operations have reduced the amount of grass clippings that make their way to landfills, planting more ground covers could reduce it even further. In addition, the Audubon Society estimates that if each of the 49 million households in the United States replaced only one square yard of their lawn with ground covers or other plants, as a nation we'd save 1.2 million hours of time spent mowing annually, plus the associated saving of fossil fuel or electricity used. There also would be a corresponding decrease in the amount of pesticides, herbicides, and fertilizers — plus water — required to maintain a lawn.

As beneficial as they are, ground covers can have a dark side, so it's important to select and manage them carefully. Many popular ground

Ground covers aren't just problem-solvers; these hardworking plants have personality and character in their own right.

While they're reducing maintenance for harried homeowners, ground covers can also help the environment. According to the Audubon Society, home lawns cover 21 million acres in the United States, with the average lawn consisting of only a third of an acre. Lawngrass requires two to four times more water than ground covers, trees, or shrubs, and the average lawn generates almost 2 tons of clippings (over 330 trash bags

covers are overachievers, to put it mildly. Kudzu (*Pueraria lobata*), a rampant vine determined to blanket the South, is probably the best-known example of a ground cover gone bad, but there are others. In the pages that follow, you'll learn how to avoid the thugs. More importantly, you'll learn how to use ground covers effectively, save on maintenance, and reap all the other benefits they can bring to your garden.

Rolling Out the Carpet

1

WHY GROUND COVERS?

Ground covers are an underappreciated lot. All too often, they're plopped in as plants of last resort simply to fill an area where lawn grass won't grow — or where lawn mowers fear to tread. Yet ground covers have lots more to offer than the ability to fill bare spots or cover steep slopes, although they can do both superbly. In fact, any time you replace at least a portion of your lawn with well-chosen ground covers, you not only reduce mowing time but also save the amount of time it would take to water, rake, fertilize, and perform other lawn care chores.

Slopes aren't the only hard-to-mow sites that benefit from ground covers. For example, replacing lawn grass under trees and shrubs with beds of ground covers makes it possible to zip around each planting much more quickly with the mower and can eliminate trimming altogether. Better still, create beds of ground covers that surround several trees or shrubs to create an island bed that is a breeze to mow around. Design the edges of the bed carefully, and you can completely eliminate trimming at the same time. (See Edges that Stick on page 188 for information on designing perimeters that don't require trimming.) If the site is shaded, so much the better: Lawn grass doesn't grow well on shaded sites anyway, but many ground covers thrive in shade.

Adjusting the overall shape of the lawn with ground covers is another way to reduce lawn care chores. Odd corners and patches of grass, along with awkwardly shaped areas at the edges of the lawn, usually require pushing or pulling mowers back and forth several times to cut completely. They're big time wasters. Replace lawn in these areas with ground covers to create a smooth mowing edge and reduce overall mowing time. Ideally, plan on a lawn with a free-form shape and gentle curves so you can cut it without having to back up and reposition the mower.

Ground covers can reduce time spent trimming and edging around trees and shrubs too. Replace grass around trees and shrubs with large masses, or drifts, of ground covers to eliminate tedious trimming. Also consider using ground covers to take the place of weedy grass along drainage ditches, around the edges of your property, next to buildings and fences, and along stairways, patios, walkways, and utility areas. There also are plenty of ground covers that will grow happily in wet spots, where mowers bog down, as well as in the damp soil around ponds and along streams.

In addition to saving time and effort, ground covers make it possible to create a lush, gardenlike feel without adding the maintenance that perennial beds and borders typically require. Ground covers are traditionally planted in large sweeps of a single species, but that's only one option. Consider planting small drifts — three or five plants of a single species, or plan on "drifts of one" if you like growing as many different plants as possible. Such plantings can closely resemble traditional flower beds but will require far less maintenance; good ground covers are tough and vigorous and look their best with minimal care.

Drought-tolerant snow-in-summer (*Cerastium tomentosum*) bears woolly white evergreen leaves and makes a fine lawn substitute. Higan cherries (*Prunus × subhirtella* 'Autumnalis') cast light shade over the site in summer, which helps plants cope with summer heat.

There are also environmental reasons for choosing ground covers instead of lawn, or at least for reducing the size of your lawn by replacing some of it with ground cover plants. Well-chosen ground covers reduce the need to water, thus saving a precious resource as well as the time and money spent distributing it — whether you're hauling hoses or maintaining an in-ground sprinkler system. They also require less fossil fuel — and fewer pesticides, herbicides, and fertilizers — to maintain. Compared with hard surfaces such as brick, bluestone, and asphalt, which reflect heat, ground covers provide relief from glare and help cool the air in the same way that lawns do. Beds of ground covers also provide a permeable surface that allows rainfall to percolate into the soil, thus reducing runoff. Plus, ground covers are friendlier to most living creatures than a conventional lawn

is. They can attract birds, butterflies, and other wildlife, including beneficial insects, and provide shelter plus flowers and fruit for food.

While ground covers are worth growing for purely practical reasons, they also play a vital role in the overall design of the landscape. Like lawn, beds of ground covers can visually unify disparate elements in the landscape to create a pleasing whole. Ground covers can serve as a foil to highlight specimen plants or sculpture. Or they can direct traffic through the landscape, edge a path, highlight a shrub border, or add interest to a shed or other outbuilding. They can define space by surrounding a special sitting area, a fire circle, or a shady retreat. Handsome, well-designed beds of ground covers add value to a home by making the landscape look lush and green — without adding the maintenance that lawn requires.

Tough and drought tolerant, hardy ice plant (*Delosperma cooperi*) makes an effective ground cover for any rough, hard-to-mow site.

MAKING THE MOST OF GROUND COVERS

Lawn is the knee-jerk landscaping option for the vast majority of homeowners in North America. Cheap and easy to install, it's planted everywhere in landscapes, both on sites where it grows well and many more where it does not. Granted, it provides a cushiony green surface that takes considerable foot traffic, but lawn comes with a substantial lifetime maintenance obligation. It needs weekly mowing and trimming, plus watering, raking, dethatching, fertilizing, pest control, and all manner of other attention to look its best. Nevertheless, not many gardeners want to eliminate lawn altogether, and lawn may be the best choice on some sites, depending on the planned use of the area or design of the landscape. See Lawn Grass Solutions on page 19 for more on deciding where to grow lawn.

Reducing the overall size of the lawn, on the other hand, makes a lot of sense, as does using ground covers for all the other benefits they bring to the landscape. Like lawn, ground covers require up-front planning. Popular choices such as English ivy (*Hedera helix*), variegated bishop's weed (*Aegopodium podagraria* 'Variegata'), and common periwinkle (*Vinca minor*) provide seemingly easy answers to the what-to-plant quandary. Not only are they the least expensive choices, they also are marketed as one-plant-fits-all-gardens solutions. Unfortunately, as many beginning gardeners find out, the quickest, cheapest, and easiest solution isn't always the best. All of these species can be very invasive and difficult to keep in check once they're established and decide they want to annex another chunk of real estate. They're also very difficult to remove where they are not wanted. There are many better, far more interesting ground covers to choose from that perform well, look great, and have less potential for escaping the bounds of the garden.

The best ground cover choices will vary from site to site and from garden to garden. What you choose will depend on how you want to use the ground covers in your landscape and, just as important, the exposure, soil, and other conditions of the site where you want to grow them. It pays to look for just the right plants, because once they're established, good ground cover plantings will solve landscape problems for years to come — and they'll look great doing it. And while ground cover plantings are not maintenance free from the get-go, the work to get them established is a good investment because of the maintenance they'll save over the long run.

For more on selecting the specific plants that will grow on the sites you want to cover, see the plant lists for specific situations in part 2, Perfect Plants for Every Site.

Blue fescue (*Festuca glauca*) is a clump-forming ornamental grass that can be mass-planted to cover ground. Here, it's used as a lawn substitute that never needs mowing.

Designing with Ground Covers

The style of your garden will help determine the shape of ground cover beds, an important consideration when reducing lawn size or planning any new plantings. Style — whether the garden is formal or informal — will also help determine the way ground covers are arranged in a bed and, to some extent, how many different ground covers you will need as well as which ones will work best.

FORMAL GARDENS. Plantings in geometric shapes — squares, rectangles, or circles — are the hallmark of formal gardens, in which balance, repetition, and proportion are the most important design elements. Measured and predictable, formal gardens have a peaceful, serene feel. Formal gardens generally feature fewer species of plants than informal ones, since they rely on repetition as a unifying element.

Formal gardens also have obvious structure — gravel or brick paths and edged beds, for example — and elements are balanced symmetrically, so a bed of ground covers on one side of a path is repeated on the other. For example, a classic formal design might consist of four beds that are divided by pathways. The beds could be square or rectangular, or their nearest corners could have a concave edge to create a circular area where the beds meet in the center to accommodate a fountain, statue, or sundial. In a classic formal design, the beds could be planted with a single ground cover, such as creeping lilyturf (*Liriope spicata*). Or ground covers could be arranged in concentric squares or rectangles — a central square of Lenten roses (*Helleborus* × *hybridus*), for example, surrounded by concentric plantings of American barrenwort (*Vancouveria hexandra*), hostas (*Hosta* spp.), and Allegheny foamflower (*Tiarella cordifolia*).

Formal plantings don't have to be monochromatic, though. To liven them up but keep the formal design, add plants with variegated leaves to the composition: a variegated lilyturf such as *L. muscari* 'Silver Dragon' or 'Variegata', for example,

or variegated hostas (*Hosta* spp.) such as 'Patriot', 'Golden Tiara', or 'Francee'. Or reserve a section of the design for a solid carpet of flowering impatiens for summerlong color. There's no reason why two or more of the plants mentioned here couldn't be a combination: American barrenwort (*Vancouveria hexandra*) interplanted with creeping phlox (*Phlox stolonifera*), for example.

Symmetry and repetition are the hallmarks of formal gardens. Here, a round bed planted up with liriope (*Liriope* sp.) echoes the shape of a central planter.

Carpets for Containers

Alone or in combinations, ground covers are effective in containers.

If the pot is filled with annuals and tender perennials that will be discarded at the end of the season, it's best to plant nonhardy ground covers — or plan on moving hardy types from the container to the garden at the end of the season. Plants like bacopas (*Sutera* spp.), Persian violet (*Exacum affine*), licorice plant (*Helichrysum petiolare*), and creeping zinnia (*Sanvitalia procumbens*) all could be used to carpet containers. Cultivars of ornamental sweet potato (*Ipomoea batatas*) such as 'Blackie', with dark purple-black leaves, work well in mixed containers ('Margarita', with chartreuse leaves, tends to be too vigorous for a container but makes an excellent annual

A handsome container becomes an eye-catching garden accent when planted with Corsican pearlworts (*Sagina subulata* and *S. subulata* 'Aurea') arranged in a checkerboard pattern.

ground cover for flower beds). Keep in mind that houseplants can be underplanted with some tender ground covers: strawberry geraniums (*Saxifraga stolonifera*), baby's tears (*Soleirolia soleirolii*), and wandering jew (*Tradescantia* spp.) are just three possibilities. Be sure to match ground covers with houseplants that require the same amount of water and other care.

To complement a single specimen plant in a pot, a ground cover that is all-green or has flowers in only one color is often the best choice, since it won't detract from the topiary or other plant that is the main event. Consider sweet alyssum (*Lobularia maritima*) — dwarf cultivars are 2 to 4 inches tall, but all cultivars can be trimmed to keep them neat — or edging lobelia (*Lobelia erinus*). Or use several plants of 'Spicy Globe' basil (*Ocimum basilicum*), which is 6 to 8 inches tall. Curly-leaved cultivars of parsley also can be massed to cover soil in containers.

For hardy plants in containers, or tender plants that are overwintered indoors, look for perennial ground cover companions. To accompany specimen plants — as well as bonsai that is kept outdoors or in a cool greenhouse — compact, all-green plants usually are most effective. Consider ophiopogon (*Ophiopogon japonicus* 'Compactus') plus many of the plants listed under Ground Huggers for Paths and Stepping-Stones on page 89. Moss also is a traditional ground cover for bonsai.

Ground covers also can be handsome grown alone as specimen plants in containers. Try planting a collection of ornamental pots, each with a separate ground cover. (This is a great way to use especially eye-catching containers without drawing attention away from the containers themselves.) European ginger (*Asarum europaeum*), lilyturfs (*Liriope* spp., especially variegated cultivars), sedums (*Sedum* spp.), thymes (*Thymus* spp.), and many other plants listed throughout this book can be effective when grown as specimens.

INFORMAL GARDENS. These lack the structure characteristic of formal gardens. While an informal garden may have elements such as steps or pathways, these elements tend to have more organic shapes. Paths snake around trees, for example, or low walls flow along the base of an existing slope. Beds are apt to be more free-form too. Informal gardens feature beds with undulating edges, such as island bed plantings that look as if they were surrounded by a sea of lawn or curved beds that conform to the shape of a slope or meandering walkway.

Balance is important in informal designs, as it is in formal ones, but in this case it is asymmetrical rather than symmetrical. A large bed of low-growing ground covers might be balanced by a smaller bed filled with taller or bolder plants. Plant collectors love informal designs, which don't depend on repeating plants to balance a design. Edging plants may or may not be repeated from bed to bed, and filling an area with a crazy quilt of drifts consisting of many different species fits right into an informal design.

Although informal designs are more common than formal ones in the United States, sometimes using elements of both makes sense. In a small front yard, beds of ground covers in a formal arrangement may be easier to care for and give the entranceway a handsome, orderly appearance. Formal elements also are useful for giving order to an otherwise informal design — and reducing maintenance in one area so you can spend time in the part of the garden you love the most. Matching beds of ground covers under posts located on either side of a path could formalize the entrance to a wild, informal cottage garden, for example.

Flower beds and walkways in free-form shapes along with natural materials like gravel and bark mulch are the hallmarks of an informal design. These informal beds of ground covers are planted with lamb's ears (*Stachys byzantina*), sunrose (*Helianthemum* sp.), and sedge (*Carex* 'Western Hills').

ADDRESSING PROBLEM SPOTS

You may already know which parts of your yard give you headaches. Perhaps it's the steep slope along the sidewalk that's so hard to mow, or maybe the barren area next to the house that never gets much sun. Knowing about problem spots is a good start, since filling such sites with easy-care ground covers pays big dividends. To get even more benefit from ground covers, and to plan your attack for covering the ground, take a hard look at your landscape to identify potential sites for ground covers that you hadn't thought of before.

Start the process by taking a walk around your yard to look for spots where you could plant ground covers. Keep a mental list of the site opportunities you find, write them down, or draw a map to scale of your property and note them on the map. While walking around your yard, look for both long- and short-term solutions to problem areas. For example, at a site along a walkway where compacted soil and trampled plants are a constant eyesore, a few bags of mulch can offer an easy, quick fix. Just cover the site with a thick layer of mulch until you can fix the problem for good. See Prioritizing Projects at right for ideas on the types of landscape solutions ground covers can offer.

Prioritizing Projects

Try to rank the importance of the sites you identify. Decide which ones will save loads of time right away or pay the biggest dividends by enhancing the overall look of the landscape. Use this information to create a landscape plan that can be phased in as time and money allow. You may find that you come up with a combination of do-it-yourself projects and areas that need the attention of an expert contractor. For example, building a series of permanent terraces on a steeply sloping site may be a project for a contractor, while planting shade-tolerant ground covers in a barren area under trees where grass won't grow may be something you can tackle alone.

If any part of your design requires grading or landscape construction, plan for that from the outset. Leave room so that heavy equipment can deliver any brick, sand, gravel, or soil you will need to have on hand as close to the construction site as possible. If you can't direct traffic around existing plantings, have a plan for moving plants to make room for equipment and materials before construction begins.

Here are some things to look for and ideas to consider in your own yard.

SMOOTH OUT LAWN EDGES. Instead of having a lawn that is a ragged shape with uneven edges and takes a long time to mow, plan beds of ground covers that will smooth out the curves and make mowing and trimming simpler and faster. A lawn that has uneven edges takes longer to mow. That's partly because you can run the mower faster in a straight or gently curved line than along a twisty, curvy route. Also, a jagged perimeter requires lots of slow, back-and-forth mowing along the edges. Your landscape can profit as well: a lawn with a strong, clearly defined shape and gentle curves makes a handsome design element. Use drifts of ground covers planted around the lawn to smooth out the edges, define the shape, and frame the lawn. Also plan on installing edging strips to keep lawn and ground covers apart. (See Edges that Stick on page 188 for more on edging strips.)

REDUCE OVERALL LAWN AREA. Replacing lawn grass with ground covers reduces time spent on mowing and other lawn care chores. Conventional low-growing herbaceous ground covers are an obvious choice for replacing lawn, but many shrubs make great ground covers as well. Mat-forming shrubs that stay under a few inches in

LAWN GRASS SOLUTIONS

LAWN IS THE BEST GROUND COVER CHOICE in some situations. No other planting withstands traffic and wear the way lawn grass does. For play areas, it's a natural choice because its soft, springy surface cushions falls, and a game of flag football or volleyball won't destroy it. (Use mulch under swing sets and jungle gyms to eliminate trimming around posts and poles.) Hybridizers are introducing new lawn grass cultivars every year, and now there are many that resist diseases, plus some that require less frequent mowing. Obviously, hard surfaces like brick or stone wear better, but lawn has the added advantage of not reflecting heat. Ground covers like creeping thyme (*Thymus serpyllum*), Roman chamomile (*Chamaemelum nobile*), and dichondra (*Dichondra micrantha*) can withstand some foot traffic and are suitable substitutes in some sites, but they don't take as much traffic or wear as lawn grass.

height — like some junipers (*Juniperus* spp.) — are fine choices, but if you have considerable ground to cover, don't be afraid to think taller and larger. Shrubs and even small trees that are wider than they are tall, make handsome ground covers. See part 2 for ideas, including using large shrubs (see Mega Ground Covers on page 132 and Shrubs that Travel on page 136) and even weeping trees (see page 143).

COVER SLOPES AND HARD-TO-MOW SPOTS. It just makes sense to clothe steep slopes, drainage ditches, and other spots where mowers bog down with easy-care ground covers. When planting these sites (or any sites, for that matter), be sure to select plants that will grow because they happily thrive in the existing conditions on the site. See Knowing Your Site on page 26 for more on matching plants to a site. Consider herbaceous perennials, to be

Tuning Up Tired Plantings

Even a mature landscape with established beds of ground covers can benefit from a critical examination.

Try to look at plantings with a new set of eyes. Are the sweeping beds of Japanese pachysandra (*Pachysandra terminalis*) monotonous? Is the English ivy (*Hedera helix*) escaping the garden and beginning to blanket a nearby woodland or shade garden? Which large established shrubs would benefit from an underplanting of ground covers? Have certain plantings survived but never really managed to thrive?

While you inspect a mature landscape, don't just look for problems and sites to fix. Pay attention to combinations you like and plantings that appeal to you. Also note which styles are most pleasing to your eye — formal or casual, wild looking or cultivated.

Identify ground covers that have become or are becoming seriously aggressive and make a management plan. Either replace them entirely with less aggressive species, or drastically reduce the amount of space they occupy. See Aggressive & Invasive Ground Covers on page 50 for suggestions on handling especially troublesome plants.

Large masses of a single species of ground cover can be downright boring. If you have a healthy planting of one species, consider adding edging plants that have a different texture or perhaps sport variegated foliage. Another option for brightening up a boring monoculture (a mass planting of a single species) is to replant some of the area — patches, even — with ground covers that will add contrast. (Share the plants you have removed with ground-cover-poor friends and neighbors.) Adding a specimen plant, such as a showy shrub, in the center of a bed also will help brighten it up. Or add a sculpture, a container filled with annuals, or even a bird bath to create an area that's about more than just the single ground cover.

To make a better plan for areas where ground covers (or other plants, for that matter) have survived but have never really grown well, start by examining the soil and other growing conditions in that spot. Then identify other plants that may grow better there. Either replant the area entirely or add one or two more species to the planting already there. Often several types of plants growing together will cover an area more thickly and luxuriantly than one species growing alone.

Also look closely at sites where existing ground cover plantings are growing to see if they need extra care to keep them lush and happy. Note whether they need to be cut back for rejuvenation, could benefit from topdressing with compost or soil, or might grow better with a layer of mulch to help suppress weeds.

This planting of horsemint (*Mentha longifolia*) would be handsome alone, but the addition of a simple sculpture highlights it, creates a focal point, and really makes it pop.

sure, but don't overlook shrubs for the job. Other candidates are vines, which can be trained to grow along the ground. Even weeping trees can cover ground, and for temporary cover, annuals may be a great short-term solution. Finally, don't overlook hardscaping for permanent fixes for tough spots. A series of terraces that level out a steep slope will eliminate hillside mowing forever, for example, and a ground-level deck can carpet the area under shallow-rooted maple trees (*Acer* spp.) where little more than weeds will grow.

PLANT ROUGH GROUND. Areas where the soil surface is bumpy or studded with boulders, rock outcrops, or other obstructions are a nightmare to care for. They can be nearly impossible to mow, leaving tedious string trimming as the only option. Eliminating lawn grass on such sites and planting ground covers instead transforms rocks into garden accents and bumpy topography into an attractive, easy-care part of the landscape.

CONNECT THE DOTS. Link individual trees and shrubs in the landscape with beds of ground covers. Underplanting shrubs and trees not only reduces the overall size of the lawn and eliminates the need to trim around each individual plant, but it also protects tree trunks from mower damage. Furthermore, it creates a more unified landscape that is lusher, richer, and more appealing than one covered by lawn alone.

FILL BARREN SPOTS. Closely inspect spots where nothing seems to survive for long or where plants are unhealthy looking. Dig up a shovelful of soil and examine it. If you can't push a spade or garden fork into the soil without standing on it and jumping a bit, at least one of the site's problems is compaction (assuming you haven't hit a rock, of course). Terrain can also cause problems. A mower will scalp grass on a bump that's higher than the rest of the area, leaving a bare spot. A rock outcrop just under the surface will create droughty conditions that lawn grasses won't tolerate. Also watch how friends and family use the site. The problem could be foot traffic, or overflow from a play area.

Many ground covers, including this hardy ice plant (*Delosperma nubigenum*) will fill in around rocks, along steps, and over other types of uneven sites.

Once you have figured out the problem, take steps to correct it. See Get to Know Your Soil on page 30 for ideas on dealing with compacted soil. If mower scalping is the culprit, dig up the grass and remove enough soil to smooth out the bump, then replant or resow. If a large rock or rock outcrop is causing the problem, replacing the lawn grass with drought-tolerant ground covers is an option. Another is to uncover the rock or outcrop altogether, plant around it, and enjoy it as a garden accent.

DIRECT TRAFFIC. Fixing spots where grass is worn thin by foot traffic takes a bit of planning. If the problem is caused by kids cutting through the back border to a friend's house, stepping-stones surrounded by adaptable ground covers may be the best solution. (Blocking traffic with a fence or large shrub will likely only move a shortcut from one place to another. It's better to accept impromptu pathways and adjust the landscape accordingly.) For more established walkways — for example, the front walk, the path to the garage, or the walk to a terrace that's set away from the house — some combination of hardscaping and ground covers may be in order. See Covering the Ground with Hardscape on page 57 for information on creating practical and attractive paved areas in your yard. Plan on using ground covers along the edges of hardscaped walkways to encourage feet to stay on the path. If visitors are cutting corners along a particular pathway, you can use larger shrubs or a small decorative fence to keep them on the path. Or redesign the walkway to eliminate unnecessary curves.

PLAN FOR PLAY. If you have kids, set aside ample space for them to play. Lawn is the best ground cover for nearly every sort of outdoor game. A good-size lawn gives adults room for a game of touch football or an impromptu round of badminton or volleyball. Lawn also is the best option for a play session with your dog. For plantings to surround a lawn used for games, choose tough ground covers that don't have brittle stems and can take a little bit of foot traffic so that participants can retrieve wayward balls with minimal fuss and without damaging the plants. Consider installing mulch under swing sets and other children's play equipment (see Walkways, Terraces & Play Areas on page 64) to eliminate the need to trim grass.

CREATE NEW SPACES. While surveying your property, always be on the lookout for new spaces and creative ways you can use your landscape. Perhaps you will find room for a small sitting area that could be surrounded by low-growing ground covers. Look for a spot where the kids can build a fort, where you can start a butterfly or water garden, or where a compost pile can go. Ground covers can play a part in all of these landscape features and more, whether they carpet the ground along the path that leads to them, enclose the feature in some way, or cover the ground in the actual space. If you have a picnic table or group of chairs that routinely sit on the lawn, think about installing some type of ground cover under them that does not require mowing or trimming. You can use ground covers that tolerate some foot traffic, but a thick layer of mulch is a perfect flooring choice, because it is inexpensive, easy to install, and eliminates the need to trim grass under and around furniture.

WELCOME GUESTS. Neat beds of ground covers along the front walk make the entrance to your home welcoming and appealing. (They also reduce the overall lawn size and cut down on mowing and trimming chores.) For a gardenlike look without all the maintenance, consider small drifts of ground covers that feature interesting and colorful foliage. Combine herbaceous perennials and shrubs, and feature plants with evergreen foliage. For extra color, underplant with spring or summer bulbs. Also include some ground covers that boast handsome flowers, particularly ones with long bloom seasons to maximize color and interest from each plant selected.

Filling an area with small drifts of several different ground covers keeps maintenance to a minimum and ensures that there are always a few plants that look attractive and add color to the planting. When combining ground covers, though, try to stick with plants that grow at similar speeds: Fast-growing English ivy (*Hedera helix*), for instance, will suffocate slower-growing ground covers like foamflowers (*Tiarella* spp.). Keep an eye on the plantings, and be prepared to do some trimming or even transplanting if one plant shows signs of overwhelming its companions. Plan on installing edging strips between lawn and ground cover beds to make sure the overall effect remains neat and well cared for.

Outdoor Carpets

A PATCH OF LAWN OR AN UNUSED CORNER OF YOUR YARD is more than just an opportunity for planting ground covers. Consider transforming that awkward spot into a new outdoor living space. In the garden pictured above, a combination of pinks and blue star creeper carpet an outdoor space that features a birdbath, pavers, and comfortable seating in a shady spot on the edge of a woods.

1 Pinks
(*Dianthus* sp.)

2 Blue star creeper
(*Pratia pedunculata*)

3 Columbine
(*Aquilegia* sp.)

Lawn Alternatives

Ground covers can be planted en masse and used in much the same way as lawn.

Whether planted with fescue or St. Augustine, a conventional grass lawn contributes a uniform carpet of green to the garden that can be very appealing and restful to look at. Ground covers can be planted en masse and used in much the same way as lawn — to carpet the ground, set off specimen plants and sculpture, ease transitions between different parts of the garden, and fill space to the edges of your property. They can either be used to create a uniform all-green carpet or a more colorful covering, thanks to silver or variegated foliage as well as flowers in any number of colors.

When planning a ground cover lawn, keep in mind that no ground cover will withstand the amount of foot traffic lawn grass can tolerate. Plan pathways or stepping-stones to traverse a ground cover lawn if traffic will be an issue. Also select plants carefully, so they will thrive in the conditions available and won't end up requiring more attention than lawn grass would. See Ground Huggers for Paths & Stepping-Stones on page 89 for ground covers that can withstand light foot traffic.

Flowering ground covers such as low-growing thymes and speedwells, including *Veronica pectinata* shown here, add a colorful burst of color in summer when they bloom. This garden features a convenient sitting area next to the lawn where visitors can enjoy the show.

Tough and drought tolerant, yarrows (*Achillea* spp.) are fast-spreading perennials that can be used to cover considerable ground. They tolerate very occasional foot traffic, too. Deadhead lawn plantings — by hand or with a string trimmer — to keep them neat. Dig and divide plants anywhere they seem to be dying or thinning out.

This colorful, drought-tolerant carpet features two flowering ground covers, snow-in-summer (*Cerastium tomentosum*) paired with rock roses (*Helianthemum* spp.). Also called sun roses, Helianthemum species are evergreen shrubs that require very well-drained neutral to alkaline soil. They are generally hardy in Zones 6 to 8.

On a hot, dry sloping site like this one, mowing would be a treacherous undertaking and conventional turfgrass would simply burn out. This lawn consists of a drought-tolerant combination of thymes (*Thymus* spp.) and buffalo grass (*Buchloe dactyloides*). Beds of drought-tolerant perennials frame the lawn in this low-maintenance garden.

To use clump-forming plants as a substitute for lawn grass, mass plant them with fairly close spacing. This hybrid sedge (*Carex* 'Ice Dance'), which reaches about 1 foot and spreads as far, is evergreen in the south, semievergreen in the north. Cut plants back in late winter.

For a site with poor, acid soil and shade, consider a moss lawn. One good sign that moss will be a good ground cover choice is if it is already a problematic weed in your lawn. See Moss Gardens for Acid Shade on page 182 for more information.

A moss lawn adds handsome elegance to this shady slope It also speaks volumes about the site itself. That's because moss thrives on poor, moist soil that has a very acid pH. Moss also indicates that a site receives very little direct sun. See page 182 for more information on starting a moss garden.

KNOWING YOUR SITE

Although many gardeners (this author included) enjoy wandering around the garden — a plant in one hand and a trowel in the other — looking for likely spots to pop in an extra perennial, that's really not the best approach to take with ground covers. Certainly, good ground covers are an adaptable lot. Many tolerate an amazingly wide range of soils or thrive in any site, from sun to shade. However, your job as the gardener is to make them as happy as possible, so they can grow vigorously and do the job you want them to do. That means knowing the site and selecting the best ground covers for that site.

Matching plant to site is actually the secret to *any* low-maintenance garden, because it is far easier to grow a garden full of vigorous, healthy plants when you start with species that will thrive there, not just tolerate the available conditions. Devoting time and effort to changing the conditions on a site isn't a low-maintenance proposition. For example, azaleas (*Rhododendron* spp.),

many of which make great ground covers, thrive in moist, well-drained, humus-rich acid soil. To accommodate them in a site that has predominately clay soil and a slightly alkaline or even neutral pH requires an enormous initial undertaking, plus annual attention to keep conditions in an acceptable range. It makes far more sense to select species that will thrive in the conditions that already exist. To do that, first get to know the conditions available on the site or sites you want to plant, then select ground covers accordingly. This section covers how to identify and learn about site conditions in your garden. You'll find lists of ground covers for different types of sites in part 2, beginning on page 66.

The amount of sun or shade a site receives, along with the soil type, are obvious factors in selecting plants, but there are others. Consider existing soil moisture — how well the soil holds moisture as well as how quickly or slowly it drains. Annual rainfall may be a factor: Species native to areas that experience rainless summers are much better choices for gardens in dry western climates than ones from regions that average an inch or two of rain a week. If your summers are rainless or nearly so, planting drought-adapted species means your plants are more likely to succeed, and you won't need to worry about supplemental watering once they are established. Plants matched to site also tolerate other characteristics a site may offer, like prevailing winds, reflected heat, salt, periodic flooding, or other adverse conditions.

Read Your Plants

Speed readers will appreciate this method for learning about a site: look at the plants that are already growing there and learn about the conditions they need to thrive. Although observing and identifying existing plants won't provide all the site information you need to grow great ground covers, the process can be revealing. With time and experience, you'll be able to simply look at the plants on a site and know a good deal about existing conditions. This is a valuable gardening skill you can use when selecting plants for any part of your garden, from beds of ground covers to perennial borders.

Even if you don't know what species are growing on a site, you can learn a lot just by observing their condition. For example, if a site is covered with a thin growth of sparse, stunted plants, a quick glance tells you to suspect poor, dry, or compacted soil. Lush growth often indicates a damp spot, but it also can indicate rich, evenly moist soil. A scraggly patch of plants under a tree can indicate shallow tree roots, little growing space for roots of other plants, or dense shade. A spot under a deep eave of the house — or between two houses — may be barren because rain doesn't reach the ground or because the site is shaded throughout the day.

Identify which plants already grow well on your site — or a similar site in a neighbor's yard — and which ones don't look healthy. If azaleas and rhododendrons thrive without much care, for example, the soil is probably acid, moist but well drained,

WEEDS MAKE GOOD READING

PAY ATTENTION to the weeds that are growing in your area, and you'll be able to use what they are telling you. Although most weeds will grow in a variety of soils, here are a few species to look for and the conditions they may indicate. Bear in mind that one or two weeds don't mean much: This technique works best when weeds occur in large drifts. Stunted, sickly weeds may indicate low soil fertility.

Bindweed (*Convolvulus arvensis*). Light-textured, sandy soil that has a crusty surface or hardpan, a dense, nearly impenetrable layer of soil beneath the topsoil.

Bracken fern (*Pteridium aquilinum*). Poor, acid soil.

Chickweed (*Stellaria media*). Deep, humus-rich, fertile soil.

Chicory (*Cichorium intybus*). Rich, heavy clay soil.

Creeping buttercup (*Ranunculus repens*). Moist to wet clay soil that is poorly drained.

Dandelion (*Taraxacum officinale*). Deep, acidic, heavy clay soil.

Joe-pye weeds (*Eupatorium* spp.). Wet or constantly moist soil.

Mullein (*Verbascum thapsus*). Poor, acid soil that is low in organic matter and hasn't been turned or dug recently.

Pineapple weed (*Matricaria matricarioides*). Compacted soil or soil with a crusty surface or hardpan, a dense, nearly impenetrable layer of soil beneath the topsoil.

Plantains (*Plantago* spp.). Acid, constantly wet or poorly drained, heavy clay soil.

Many ferns are surprisingly vigorous spreaders on the right site, especially on a spot that offers rich, moist, well-drained soil.

and fairly high in organic matter. All the plants on a site give you clues, so look at trees and shrubs as well as herbaceous plants. Rich, deep green leaves on a pin oak (*Quercus palustris*) signal acid soil; in neutral to alkaline soil, the foliage is often yellowish due to iron chlorosis. Pin oaks also grow well in moist to wet soil, as do sweet gum (*Liquidambar styraciflua*), tupelo (*Nyssa sylvatica*), and eastern arborvitae (*Thuja occidentalis*).

If you are starting with cultivated garden beds, use a perennials encyclopedia with lots of photographs to identify the plants. Sprawling drifts of gooseneck loosestrife (*Lysimachia clethroides*), for

instance, indicate rich, moist soil (and a laissez-faire gardener), while thriving plantings of lavenders (*Lavandula* spp.) and thymes (*Thymus* spp.) indicate well-drained conditions plus full sun. Huge clumps of hostas (*Hosta* spp.) and ferns generally indicate rich, moist soil and shade.

Use a field guide to identify wildflowers in uncultivated areas. A good one will contain pictures and descriptions of native as well as nonnative species that have escaped cultivation. In addition to learning their names, pay attention to the sites where they are found growing naturally — the field guide will have brief descriptions that give clues. If you find a ground-hugging cover of partridgeberry (*Mitchella repens*) and moss, and perhaps blueberries (*Vaccinium* spp.), there's no doubt you are dealing with acid soil. Joe-pye weeds (*Eupatorium* spp.) and queen of the prairie (*Filipendula rubra*) indicate rich, moist to wet soil, while butterfly weed (*Asclepias tuberosa*) and purple coneflowers (*Echinacea purpurea*) generally signal dry, well-drained soil.

The Essentials of Climate

Are you in a region that has cool, rainy summers or hot, dry ones? How about hot, humid ones? There are ground covers that thrive in all of these conditions. The best plants for your garden are those that can tolerate the amounts of heat, cold, rainfall, and humidity in your area — not species you admired on a visit to a garden in a far-off climate with different conditions than your own. Gardeners in your area, along with experts at local botanical gardens or reputable garden centers, will be able to tell you which climate factors most affect plant growth in your area.

HARDINESS. Plant hardiness — how much winter cold a particular species can survive — is an important consideration. Since vigorous growth is essential for a ground cover to do its work, it's best to stick with species that are completely hardy in your area. Although it's fine to experiment with herbaceous plants that may or may not survive the winter, losing an entire bed of ground covers

after a particularly severe winter can be a real blow. Even if a bed isn't killed outright, cold-damaged ground covers are likely to be slow to start growth in spring and may struggle to survive for months. Plantings may die out in patches, allowing weeds an easy foothold, even in established plantings, when ground covers aren't in the peak of health. All the plant descriptions in this book include hardiness zones; see the USDA Hardiness Zone Map on page 212. If you're putting in a large planting or want to be absolutely safe, choose ground covers that are hardy to a zone colder than the one you live in.

Keep in mind that winter temperature isn't the only factor that affects plant survival rates. Snow cover plays a big part as well. Many plants can survive very cold winter lows provided they are covered by an insulating blanket of snow. If you plant them in a warmer zone, they may not come through the winter if snow cover is not dependable. Soil drainage also is important, since wet soil in winter causes crown rot and other problems in many plants. Try growing the same species in two spots in your garden — one that is poorly drained in winter and another that features perfect drainage (such as a spot with sandy or gravelly soil behind a rock wall) — and you can observe the effect of winter soil moisture yourself.

HEAT. Summer heat affects plant survival rates — and not just in hot weather. Obviously, plants unable to tolerate toasty weather can die in summer from any combination of heat, humidity, or drought. However, species that survive summer heat but don't really thrive in it very likely will be weakened by season's end. Weakened plants are more likely to be killed or damaged by winter weather than vigorous ones are. The hardiness zones in this book are given in ranges to indicate the southernmost areas where plants can be grown successfully. In the Southeast, these ranges are very helpful, but gardeners in the West may find them misleading. That's because many plants that can't survive the hot, humid summers in the Southeast thrive in the cooler summer weather along the Pacific Ocean. Or they may be able to tolerate heat in desert areas as long as it doesn't come hand-in-hand with high humidity

While climate plays a major role in what ground covers will perform best in your area, many plants thrive in a wide range of areas. The liriopes (*Liriope* spp.) and impatiens (*Impatiens walleriana*) that carpet the ground in this tropical garden also grow well much farther north.

Succulents are great choices for sites where drought tolerance is essential. Here, echeverias (*Echeveria* spp.) and blue *Senecio mandraliscae* surround golden barrel cactuses (*Echinocactus grusonii*). Hardier succulent species for northern gardens include sedums (*Sedum* spp.), hens-and-chicks (*Sempervivum* spp.), and houseleeks (*Jovibarba* spp.).

and rainfall. This is another example of why it is so important to consult local sources for ideas about which ground covers will do best in your area.

RAINFALL. Knowing how much rain you can expect, along with when it is likely to fall, can determine success or failure with a particular species. Planting ground covers that require more rain than a site naturally receives means adding extra watering chores to your gardening agenda. Trying to grow plants that require a hot, dry summer dormancy in an area with regular summer rainfall also can be problematic.

If finding ground covers that match your climate and soil seems too complicated, opt for the ready-made list of species that are likely to thrive on your site: native plants. Plants native to your local area are most likely to survive wet years and dry ones and tolerate whatever your climate throws at them, whether it's sopping wet winters or hot summer droughts. Unfortunately, native plants are still often overlooked in favor of nonnative species that suppliers can market widely, so you may have to search a bit to find some of the less available ones. See Native Carpets on page 47 for more on finding sources for native plants.

Although studying site conditions is essential in choosing great ground covers, selecting the specific plants you want to grow gets to the heart of why gardening is so fascinating. Site conditions commonly narrow the list of appropriate plants for a given spot, but in most cases there are still many plants to choose from and a number of ways they can be arranged in the garden. Jot down key features of your site before you start listing specific ground covers. A list will help keep you focused when you visit garden centers or discuss possibilities with local experts. If you tend to be an impulse shopper, use the list to verify that each plant you choose really has a chance of growing successfully where you want it to.

A single ground cover may be just the ticket for a small site, but you'll likely be looking for more than one. Single species of ground covers can be arranged in large drifts, or they can be planted in small drifts of just one to a couple of plants. As an alternative, two or more species can be planted in combination to form a ground cover. Read on for tips on selecting plants, and see Creating Combinations on page 42 for ideas on creating mixed plantings.

Get to Know Your Soil

Even though most popular ground covers tolerate a range of soils, it pays to be familiar with the specific soil conditions your garden offers plants so you can match your ground cover choices as closely as possible. Fortunately, with a few simple tests, you can determine enough about your soil to select plants that will thrive in it. Keep in mind that conditions will vary throughout your property, so look at the individual sites you want to plant, and keep notes about the conditions you find in each.

SOIL TEXTURE. This term refers to the relative proportions of sand, silt, and clay a soil contains. The texture affects not only how well or how poorly the soil holds moisture and nutrients but also the amount of air in the soil. The texture of your soil determines many of the problems you may encounter: soils with a high percentage of clay, for example, compact easily, form concrete-like clods when dry, and are cold and wet in spring; soils containing a large percentage of sand, on the other hand, dry out very quickly and tend to be low in nutrients.

SOIL STRUCTURE. Sand, silt, and clay particles don't exist independently: they clump together to form a soil's structure. The structure can range from loose and crumbly (good for plant growth) to dense and compacted. Soil described as being friable or having good tilth has good structure. That doesn't just mean a soil is easy to dig, though. Soils with good structure can hold up to twice as much moisture as ones without it. Good structure also means roots can penetrate the soil easily and will find plenty of oxygen and nutrients.

Ideally, soil particles clump together to make both large and small pore spaces. In soils with good structure, fully half the volume of the soil consists of pore spaces. Large pores fill with water during a rain, and then the water drains through them quickly, leaving air. Small pores hold water in the soil, making it available to roots and other soil organisms. Pore spaces are interconnected; water can actually move up through the soil via pore spaces in a process called capillary action. The percentages of sand, silt, and clay in a soil affect the size of the pore spaces: sandy soils tend to have too many large pores and not enough small ones, so they are droughty; clay soils tend to have too many small pores and not enough large ones, making them heavy and wet once the soil pores are filled in rainy climates. Clay soils form cementlike clods if worked when they are too wet, and once they dry out, they can be very difficult to re-wet.

COMPACTION. The drainage tests mentioned on page 32 are helpful in determining whether or not your soil structure is in trouble. Compacted soil does not drain well, and soil with a high clay content that is compacted drains especially poorly. An even simpler way to judge soil compaction is to plunge a garden fork into the soil after a heavy rain. If you can't get it all the way in without stand-

SQUEEZE YOUR SOIL

TRY A QUICK-AND-EASY TEST to get a good idea of where your soil falls. A couple of days after a rain, dig down and place a sample of soil the size of a Ping-Pong ball in the palm of your hand. Gently squeeze it with your thumb. Sandy soil feels gritty, silty soil feels a bit like moist flour or talcum powder and somewhat greasy, and clay soil feels sticky and slippery. Press down on the sample of soil, then release: if it crumbles, it has a fairly balanced texture. Soil that holds its shape has a high clay content. If you can roll it into a snake, it has even more clay. Next, roll out a ribbon of soil with your fingers and notice what happens.

- If the soil feels gritty and you can't make a ribbon at least 1 inch long, you have sandy loam soil. A 1- to 2-inch ribbon that feels somewhat gritty indicates sandy clay loam, while one that exceeds 2 inches indicates sandy clay soil.

- If your ribbon of soil feels smooth for the most part, you have silty loam if you can only make a ribbon less than 1 inch long. You have silty clay loam if your ribbon is between 1 to 2 inches, and silty clay if it exceeds 2 inches.

- If your ribbon feels both gritty and smooth, you have loam soil if you can only make a ribbon less than 1 inch long. You have clay loam if your ribbon is between 1 and 2 inches, and clay soil if it exceeds 2 inches.

A soil with balanced amounts of all three ingredients is ideal. Trying to change the texture of your soil — by adding sand to a clay soil, for example — isn't practical, however, because the quantities necessary to change soil texture are simply enormous. Fortunately, adding organic matter to any soil helps improve it.

ing on it, your soil is at least somewhat compacted (as long as you haven't hit a rock, of course.)

Although you can select ground covers that will grow in less-than-ideal conditions, it pays to take steps to improve structure and reduce compaction. Loosen the soil and add plenty of organic matter at planting time, and start a regular program of adding more organic matter in the form of well-rotted compost every time you dig. Mulching also adds organic matter: A layer of compost topped by longer-lasting bark mulch is an excellent way to hold moisture in the soil and add organic matter at the same time. Other options for dealing with compacted sites include installing hardscape,

THE IMPORTANCE OF ORGANIC MATTER

NOT ONLY DOES ORGANIC MATTER play a crucial role in forming soil particles and structure, but it is also the great equalizer when it comes to soil improvement plans. Adding organic matter improves any soil: it helps sandy soil hold onto moisture and nutrients, and it increases pore space in clay soils and helps them drain better. Gardening practices can either improve or destroy structure, so make good soil management part of your everyday gardening habits. What bad habits destroy structure? Something as simple as walking on soil crushes pore spaces, as does working soil when it is too wet. Adding organic matter, on the other hand, is always beneficial. Get into the habit of working it into the soil when you prepare new beds and at planting time, as well as by routinely mulching.

building raised beds, or covering the site with deep mulching for a season or even two before planting. See Smothering and Solarizing on page 190 for more information on deep mulching.

DRAINAGE AND SOIL MOISTURE. Testing soil drainage is a fairly simple matter: dig a hole that's about 6 inches wide and 1 foot deep. Fill it with water, then let the water drain away. As soon as the water has seeped away completely, fill the hole again and keep track of how long it takes for the water to drain away. In sandy soils, it will drain quickly, but in clay soil, the water will disappear more slowly. In poorly drained soil, the water can take more than 8 hours to drain.

Plants can have problems if the soil drains too quickly or too slowly. To determine how well your soil retains moisture, two days after a good, hard rain, dig a 6-inch-deep hole and feel the soil at the bottom of it. If it's dry, your soil drains too quickly, and selecting drought-tolerant plants is a good idea. If you feel some moisture, squeeze a soil sample in your hand. If it's damp but not wet, your soil both drains and retains moisture fairly well. If water squeezes out of the sample and your hand gets wet, the soil drains poorly. Poor drainage may be caused by soil compaction and is also commonly associated with soils that are high in clay content. (Clay soils also are called heavy soils, because they hold moisture and weigh more than

better-drained soils and thus are physically heavy when dug or turned.)

Whether your soil drains too quickly or too slowly, select ground covers that will grow in the existing moisture level. Also start a program of adding organic matter every chance you get to improve soil conditions, no matter which ground covers you are growing.

One particularly frustrating soil moisture condition to watch for is dry shade. Trees block rainfall on shaded sites, and shallow tree roots can soak up whatever moisture does reach the ground, making it difficult for many shade-loving plants to survive. Sites under deep roof eaves — especially spots that are on the lee side of prevailing winds — also can be very dry because rainfall doesn't reach the ground. The area between houses that are spaced close together can have the same problem. In all of these cases, look for ground covers that tolerate dry, shaded sites. Another option is to install soaker hoses at planting time and water these sites regularly.

ACIDITY AND ALKALINITY. A soil's pH — whether it is acid, neutral, or alkaline — affects how available nutrients are to plants. The good news is that plants adapt to a wider range of soil pH levels than most gardeners think they do, and it's fine if you only have a general idea of your soil's pH. (In this book, pH requirements are mentioned only when a plant must have a particular pH level.) Most areas of the country that get high amounts of rainfall have slightly acid soil. Midwestern prairie states that get less rainfall have soils with near neutral pH, while in dry western states, the soil is likely to be alkaline. If you don't want to bother testing your soil — and many good gardeners have never had their soil pH tested — ask neighbors who garden, experts at garden centers in your area, or your local Cooperative Extension office about pH ranges in your area. Your Extension agent also will be able to help you get your soil tested. Keep in mind that the construction history of a site also can affect pH. Soil may have been brought into your yard or subsoil may have been mixed with topsoil during grading.

Sun and Shade

A site's exposure — the amount of sun or shade it receives — obviously affects which plants will grow there. Watching a site and jotting down notes or simple diagrams of areas that are in sun or shade at different times of the day is a good way to get a true picture of the site. Try to look at a site hourly throughout the day, and ideally, check it during different seasons of the year as the sun changes its angle. Plants that perform best in full sun generally need a minimum of eight hours of direct sun daily. Plants that need full shade are best grown on sites that never receive any direct sun at all. In between those two extremes is a large gray area that the term "partial shade" doesn't adequately describe. Here's where notes about a particular site are helpful. Think about the following sun and shade patterns and the types of partial shade they supply.

MORNING SHADE, AFTERNOON SUN. Plants that thrive in full sun but tolerate partial shade tend to do well in this sort of partial shade. It's also a good place for species that thrive in full sun as well as heat and drought, if you don't have a site in full sun to give them. Sites that are sunny in the afternoon tend to be hotter than ones that are sunny in the morning.

MORNING SUN, AFTERNOON SHADE. A site offering this type of partial shade is generally cooler and gentler than a spot that is sunny in the afternoon, especially if the sun comes early in the morning. It's good for growing plants that do well in full sun and tolerate partial shade but need protection from heat. Provided the area is shaded by about 11:00 a.m. and the soil isn't too dry, it's also usually fine for plants that thrive in full shade.

Massive drifts of ferns create a thick, lush blanket for this shaded site.

MORNING AND AFTERNOON SUN, MIDDAY SHADE. Another beneficial pattern you may find is a site that receives sun in the morning and late afternoon but is shaded during the hottest part of the day. Such a site is suitable for plants that like full sun but need protection from heat.

STREETSIDE PLANTINGS

BEDS THAT ABUT STREETS — or run along driveways, for that matter — can be difficult to plant for a variety of reasons. First, in areas where salt is used during the winter months, plantings need to be salt tolerant. In areas with significant snowfall, herbaceous species often are best, because they die to the ground in winter, leaving room for piling up plowed snow. Streetside sites also tend to have poor soil. Not only is it commonly compacted from foot traffic and construction, but it also may contain a high percentage of clay because subsoil is often used to fill in along sidewalks and curbs. When creating beds in the strip between street and sidewalk, along driveways, in traffic or parking lot islands, or in the front yard next to the road, make an effort to improve the soil before planting.

Work in plenty of well-rotted compost, along with topsoil if the soil is particularly bad. Then plant some of the tough, salt-tolerant perennial ground covers listed here. If the site doesn't need to accommodate piles of snow in wintertime, shrubs make fine additions to sidewalk plantings. See Ground Covers for Seaside Sites on page 110 for a list of salt-tolerant shrubs. For more information on any of the plants listed here, see the page numbers listed.

Ajuga spp. Ajugas, bugleweeds. See page 148.
Armeria maritima. Common thrift. See page 98.
Festuca glauca. Blue fescue. See page 86.
Hemerocallis spp. Daylilies. See page 118.
Hosta spp. and hybrids. Hostas. See pages 71, 152, and 161.
Iberis sempervirens. Candytuft. See page 83.
Leymus arenarius. Blue lyme grass. See page 172.
Liriope spicata. Lilyturf. See page 183.
Ophiopogon japonicus. Mondo grass. See page 84.
Paeonia spp. Peonies. See page 109.
Sedum spp. Sedums, stonecrops. See pages 84 and 109.
Sempervivum spp. Houseleeks, hens-and-chicks. See page 101.
Stachys byzantina. Lamb's ears. See page 87.

DAPPLED SHADE. This is the bright, patchy shade cast by high-branched trees, such as oaks (*Quercus* spp.). Beams of sunlight reach the soil surface, but there is an even pattern of sun and shade on the site all day long. If you notice areas that are brighter than others, plant accordingly: place species that need full shade firmly in the shadows and reserve the patches of sunlight for plants that need some good light for best performance. Many plants that thrive in partial to full shade actually need good bright light to bloom well. Plants with variegated leaves often produce the brightest foliage when sited in a spot that receives good light but not direct sun, which can burn leaves.

FULL SHADE. A site that is in full shade receives no direct sunlight from morning until night. It can be tricky, but not impossible, to plant. Stick with species that tolerate full shade, since ones that need even partial shade will probably be lanky at best. A site under a deciduous tree is perfect for a planting of ground covers mixed with spring ephemerals, which often sprout, flower, and die back before the tree has fully leafed out. An area that is in shade cast by evergreens or that is located on the north side of a building is the toughest to deal with because few plants will grow there. In the darkest spots, a thick layer of mulch may be the best option.

SHADE GRADATIONS. Determining the type of shade a particular site receives isn't as simple a process as we would like it to be. Few beds — and even fewer gardens — offer a single exposure, and it's up to the gardener to determine what exposure each patch of ground offers. When scoping out a site, try to look for the gradations — bright patches of nearly full sun in a bed with dappled shade, or spots of deep shade and brighter shade in a woodland bed. Also be aware of sites that range from deep shade at one end to full sun at the other. Once you have an intimate knowledge of your site, you can select a mix of sun- and shade-loving ground covers and plant them accordingly.

Other Cultural Considerations

In many cases, knowing something about the soil and whether a site is in sun or shade is enough information to choose ground covers. Some other factors may be important in your garden, however.

TOPOGRAPHY. A sloping site covered with lawn grass or ground covers can pose a challenge because water rushes down the slope rather than percolating into the soil, where plant roots can soak it up. Anything you can do to slow the speed of the water will help increase the amount that soaks in and reaches plants. (See Planting on Slopes on page 196 for some suggestions on dealing with sloping sites.) For a permanent solution, consider installing terraces — either build them yourself or let an expert do the job — which will transform a steep slope into a series of level beds separated by walls. The walls can be made of landscape timbers, preformed building blocks, dry-laid stone, mortared stone, or brick. The size of the beds, along with the height of the walls, will vary from site to site. When filling the terraces with soil, add plenty of organic matter and fill several inches above the top edge of the wall to allow for settling. Wait for the soil to settle before planting and mulching.

WIND. Sites exposed to prevailing winds can make for some challenging gardening. Wind desiccates foliage, and plants exposed to wind dry out more quickly than ones growing in more protected spots. Tough, drought-tolerant ground covers can handle windy sites, but also consider planting a windbreak of trees and shrubs to filter and reduce wind. Fences also block wind but do not filter it, so gusts can be a problem on the lee side.

REFLECTED HEAT. Pavement is the major culprit responsible for reflecting heat, which can burn plant leaves. On sites where reflected heat is a problem — along sidewalks and driveways, for example — tough heat- and drought-tolerant ground covers are good choices. Beds even a few feet away from a spot that receives too much

reflected heat may not suffer from this problem, so one solution is a planting of heat-tolerant species along the source of the reflected heat that will protect any plants that are less forgiving. Adding organic matter to the soil at planting time and using organic mulches are steps you can take to increase moisture retention and help plants cope with excessive heat.

SALT. Ocean breezes carry salt inland, so salt-tolerant plants are a must in seaside gardens. In dry regions of the West, where soils tend to be alkaline, salt-tolerant plants are often the best choice because the ground may contain high levels of salt, either naturally or because of irrigation with water high in salts. Soils that have a high salt content can cause plant roots to dry out because water actually moves out of the roots and into the soil. High salt levels also degrade soil structure, and very alkaline conditions chemically destroy soil organic matter. See Ground Covers for Seaside Sites on page 110 for a list of salt-tolerant plants.

FLOODING. Depending on how you look at it, a site that's flooded periodically can be an interesting challenge to plant or simply a headache. If the site is along a stream, ground covers with well-branched, deep roots are essential, because part of their function is to hold the soil in place. If the site is located next to a pond or is simply a low-lying spot that is wet for part of the year, bog garden plants may be the best ground covers. See Ground Covers for Wet Soil on page 173 for plants that thrive with wet feet.

Deep red flowers of autumn sage (*Salvia greggii*) decorate the foliage of ground cover gold-and-silver chrysanthemum (*Ajania pacifica*, formerly *Chrysanthemum pacificum*), which will produce its buttonlike yellow flowers in fall.

Fragrant Foliage

For really tough spots, your selection criteria may not go beyond just finding plants that will survive in a particular site. In other areas, consider using a theme to narrow your options from the many available choices.

A variety of ground covers that have fragrant foliage are suitable for covering a sunny site, for example. 'Hidcote', 'Baby White', 'Blue Cushion', 'Munsted Dwarf', and 'Jean Davis' are all compact cultivars of English lavender (*Lavandula angustifolia*) that blend nicely in a bed with drifts of thymes (*Thymus* spp.).

Oregano (*Origanum vulgare*) also makes a fine aromatic ground cover. 'Aureum' sports chartreuse leaves and only reaches 8 to 12 inches in height. Other species are taller, but still effective. (Remove the flower stalks to keep the plants looking neat and to prevent self-sowing.) Rosemary (*Rosmarinus officinalis*) is a good choice in warmer climates. 'Arp' is the hardiest cultivar and survives in Zone 7, while 'Prostratus' is a less hardy, low-growing cultivar that usually reaches about 6 to 12 inches in height.

Other fragrant-foliage options include lavender cotton (*Santolina chamaecyparissus*), green lavender cotton (*S. virens*), calamint (*Calamintha nepeta*), and Roman chamomile (*Chamaemelum nobile*). Also consider catmint (*Nepeta × faassenii*); compact cultivars such as 'Little Titch', 'Blue Wonder, and 'Snowflake' might be best. Lemon balm (*Melissa officinalis*) makes an attractive mound of fragrant foliage and can be clipped to keep plants attractive; variegated 'Aurea' and gold-leaved 'All Gold' are especially handsome. Mints (*Mentha* spp.) make good fragrant-leaved ground covers provided they are given a spot where they can spread freely.

Ground covers that feature fragrant foliage abound in this handsome planting, including thymes (*Thymus* spp.), lavenders (*Lavandula* spp.), lavender cotton (*Santolina chamaecyparissus*), and green lavender cotton (*S. virens*).

PLANT SELECTION

Although studying site conditions is essential in choosing great ground covers, selecting plants gets to the heart of why gardening is so fascinating. Site conditions commonly narrow the list of appropriate plants for a given spot, but in most cases there are still many plants to choose from and a number of ways they can be arranged in the garden. Jot down key features of your site before you start listing specific ground covers. A list will help keep you focused when you visit garden centers or discuss possibilities with local experts. If you tend to be an impulse shopper, use it to verify that each plant you choose really has a chance of growing successfully where you want it to.

A single ground cover may be just the ticket for a small site, but you'll likely be looking for more than one. Ground covers can be arranged in large single-species drifts, or they can be planted in drifts of just one to a couple of plants. As an alternative, two or more species can be planted in combination to form a ground cover. Read on for tips on selecting plants, and see Creating Combinations on page 42 for ideas on combining them.

that go dormant in broiling summer weather or develop ugly, scorched leaves in sites subject to reflected heat may perform beautifully in a cooler location. On the other hand, heat-loving species may merely limp along in areas where cool summer weather is the norm. Use the site information you gathered to make good choices.

Whether you're planting a single species of ground cover or combining several, look for foliage colors and textures that contrast with or complement one another. Ground covers usually are meant to provide a soothing, fairly uniform background in the garden, but that doesn't mean they have to be boring. It's surprising how variable all-green foliage can be, and how interesting a planting can be just because of foliage color. Leaves can be chartreuse, light green, deep rich green, blue-green, silver-green, or silver. Leaves also can be variegated — splashed or marked with chartreuse, white, yellow, pale green, silver-blue, or even pink.

Pair plants with foliage colors that complement one another to make any ground cover bed

Handsome contrast is what gives this combination its season-long appeal. The chartreuse leaves of *Hosta* 'Zounds' set off the much smaller, green-edged silver leaves of spotted deadnettle (*Lamium* 'Beacon Silver'), which have an almost lacy texture.

Foliage First

Many popular ground covers feature pretty flowers or attractive berries, or both, but for the best-looking plantings, consider foliage first. Practical and hardworking, ground covers need foliage that looks attractive all season long — or all year-round in the case of evergreen species. Any other features — flowers, berries, fall foliage color — are bonuses. Day in and day out, it's foliage that keeps the ground covered and your garden attractive.

One way to pick good ground covers for your area is to look for species with foliage that remains appealing through the worst of your gardening seasons. If possible, look at the plants during the droughts, extended rainy spells, or other tough climatic conditions your region has to offer. If a species looks acceptable in a nearby garden in the worst of times, it's probably a good choice for yours. Knowing your site is important here: Plants

interesting to look at. For example, combine two hosta cultivars: 'Blue Umbrellas', which has large blue-green leaves with a handsome puckered texture, with 'June', which has leaves variegated in yellow, chartreuse, and blue-green. Also look for plants that add interesting leaf shapes and textures to the mix. Shade lovers like epimediums (*Epimedium* spp.), Allegheny spurge (*Pachysandra procumbens*), and foamflowers (*Tiarella* spp.) add interest and contrast, as do grasslike sedges (*Carex* spp.). All thrive in shade and will cover the ground quite nicely. For a sunny spot, it's possible to create interesting contrast simply by combining several different cultivars of junipers (*Juniperus* spp.). Or add drifts of lamb's ears (*Stachys byzantina*), sedums (*Sedum* spp.), pinks (*Dianthus* spp.), and other low growers to the mix.

Using plants with contrasting foliage colors or textures, or both, adds interest and appeal to any planting. Chartreuse foliage combined with deep green or variegated leaves, for example, can be quite eye catching; so can delicate, ferny leaves next to broad, bold foliage. Use high-contrast combinations to create plantings that are striking. Dramatic combinations can also help to draw visitors to a certain part of the garden or call attention to a particular area. Plan on more subtle contrasts for edgings or beds designed to provide a uniform backdrop for specimen plants or an attractive frame for perennial or annual flowers.

Spread and Speed

Whether you plant ground covers side by side or combine them in a single bed, it's important to know the mature spread and height of each species. Spread isn't the only factor that determines whether a particular plant is going to stay put or attempt to engulf the entire garden and surrounding neighborhood. Many ground covers spread indefinitely; how vigorous they are, or how fast they spread, determines how easy or difficult they are to control. (The types of spreading mechanism a species employs also plays a role: see How Ground Covers Spread on page 40.) For example, bugleweed (*Ajuga reptans*) spreads indefinitely and can invade lawn grass, but the plants are relatively easy to control because they spread across the soil surface for the most part and have fairly shallow roots. On the other hand, variegated bishop's weed (*Aegopodium podagraria* 'Variegatum', plus the all-green species) and variegated houttuynia (*Houttuynia cordata* 'Chameleon'), both of which also spread indefinitely, have deep, wide-spreading rhizomes that are difficult or impossible to dig out. Once you plant them, they're there for good — including in many places you didn't plant them — unless you attack the planting with herbicide. The individual plant descriptions in part 2, beginning on page 66, indicate spread and height at maturity, the speed at which plants spread, and whether or not they have a propensity to become seriously aggressive.

(Left) The soft, gray foliage of lamb's ears (*Stachys byzantina*) offer a striking contrast to any green-leaved planting.

(Center) The chartreuse-and-white leaves of spotted deadneattle (*Lamium maculatum* 'Beedham's White') set off the lacy-textured leaves of sweet woodruff (*Galium odoratum*), plus mints (*Mentha* spp.) and green-and-white *Plectranthus* species, a tender perennial, add even more interest.

(Right) This bright foliage combination consists of *Ajuga* 'Burgundy Glow' and chartreuse *Lysimachia nummularia* 'Aurea'.

Keep in mind that if you are covering ground with a combination of ground covers, it is important to select plants that are compatible in both size and vigor. Otherwise one plant inevitably will smother its bedmates. Combining ground covers does take a bit more planning than planting a vast monoculture, but it has advantages. For one thing, it is a great way to add rich texture and color to an area. In addition, if one species doesn't grow well or dies, you have another plant (or plants) already growing on the site. You can let the remaining plants fill in or can replace the one that failed easily without having to replant the entire area. Similarly, if one species spreads too fast, you can eradicate or move it before it smothers the others and takes over the garden.

The size of the site plays an obvious role in determining the best plant or plants for the job. A single ground cover may be all you need to cover a small space. Most cultivars of English lavender (*Lavandula angustifolia*) spread 3 to 4 feet at maturity, and a single plant easily will cover a 3-foot-square bed and attractively billow over the edges. On the other hand, you could substitute three plants of dwarf white English lavender (*L. angustifolia* 'Nana Alba'), which spreads 1 foot wide. For added interest and a denser ground cover, try combining the lavender with thyme; tiny mother-of-thyme (*Thymus serpyllum*), for example, reaches 1 to 4 inches tall and spreads to 1 or 2 feet.

Remember that the size of the ground cover plants you purchase isn't the size they'll end up being, so do you homework *before* you buy. On a small site, even a single juniper can get much too large, regardless of how little and cute the plant looks potted up at a garden center. Read the small print on the label, and you'll find that creeping juniper (*Juniperus horizontalis*) spreads to at least 8 feet at maturity, and many have an indefinite spread. That makes them a good choice for a large site, perhaps, but not for a 3-foot square spot where they'll need constant pruning to keep them in bounds. See Spacing Patterns on page 196 for guidelines on positioning plants.

The ideal height for a ground cover depends on both the site and your gardening style. For a low ground cover to replace a section of lawn, plants that remain under a foot high are typical for a small yard. Plants that grow to 2 feet tall are fine for larger sites on most properties. Ground covers that reach as high as 3 feet will still "read" as lawn in large yards or in ground cover plantings in front of shrub borders or woodlands.

For an edging, a good rule of thumb is to select plant heights that do not exceed half the width of the path. So for a 3-foot-wide path, select plants that are under 1½ feet at maturity. Shorter is better if you prefer that plants not hang over the path's edge. In some cases, shrubs and even weeping trees make outstanding ground covers. Even large plants like these can seem like horizontal ground covers provided they're given enough space to spread.

The woolly white leaves of lamb's ears (*Stachys byzantina*) soften the edge of the brick paving that separates this handsome combination from the lawn. Needlelike, blue-green foliage of pinks (*Dianthus* spp.) add contrast, while tiny, rich magenta flowers add spots of color.

How Ground Covers Spread

Knowing how a particular species spreads is a very useful piece of information to have when selecting and planting ground covers.

Those that spread by deep, fast-growing, widely spreading rhizomes can be very drought tolerant, for example, but they also can be very difficult to dig up and remove if they don't turn out to be the plants you want for a particular site. Species that spread by stolons or runners are great for filling in around other ground covers — or filling an area all their own. Certain plants cover the ground by trailing, weeping, or spreading branches; some self-sowing species can be used as ground covers too.

Understanding root structure can be helpful when selecting companion plants. Pair hostas, which are clump formers, with ground covers that spread by stolons — foamflowers (*Tiarella* spp.), for example — or by slowly creeping rhizomes — wild blue phlox (*Phlox divaricata*), for example. The foamflower or phlox will fill in around the hostas. In many cases, the way a species spreads also determines how to propagate it; see Growing Your Own on page 203.

RHIZOMES. These are specialized stems that are horizontal to the soil surface and either run along the surface or underground. While rhizomes range from long and thin to thick and fleshy, all have nodes and internodes and produce roots at the nodes. Rhizomatous plants can have short, slow-growing rhizomes that creep and fill a space slowly, or they can produce very long, wide-ranging rhizomes that spread very quickly. Epimediums (*Epimedium* spp.) and wintergreen (*Gaultheria procumbens*) are two ground covers that spread slowly by rhizomes. Mints, (*Mentha* spp.), bishop's weed (*Aegopodium podagraria*), and yellow archangel (*Lamium galeobdolon*) are all very fast-spreading rhizomatous plants. Woody plants, including cowberry (*Vaccinium vitis-idaea*), can spread by rhizomes too.

RUNNERS AND STOLONS. Although gardeners often use these terms interchangeably, a runner is a slender rhizome, a long, horizontal, aboveground stem that runs along the soil surface and produces roots and small plantlets at the tip and at leaf nodes. True stolons produce roots and plantlets only at their tip. Strawberries (*Fragaria* spp.) and strawberry geraniums (*Saxifraga stolonifera*) produce true stolons, while Aaron's beard (*Hypericum calycinum*) spreads by runners.

SUCKERS. These are short shoots that arise from either the roots or crown of a plant. For instance, mahonias, including creeping mahonia (*Mahonia repens*), spread by suckers; so does inkberry (*Ilex glabra*). Snowdrop anemone (*Anemone sylvestris*) is an herbaceous plant that spreads by root suckers.

Hen-and-chicks (*Sempervivum tectorum*) spread slowly but steadily by producing small rosettes at the ends of short runners. Although the parent plants (the hens) die after flowering, the clumps cover ground as new rosettes (the chicks) root.

'Silver King' white sage (*Artemisia ludoviciana* 'Silver King') spreads by rhizomes. Plants cover ground especially quickly in rich, well-drained soil, and they can easily become invasive.

SPREADING, CLUMP-FORMING PLANTS. Both herbaceous and woody plants with clump-forming roots and spreading tops can be used as ground covers, provided they grow at a steady rate and have a fairly horizontal habit. Hostas are a good example of clump formers that make fine ground cover plants. A good many shrubs fall into this category, from low-growing forms of rhododendrons and azaleas (*Rhododendron* spp.) to creeping juniper (*Juniperus horizontalis*) and Rocky Mountain juniper (*J. scopulorum*), both of which have wide-ranging branches that cover a considerable distance.

TRAILING STEMS. Actually rhizomes, this term is used to refer to less vigorous horizontal stems that are somewhat vinelike and that grow along the soil surface and produce roots at the nodes. Partridgeberry (*Mitchella repens*) is an example of a ground cover with trailing stems.

VINES. Although most often thought of as climbing plants, vines used as ground covers spread their thin, flexible branches along the soil. They are especially useful for training over rocky slopes and other obstacles where other types of ground covers are hard to grow. English ivy (*Hedera helix*) is among the best-known vining ground covers, but some other vines, including climbing hydrangea (*Hydrangea anomala* subsp. *petiolaris*) and wood vamp (*Decumaria barbara*), can be used in the same way.

ARCHING AND WEEPING BRANCHES. Some of the best ground cover shrubs produce branches that arch over the ground, creating a blanket of layered branches and leaves. They may take root if they touch soil. Cotoneasters (*Cotoneaster* spp.), including rockspray cotoneaster (*C. horizontalis*), fall into this category. Cultivars of shrubs and even trees that have cascading or weeping habits also make handsome and unusual ground covers.

SELF-SOWING. A number of plants can spread and cover the ground densely just from self-sown seeds. Weeds are an obvious example, but cultivated plants that self-sow and can be used to cover the ground include several species of violets (*Viola* spp.), yellow corydalis (*Corydalis lutea*), lady's mantle (*Alchemilla mollis*), wild geranium (*Geranium maculatum*), as well as money plant (*Lunaria annua*).

CREATING COMBINATIONS

This lush, green-and-chartreuse combination makes a handsome cover for a shady bed. It features a bed of native maidenhair ferns (*Adiantum pedatum*) edged with variegated hakone grass (*Hakonechloa macra* 'Aureola'), both of which need rich, moist soil to thrive.

Drifts, of course, are the most common ground cover planting pattern. They can be any size, from one plant to a hundred or more, and can be planted with a single species or several different ones. Although traditional ground cover monocultures make sense in some cases, other planting options are more exciting. Think of ground covers as the rugs of your garden. You probably decorate different rooms with different colors and patterns of carpet, so why not do that in your garden? Indoor rooms are enhanced with a mixture of floor coverings in a harmonious blend of colors, textures, and patterns, and outdoor ones can be as well.

Your personal sense of style, along with the style of your house and garden, will determine the choices you make. Do you want low-growing ground covers that suggest the texture of a modern Berber carpet, or a series of formal rectangles or squares in a solid color to set off a sculpture or sundial? Or is your garden informal and cottagey? Perhaps ground covers arranged in small drifts of two or three plants will look best — or even drifts of one, in the event that you are a plant collector and want to grow a little of everything. Other options to consider include annuals for temporary cover, plantings that consist of all native plants, and mixed plantings that attract wildlife.

Ground Cover Gardens

If you want to add some low-maintenance plantings to your yard but don't like the usual ground cover monocultures, consider creating ground cover gardens. These resemble traditional flower beds but are planted with a mix of ground covers arranged in small drifts or good-size clumps of a single species. Plantings combining both perennials and woody plants are fine. Ground cover gardens aren't plantings for control freaks: they're easiest if you let plants intermingle and form their own interesting combinations. The end result is a planting that has the feel of a flower bed, but with much less maintenance.

Ideally, select plants that spread with similar speeds. Avoid combining really vigorous spreaders, which will simply blanket the entire bed, with less-vigorous species. Otherwise they will simply crowd out all the other plants. Fast-spreading species like English ivy (*Hedera helix*) or crown vetch (*Coronilla varia*) will quickly overwhelm nearly anything they are planted with, for example. If you do end up with one plant that seems to be spreading too fast, either dig it up and remove it, or take out nearby bedmates and give it more space.

The plants you choose for combinations should have interesting foliage, and you'll want at least some ground covers that bear flowers too. For example, in a site with partial shade, combine clumps of any of the epimediums (*Epimedium* spp.) with Japanese painted fern (*Athyrium niponicum* var. *pictum*), Chinese astilbe (*Astilbe chinensis*), bleeding hearts (*Dicentra* spp.), heucheras (*Heuchera* spp.), crested iris (*Iris cristata*), spotted deadnettle (*Lamium maculatum*), medium-size hostas (*Hosta* spp.) such as 'Radiant Edger' or 'Golden Tiara', and variegated common periwinkle (*Vinca minor* 'Argenteovariegata'), which isn't as vigorous as its all-green cousin. European ginger (*Asarum europaeum*) makes a nice edging for this group. Several dwarf shrubs would work well also. Consider incorporating shrubs such as 'Little Henry' sweetspire (*Itea virginica*), which reaches 2 feet high, as well as 'Hummingbird' summersweet (*Clethra alnifolia*), reaching about 3 feet high.

In a sunny spot, consider Carpathian bellflower (*Campanula carpatica*), Dalmatian bellflower (*C. portenschlagiana*), calamint (*Calamintha nepeta*), pinks (*Dianthus* spp.), bloody cranesbill (*Geranium sanguineum*), dwarf bearded irises (*Iris* spp.), moss pink (*Phlox subulata*), and lamb's ears (*Stachys byzantina*), to name a few. Shrubs such as bearberry (*Arctostaphylos uva-ursi*) and dwarf conifers make interesting additions.

Drifts of compatible ground covers can be used to create a gardenlike planting for nearly any site. The colorful blanket for this sunny slope consists of 'Silver Queen' white sage (*Artemisia ludoviciana* 'Silver Queen'), black-eyed Susans (*Rudbeckia* 'Goldsturm'), and *Amsonia hubrectii*.

Temporary Fillers

Annuals are an inexpensive option for filling an area temporarily. Used as ground covers around perennials in a newly planted flower bed, they'll cut down on weeds and cover the soil too.

Just as important, their flowers or foliage will add color and give the planting a lusher, fuller look for the first season or two. Once you see the effect, you may find you want to add some annuals to perennial plantings beds every year. Fill spaces between larger perennials with impatiens (*Impatiens walleriana*), begonias (*Begonia* spp.), sweet alyssum (*Lobularia maritima*), mountain spinach (*Atriplex hortensis*), ornamental sweet potatoes (*Ipomoea*

Grown as annuals in northern zones, gazanias (*Gazania ringens*) can be used for temporary cover where they are not hardy. In this warm-climate garden, though, they make a striking permanent ground cover.

batatas 'Margarita' or 'Blackie'), or licorice plant (*Helichrysum petiolare*). Gazanias (*Gazania ringens*) also make fine temporary ground covers in northern climates (the plants are hardy in Zones 8 to 10); use gazanias in drifts or as a colorful edging on sunny sites. Annual vines commonly found in vegetable gardens, such as pumpkins and gourds, are another great option for blanketing a large area for a season. Use them to fill in around shrubs or to cover a newly dug bed to keep the soil covered, combat weeds, and add some organic matter in the process.

Cover crops, another group of plants primarily used in vegetable gardens, are an option for covering the ground in a newly dug but not-yet-planted flower garden. They'll hold the soil in place and help crowd out weeds until the soil has settled and you are ready to plant. Cover crops also add loads of organic matter to the soil — there's a reason they're also called green manures. Seed for these plants is most often available from companies that sell vegetable garden seed. Select annual species, so eradicating them doesn't become a problem, and sow in a prepared seedbed that has been cleared of weeds and loosened. Typically, cover crops are mowed if they grow more than a few inches tall and are then tilled into the soil before planting. Cover crops to consider include soybeans (*Glycine max*), hairy vetch (*Vicia villosa*), annual ryegrass (*Lolium multiflorum*), buckwheat (*Fagopyrum esculentum*), and winter rye (*Secale cereale*).

Don't overlook low-growing tender bulbs for filling in as well. Caladiums (*Caladium bicolor*, formerly *C.* × *hortulanum*), also commonly known as angel's tears or elephant's ears, are hardy only in Zones 10 and 11 but can be used for summertime color in the North.

Mulching with Plants

Low-growing ground covers can take over the soil protection chores that mulch ordinarily handles. They'll also add extra color to beds and borders in the process. Instead of dealing with grass or weeds in a shrub border or along a hedge, fill the area under the shrubs with ground covers to take the place of grass or crowd out the weeds.

Tough, vigorous ground covers are usually best for this purpose, since they compete quite well with the roots of commonly grown shrubs, such as viburnums (*Viburnum* spp.), forsythias (*Forsythia* spp.), hydrangeas (*Hydrangea* spp.), and hollies (*Ilex* spp.). Even rhododendrons and azaleas (*Rhododendron* spp.) can be underplanted, but because of their shallow roots, choose carefully and stick with less vigorous woodland wildflowers unless the shrubs are particularly vigorous and healthy.

Before deciding what to plant, study the sun and shade patterns around the shrubs, since the exposures will vary. Sites on the south side of a shrub border may be dry and sunny, while those on the north side may be quite shady. Adaptable plumbago (*Ceratostigma plumbaginoides*) grows in partial shade to full sun; it thrives in rich, well-drained soil but also tolerates poor, dry soil. Bugleweed (*Ajuga reptans*), lily-of-the-valley (*Convallaria majalis*), lilyturf (*Liriope spicata*), and Lenten roses (*Helleborus × hybridus*) also are good candidates for a spot in partial shade. Fast-spreading epimediums such as *Epimedium × perralchicum*, *E. perralderianum*, and *E. × warleyense* are other good choices for partial to full shade, as are hostas (*Hosta* spp.) and sweet woodruff (*Galium odoratum*). For a dry spot in full sun, consider drifts of daylilies (*Hemerocallis* spp.), snow-in-summer (*Cerastium tomentosum*), common pussytoes (*Antennaria dioica*), and sedums (*Sedum* spp.). Avoid ground covers that will climb and blanket shrubs, such as wintercreeper (*Euonymus fortunei*) and English ivy (*Hedera helix*).

Compact shrubs make good ground covers under taller shrubs, so feel free to experiment. For sunny spots, try plants such as bearberry (*Arctostaphylos uva-ursi*), sweet fern (*Comptonia peregrina*),

(Left) Silver-leaved spotted deadnettle (*Lamium maculatum* 'White Namcy') forms a dense living mulch for lilac (*Syringa meyeri* 'Palibin').

(Right) Underplanting shrubs with ground covers helps crowd out weeds, protects the soil, and eliminates the need to mulch. Here, red osier dogwood (*Cornus stolonifera* 'Flaviramira') is underplanted with a thick carpet of *Ophiopogon planiscapus* 'Nigrescens'.

ADDING POP-UP COLOR

TO PUNCH UP THE APPEAL of a ground cover planting, underplant it with bulbs for extra color. Daffodils (*Narcissus* spp.) are perfect for this purpose. Like other spring bulbs, they're inexpensive, and they bloom before most deciduous perennial ground covers really get growing in spring. Many are tall enough to carry their flowers above a 6- or 8-inch-tall bed of evergreen ground covers. Spanish bluebells (*Hyacinthoides hispanica*) hold their flowers 16 inches in the air and also are suitable for planting through beds of taller ground covers, as are summer snowflakes (*Leucojum aestivum*), another good, taller candidate that reaches 2 feet high and blooms in spring, despite its common name. See Bulbs for Adding Color on page 102 for a list of hardy bulbs to decorate plantings of low-growing ground covers like creeping mazus (*Mazus reptans*) and mondo grasses (*Ophiopogon* spp.).

For adding summer color, try hardy amaryllis or magic lily (*Lycoris squamigera*), or drifts of ornamental onions such as star of Persia (*Allium cristophii*), giant onion (*A. giganteum* and *A.* hybrids), *A. schubertii*, and drumstick chives (*A. sphaerocephalon*). For fall color, consider colchicums (*Colchicum* spp.), fall-blooming crocuses (*Crocus* spp.), and autumn or winter daffodil (*Sternbergia lutea*).

Tiny snowdrops (*Galanthus nivalis*) add their dainty late-winter to early spring flowers to a planting of *Ajuga pyramidalis* 'Metallica Crispa'.

cotoneasters such as *Cotoneaster adpressus* or *C. dammeri*, low-growing junipers (including cultivars of *Juniperus chinensis, J. horizontalis,* and *J. squamata*), and dwarf forms of Japanese spirea (*Spiraea japonica* 'Goldflame', 'Little Princess', and 'Nana', among others). For shade, consider dwarf Himalayan sweet box (*Sarcococca humilis*), low-growing mahonias (*Mahonia nervosa* and *M. repens*), and prostrate forms of yew, including *Taxus baccata* 'Repandens' and *T. × media* 'Everlow'.

Planting ground cover mulches in flower beds — under large perennials such as peonies (*Paeonia* spp.) or giant hostas (*Hosta* spp.), for example — also is very practical. They will not only control weeds but also help protect the soil, as mulch does. They have an added advantage that conventional mulch doesn't, though, since they don't need to be replenished each season. For underplanting perennials, you'll want less vigorous plants than the ones used under or near shrubs, since they won't need to compete with shrubs roots. Perennial ground covers for flower beds in shade include wild gingers (*Asarum* spp.), foamflowers (*Tiarella* spp.), sedges (*Carex* spp.), green-and-gold (*Chrysogonum virginianum*), spotted deadnettle (*Lamium maculatum*), and European strawberry (*Fragaria vesca*). For sun, consider plants such as creeping baby's breath (*Gypsophila repens*), candytuft (*Iberis sempervirens*), creeping Jenny (*Lysimachia nummularia*), creeping mazus (*Mazus reptans*), thymes (*Thymus* spp.), and gold-and-silver chrysanthemum (*Ajania pacifica*).

GOING WILD

Ground covers are more than just practical problem solvers: they offer many benefits to the ecologically minded gardener. Many native plants, for example, make outstanding ground covers. Beds of both native and nonnative plants play an important role in landscapes designed to attract birds, butterflies, and other wild creatures.

Native Carpets

Gardening with native ground covers is an excellent option whether you have sun or shade. Native species are indicated in plant descriptions in part 2 of this book. You will have to decide what the word "native" is going to mean for your own garden. Are you going to consider plants that are native to any part of North America? What about naturalized species that have been here so long we forget they are not native — creeping Jenny (*Lysimachia nummularia*) is originally a native of Europe, not North America, for example. Or are you going to grow only plants native to your region or local area? Either way, research is in order. Consult with local botanical gardens and arboretums, as well as local parks and natural areas, to see if they have lists or displays of native plants. Local or state native plant societies also are good sources of information. All of these organizations commonly have plant sales, which are good places to find native plants. They also will likely be able to provide information on local nurseries that sell plants that have been nursery propagated, not collected in the wild.

NATIVE GROUND COVERS FOR SHADE. Native wildflowers are among the most popular shade garden plants available, and many make excellent ground covers. See Native Plants for a Woodland Floor on page 165 for a list of species to consider. Keep in mind that just because a garden is planted with natives doesn't mean the plants have to be mixed all together in a naturalistic style, as they would grow in the wild. Large free-form drifts arranged in a flowing informal pattern to blanket the ground under trees and shrubs can be just as handsome and may be more suitable for your purposes. Native ground covers also can be used in a more formal design. Fill rectangular or square beds with them, and repeat species to create an attractive composition that is balanced.

NATIVE GROUND COVERS FOR SUN. Here, too, sun-loving ground cover species can be planted in a casual, cottagey mix or a more formal arrangement. Another option for covering the ground with natives is a meadow- or prairie-style planting, which doesn't necessarily fit the conventional definition of ground covers — for one thing, it's usually far taller than most ground cover plantings. However, when the plants are allowed to grow together as they would in the wild, they cover the ground with dense, weed-suppressing growth. They also are very low maintenance once established.

Meadow and prairie plantings can be established from seed or plugs. Plugs, also called starts, are small plants grown in specially designed flats of individual cells. Or you can sow seed the first year and then in subsequent years add plugs of individual species like purple coneflowers (*Echinacea purpurea*) or butterfly weed (*Asclepias tuberosa*) to create a planting that features more flowers that a typical meadow or prairie planting would. When

LETTING LAWN GROW UP

HERE'S A SIMPLE WAY TO CUT DOWN ON MOWING: Let a section of your lawn grow long, and create a meadowlike area in your yard. This works best when the spot you select is away from neighbors' yards — perhaps out at the back of your property. For the best results, cut defined edges around the area, and also cut a path through it to make it appealing to walk though. You may be surprised at the flowers that appear (get rid of weeds like dandelions to keep criticism from neighbors to a minimum), and you can also pop in perennials if you like. Patches of long grass are fascinating to walk though because they'll attract butterflies along with all manner of insects, spiders, and other wildlife. Grass and flower seed heads also will be attractive to birds. So, spend some of the time you save mowing enjoying the wildlife.

buying a seed mix, look for one with species native to your area and that doesn't contain nonnative plants. A good mix will contain mostly perennials along with some annuals to help cover the ground and provide color the first year. Grasses are important components and should be included in any meadow or prairie mix you purchase. Consult local experts or your local Cooperative Extension Service to determine the best time to plant. You'll have to kill existing vegetation to sow or plant, and the plantings will need regular weeding until they are established. After that, they'll survive with little more than an occasional weeding to remove woody plants and an annual mowing or burning, a method used to revitalize prairie plantings, which burn periodically in nature.

Attracting Wildlife

Beds of ground covers aren't the first things that spring to mind when discussing gardens designed to attract wildlife, but there's no reason they can't play a role. Species that produce berries are great for feeding many kinds of wildlife from birds to box turtles. Winged wildlife such as butterflies and hummingbirds also are attracted to flowers, so include blooming ground covers in your plantings. Sedums (*Sedum* spp.), catmints (*Nepeta* spp.), and yarrows (*Achillea* spp.) all attract butterflies, while hummingbirds visit the flowers of hostas (*Hosta* spp.), daylilies (*Hemerocallis* spp.), and salvias (*Salvia* spp.), to name a few.

Vines are effective, if nontraditional, ground covers when allowed to scramble horizontally instead of climb vertically. Various species produce berries that will feed wildlife and also provide shelter. Virginia creeper (*Parthenocissus quinquefolia*), wild grapes (*Vitis* spp.), trumpet honeysuckle (*Lonicera sempervirens*), and American bittersweet (*Celastrus scandens*) are first-rate choices, but avoid American bittersweet's extremely invasive cousin, Oriental bittersweet (*C. orbiculatus*).

Many shrubs, including firethorns (*Pyracantha* spp.) and junipers (*Juniperus* spp.), produce berries, as do native perennials like wintergreen (*Gaultheria procumbens*). Rose hips also are good forage for birds. Several of the new Meidiland roses (*Rosa* hybrids) set hips, including 2-foot tall 'Panda Meidiland', which spreads to 4 feet, along with 'Scarlet Meidiland', which reaches 3 feet tall and spreads to 5 feet. Some other berry-bearing shrubs to put on your list for ground covers that attract wildlife include bearberry (*Arctostaphylos uva-ursi*), blueberries (*Vaccinium* spp.), cotoneasters (*Cotoneaster* spp.), fragrant sumac (*Rhus aromatica*), hollies (*Ilex* spp.), mahonias (*Mahonia* spp.), and coralberries (*Symphoricarpos* spp.).

One reason ground covers can provide safe haven for turtles, toads, and other wildlife is because creatures don't have to be on the lookout for mowers. Here, a box turtle pauses in a patch of creeping mazus (*Mazus reptans*).

One Wild Landscape

WHILE THIS PLANTING CONSISTS OF NATIVE PERENNIALS that are decidedly taller than most ground covers, a meadow planting like this one most certainly covers ground and reduces maintenance. This meadow will need to be cut or burned to the ground annually, but needs little other annual care. Drifts of both pink- and white-flowered purple coneflowers occupy the foreground. Other species in this planting include great rudbeckia, panic grass, and mountain mint.

1. Purple coneflower
   (*Echinacea purpurea* 'Ruby Star')
2. White coneflower
   (*Echinacea* 'White Swan')
3. Great rudbeckia
   (*Rudbeckia maxima*)
4. Panic grass
   (*Panicum virgatum* 'North Wind')
5. Mountain mint
   (*Pycnanthemum muticum*)

AGGRESSIVE & INVASIVE GROUND COVERS

Ground covers are, almost by definition, vigorous wide-spreading plants, and many of them can be a challenge to control. They're frequently found on lists of invasive plants, because given the chance, many will spread far beyond the bounds of the site where they were originally planted; they will even spread into natural areas and crowd out the native vegetation. The terms "invasive" and "aggressive" are often used loosely when describing fast-spreading plants, but there is a distinction. In general, aggressive is best applied to plants that spread vigorously in the garden by self-seeding or creeping; they spread to the point that they crowd out less vigorous plants. Plants described as invasive also spread quickly in the garden, but in addition they are able to establish themselves in uncultivated areas and take the place of native species.

Ground covers that can also be climbers, such as English ivy (*Hedera helix*), Japanese honeysuckle (*Lonicera japonica*), wintercreeper (*Euonymus fortunei*), porcelain berry (*Ampelopsis brevipedunculata*), Oriental bittersweet (*Celastrus orbiculatus*), and kudzu (*Pueraria montana* var. *lobata*) have a penchant for world domination and will cover your garden, engulf your house, climb your trees, and spread far beyond the bounds of your garden. Other ground covers that are often found on lists of invasive plants include crown vetch (*Coronilla varia*), creeping Jenny (*Lysimachia nummularia*), bishop's weed (*Aegopodium podagraria*), and vincas (*Vinca major* and *V. minor*). Barberries (*Berberis* spp.) have become a problem because birds relish their berries and thus spread the seed.

Variegated forms of climbers like English ivy and wintercreeper spread more slowly than the all-green species and thus are easier to control. While the same is true for variegated bishop's weed and variegated forms of vinca, all of these are plants to be wary of and to site very carefully if you grow them at all — green or variegated. (There's never any reason to plant invasive plants such as Japanese honeysuckle, Oriental bittersweet, porcelain berry, or kudzu.)

It's nearly always crazy to add a plant to your garden that you'll have to fight to keep in bounds, but there are reasons it might make sense to plant some of these very vigorous plants — provided you can do it without causing recurring headaches or environmental nightmares. In a contained bed, with a wall on one side and a sidewalk or driveway on the other, plants like English ivy will be perfectly well behaved provided you enforce the boundaries with pruning shears once or twice a season. In this case, it will do the job of a good ground cover: smother the ground with green and keep weeds at bay. Every few years, when a thick mass of ivy stems builds up on the ground, chop them down to a height of about 3 or 4 inches using a lawn mower or a string trimmer with a blade attachment. Rake out all the pieces and discard them in the trash, not the compost pile, where they are perfectly able to root.

English ivy and some of the other tough customers mentioned here also aren't bad choices for a spot where nothing else will grow, such as under shallow-rooted trees like maples (*Acer* spp.). While there's rooting space for a shady garden under deep-rooted species like oaks (*Quercus* spp.) and black walnuts (*Juglans nigra*) — and many species grow happily under walnuts, despite all the myths — most maples fill every square inch of soil with their roots. Since English ivy creeps along the soil surface, it can eke out a living in such conditions if planted around the tree just outside the drip line and trained back into the shade. Or try the ivy in shallow pots or window boxes set around the tree and let the vines cascade out and over the ground. Either way, the planting will look better than the smattering of grass and weeds that will otherwise manage to survive there. Add a layer of mulch around the tree to further smother weeds so the ivy can put down some roots. Add pots filled with annuals to supply some color in this otherwise all-green composition. Also keep the pruning shears handy and whack back the ivy regularly once it becomes established, whether it spreads out to the garden or tries to climb up the tree.

Site selection is one of the best ways to manage fast-spreading ground covers. For example, many plants spread more slowly when given less-than-ideal cultural conditions. Plant a species that thrives in rich, moist soil in a drier site, and spreading may be less of a problem. Selecting sites that have physical barriers on all sides is an even more reliable way to keep plants in check. Look for areas contained by some combination of the following types of barriers: house or other building foundations; cement, stone, or brick walkways, sidewalks, or driveways; raised beds or planters; parking lot islands; planting islands surrounded by a driveway; mowed lawn; a pond or stream; or walls, curbs, or edgings.

When offered plants from a friend or neighbor's garden, listen carefully to descriptions. Avoid plants they describe as "aggressive," or that have "grown out into my woods." Also look at the plants in the person's garden, if possible, and steer away from those that seem to be far too vigorous. If you don't, you'll be planting a headache.

COVERING WISELY

Here are some other pointers for growing ground covers responsibly.

- **SELECT** native species whenever possible.
- **SITE** aggressive ground covers very carefully. Beds that are contained on all sides are best.
- **MONITOR AND MANAGE** all of your ground cover plantings carefully. Watch plants to keep track of how fast they spread, and stop them before they get out of bounds. Prune regularly to contain their spread and cut back self-seeders immediately after the flowers fade to prevent them from increasing.
- **DON'T PLANT** invasives where they can escape the garden and colonize wild areas. If they are planted along a back lot line — to fill a waste area, for example — they will quickly spread to woodlands or other wild areas, crowding out native species.
- **AVOID** planting invasives along the edges of the garden where they can spread to neighboring yards.
- **DON'T SHARE** invasive plants with gardening friends and neighbors — especially beginning gardeners who may not know the ramifications of growing them.
- **DO NOT DUMP** pieces of stems, roots, or rhizomes of aggressive or invasive ground covers on compost piles or into waste areas, where they can sprout and spread.

The Dirty Dozen

To avoid adding troublemakers to your garden, consult local plant societies or native plant experts for lists of species that are classified as invasive in your area.

Bear in mind that plants that are invasive in one region may not be a problem in another, so local information on which plants to be wary of is by far the best. For web sites that list nonnative invasive plants and the regions where the species are problematic, see Resources, page

Aegopodium podagraria 'Variegatum'

Ampelopsis brevipedunculata

211. Here's a sampling of some seriously aggressive to invasive plants that you may want to avoid altogether, or at least think very seriously about before adding to your landscape.

❶ *Aegopodium podagraria* 'Variegatum'. **Variegated bishop's weed, goutweed.** Attractive three-part leaves margined with white, plus an ability to grow nearly anywhere, are the main reasons for this plant's popularity. This herbaceous perennial is a tough, aggressive spreader, though, and nearly impossible to eradicate once established. You might consider bishop's weed in large areas where little else will grow — it is effective in shade under trees surrounded by mown lawn. Remove the clusters of white flowers borne in early summer before seed sets, since seedlings of the all-green species will overtake variegated plantings. Mowing plantings to the ground is the easiest way to remove the flowers and also rejuvenates tired-looking foliage. Zones 4 to 8.

❷ *Ampelopsis brevipedunculata*. **Porcelain berry, porcelain ampelopsis.** This vigorous woody vine is an invasive species in many areas and generally not suitable for gardens, although it is still sold. It has lobed leaves and climbs by tendrils and spreads very rapidly. Its insignificant greenish flowers are followed by clusters of blue berries. Japanese beetles decimate the leaves in summer. Plants grow in sun or part shade and in any soil, but poor, infertile conditions help control their spread. 'Elegaus' bears variegated leaves and is somewhat less vigorous. Zones 4 to 8.

3 *Berberis thunbergii.* Japanese barberry. Most popular as foundation plants or hedges, low-growing forms of Japanese barberry are also used as ground covers for sun or part shade. Keep in mind, however, that birds relish the fruit and that these popular shrubs have become invasive in many areas due to bird-planted seedlings. Plants bear small oval, deciduous leaves, insignificant flowers, and red berries. Many cultivars are sold including purple- and yellow-leaved ones. Zones 4 to 8.

4 *Coronilla varia.* Crown vetch. Well known as a stabilizer for highway embankments in full sun, crown vetch is a vigorous, nonnative perennial. It forms loosely mounded clumps of pinnate leaves, with leaflets arranged in a featherlike fashion, topped by small clusters of pea-shaped flowers in white, purple, or pink from summer to fall. The delicate-looking foliage is misleading: this tough, often invasive spreader engulfs any perennials in its path. Zones 4 to 9.

5 *Duchesnea indica.* Mock strawberry. A mat-forming perennial that spreads vigorously by stolons, mock strawberry forms rosettes of three-leaflet evergreen leaves that resemble those of strawberries. Five-petaled yellow flowers appear from early to late summer and are followed by dry, tasteless, red berries. Plants spread vigorously and thrive in partial to full shade. They travel fastest in warmer zones. Zones 4 to 9.

6 *Euonymus fortunei.* Wintercreeper. Also called Japanese euonymus, this evergreen shrub or trailer densely covers the ground but also climbs trees, buildings, and other structures to a height of 50 or 60 feet. The species has dark green leaves with silver veins, and green-leaved cultivars are far more vigorous and more likely to become invasive than variegated cultivars, which have leaves patterned with yellow or white. Plants grow in sun to light shade. Zones 4 or 5 to 9.

7 *Euphorbia cyparissias.* Cypress spurge. An herbaceous perennial with blue-green, needlelike leaves, this species spreads vigorously via rhizomes and self-sown seeds. Plants bear showy, rounded clusters of yellow-green flowers from late spring or early summer through midsummer. They spread fastest in evenly moist soil, although they also tolerate drought. Zones 4 to 9.

Euonymus fortunei

8 *Fallopia japonica.* **Japanese fleeceflower.** Also called Japanese knotweed and formerly classified as *Polygonum cuspidatum,* this spreading, rhizomatous perennial is an invasive, vigorous thug that has been banned in several states. It engulfs everything in its path — boulders, small buildings, and abandoned cars. Plants grow in full sun to partial shade and any well-drained soil and are drought tolerant. Also invasive are its twining cousins *F. aubertii* (mile-a-minute or silver fleece vine, formerly *Polygonum aubertii* and *Bilderdykia aubertii*) and *F. baldschuanica* (mile-a-minute plant or Russian vine, formerly *P. baldschuanica* and *B. baldschuanica*), neither of which should be planted in gardens. Zones 3 to 10.

Lysimachia nummularia

Hedera helix

9 *Hedera helix.* **English ivy.** Adaptable and reliable, English ivy has earned its popularity, although it is often used when far less invasive species would make more interesting landscape additions. It provides reliable evergreen cover, thrives in sun or shade and very poor soil, and is inexpensive. The plants used as ground cover are the juvenile form, which has lobed leaves and climbs via aerial rootlets to 50 feet or more. Where English ivy has escaped or in overgrown gardens, it can entirely cover trees and buildings. The adult form is shrubby, with flowers and berries, and often appears at the tops of trees once the juvenile form can no longer climb. The species is most often grown, but many cultivars — some with both deeply cut and variegated leaves — are available. The cultivars are less vigorous than the species. Sap from the leaves can cause a rash similar to poison ivy or poison oak in some people. Zones 5 to 10. Hardiness of cultivars is variable; most are hardy only in Zones 6 or 7 to 10.

10 *Lysimachia nummularia.* **Creeping Jenny.** Also called creeping Charlie and moneywort, this rampantly spreading, weedy species bears round green leaves and yellow flowers in summer. It has naturalized widely in North America. Plants easily invade lawn areas in moist shade but can make an acceptable lawn grass substitute that tolerates some foot traffic. 'Aurea', with chartreuse leaves, is widely sold as a perennial ground cover. Zones 4 to 9. A well-behaved, ground-hugging relative, *L. japonica* 'Minutissima', is worth growing. It is about 1 inch tall and spreads to 1 foot; it is hardy in Zones 6 to 10 and also tolerates light foot traffic.

Phalaris arundinacea var. *picta*

11 *Phalaris arundinacea* var. *picta.* **Variegated ribbon grass.** This fast-spreading, wide-ranging grass features leaves striped green and white. Leaves reach 2 to 3 feet tall and often flop. Plants grow in partial shade and, spread by rhizomes, form broad drifts that will overwhelm most perennials. Plants that revert to all-green leaves are especially invasive. Zones 4 to 9.

12 *Vinca* spp. **Periwinkles, vincas.** Vigorous and fast creeping, these popular ground covers are formidable spreaders that can become very invasive. While useful for holding soil on shady slopes, cascading over walls, and filling shady waste places, unsupervised plantings will escape the garden and blanket woodlands and other areas, crowding out native plants. If you decide to use them, grow them on sites with physical boundaries or trim the edges often to keep the plants in place. Both species have creeping, vinelike stems that form mats of roots and a dense weed-smothering cover that tolerates occasional foot traffic.

Vinca major. **Big-leaved periwinkle.** Although the all-green species is seldom grown, variegated forms of this species are very popular. Plants range from 8 to 18 inches tall and have pale blue, trumpet-shaped, 2-inch-wide flowers from spring to fall. The leaves

Vinca minor

on variegated selections are green marked with pale green, yellow-green, cream, or white. They are evergreen in warm to mild climates. Zones 7 to 11.

Vinca minor. **Common or dwarf periwinkle, myrtle.** This popular 6- to 12-inch-tall species is grown for its glossy dark green leaves and 1-inch-wide, purple or violet, trumpet-shaped flowers, which are borne primarily in spring and early summer, although plants bloom intermittently to fall. Cultivars with variegated leaves spread less invasively than all-green forms. Zones 4 to 9.

Picking Your Battles

It may sound like heresy, and it certainly requires an attitude adjustment for most gardeners, but some weeds may be a viable ground cover option, at least temporarily. If it's not the best time of year to plant, or if you don't have the money to install or the time to tend a new planting, think twice before pulling up a lush patch of weeds. That drift of ground ivy (*Glechoma hederacea*), also called gill-over-the-ground, along the driveway may be a common lawn weed, but leave it be if the site is fairly far down on your garden to-do list. Weeds don't require any care whatsoever

and also tolerate periodic mowing or trimming (both good options for keeping more aggressive species in check while you wait to replace them), protect the soil, withstand foot traffic, and tolerate whatever shortcomings the site has to offer. Plus, they add free color and texture for the time being. Sure, pull them up when you have the time to plant something better, but for now, what's not to like — or at least tolerate?

Weigh the pros and cons before using weeds as temporary ground covers. Do they create lush cover? Are they behaving themselves? Site conditions may determine your course of action. In rich, moist soil, ground ivy, which belongs to the mint family, is a serious lawn invader. It is fairly shallow rooted, though, and relatively easy to pull up in most sites.

Other weeds may be suitable for temporary ground cover service. These include mock strawberry (*Duchesnea indica*), a mat-forming perennial native to India that has naturalized in North America. It spreads rapidly and indefinitely by stolons but is fairly easy to pull where not wanted. Tolerant of light foot traffic, mowing, and drought, mock strawberry is happiest in light shade, but tolerates full sun if the soil is moist.

The European native *Lysimachia nummularia*, commonly called creeping Jenny, creeping Charlie, or moneywort, also may fit into the "tolerate" category. While its gold-leaved strain, 'Aurea', is a popular perennial, the green-leaved species is considered a lawn weed. Both spread quickly in damp, rich soil and moderate shade.

Whatever weeds you decide to tolerate as temporary ground covers, keep a close eye on them. Otherwise, before you know it they'll take over the garden. For taller-growing weeds, it's a good idea to mow or cut down plants just as the flowers fade to keep them from setting seed. Other than that, an occasional session of ripping out excess plants that have spread beyond their appointed bounds may be all it takes to maintain a neat, green carpet as long as you want it to be there.

COVERING GROUND WITH HARDSCAPE

Sometimes, the best option for covering the ground isn't a ground cover at all. For sitting areas, on walkways, and in areas where the conditions are simply too difficult to get plants established, hardscaping may be the best alternative. "Hardscape" is a general term for all the nonliving parts of a landscape, including paved surfaces such as terraces and walkways, plus walls, curbs, stairs, and the like. For replacing lawn or ground cover, suitable hardscape materials include bricks, precast pavers, flagstones, gravel, concrete, and ground-level decking. All are handsome, practical options for surfacing a terrace or walkway where durable, level footing is important.

One of the obvious advantages of hardscaping is reduced maintenance. The savings in upkeep is especially great on sites where compacted soil and other problems caused by high traffic make it very difficult to care for lawn and other plants growing (or trying to grow) on such sites. Installing hardscape completely eliminates the headaches of trying to garden where growing conditions are far from optimum. With or without compacted soil, hardscaping also is an excellent option for sitting areas. While chairs arranged on the lawn are handsome to look at, hardscaped flooring (or simply mulch) is a more practical option, since moving chairs every week to mow around them is time consuming. In addition to easing maintenance, hardscaping also makes it easy to get out into the garden with dry feet even after a rain, when lawn grass is wet.

Replacing lawns and other plantings that require regular irrigation with hardscape also helps reduce water use, especially in hot, dry climates, where a lawn must be watered frequently to keep it green. In fact, hardscape plays an essential feature in landscapes that employ water-conserving features, called xeriscapes. Although xeriscaping was developed to help reduce water usage in the western United States, water-saving principles — such as replacing lawn with hardscape or drought-tolerant ground covers — make sense for gardeners throughout North America.

Whether you live in an area where hot, dry weather is the norm — and summertime watering restrictions are common — or you just want to reduce the amount of water necessary to keep your lawn lush and green, consider using a combination of drought-tolerant plants and hardscape to cover ground.

Stepping-stones planted with low-growing thymes (*Thymus* spp.) create a lush, colorful, drought-tolerant walkway.

Hardscape and plants work together in this garden to create an appealing outdoor living space. The brick squares, set in sand to minimize damage to the trees, are combined with gravel and a wealth of low-growing plants to cover ground.

Hardscape Style

Well-designed terraces and walkways add more than just practical, low-maintenance footing to your landscape. Whether you choose elegant brick or flagstone, opt for practical concrete pavers, or use a combination of materials, hardscaping adds style and appeal to any landscape. In the overall design of a garden, hardscape terraces and walkways not only pave the garden floor, but they also function as a solid horizontal plane that sets off vertical elements such as specimen plants, flower beds, container gardens, and sculpture — just as a lawn or beds of ground covers do. From a design standpoint, an expanse of thickly spread mulch functions perfectly well as a paved area.

Hardscaped terraces and walkways can be as simple or as complex as you want. They can add rich detail to a landscape, such as a brick or flagstone terrace does, but even terraces and walkways that have a very simple, plain design — such as poured concrete or raked gravel — are appealing when they are surrounded by plants spilling over the edges and accented with outdoor furniture, container gardens, sculpture, or other features. If you have room for a large terrace, consider breaking it up with beds of ground covers or higher-maintenance annuals or perennials. Or combine more than one type of hardscape — areas of brick and gravel, for example. For an even more integrated approach, combine hardscaping with ground covers that tolerate some foot traffic. Either plant ground covers in the joints between bricks or other pavers or let plants from adjoining beds self-sow in the joints or into gravel. Stick with choices that thrive in the amount of rainfall your garden normally receives to create an area that needs no supplemental watering.

Hardscaping also can be a focal point, rather than just a foil for plants. For a one-of-a-kind installation, consider a pebble-and-stone mosaic set in mortar, or combine flagstones with brick or concrete pavers to create an attractive pattern. Before getting started, consult garden construction and design books, do research on the Internet, or get help from a landscape expert so you make the right decisions and install terraces, walkways, and other hardscape elements correctly so they will be as durable and long lasting as possible.

Keep in mind that hardscape is low maintenance, not no maintenance. Landscape features such as terraces and walkways require regular sweeping or raking, plus snow removal and other housekeeping care. Hardscape also doesn't cool the air the way plants do as they release moisture from their leaves, and depending on its color, it reflects or absorbs heat.

Planning for Durable Flooring

All good hardscape installations — whether simple or complex — take planning. One reason preparation is so important is that hardscape features are permanent, or nearly so. Even an area of raked gravel is difficult to move once it's been spread in the garden, so it pays to plan and make sure the gravel is dumped in the right place the first time. Most hardscapes require heavy machinery for delivery of materials as well as for grading and installation, whether you have them installed by experts or rent the equipment and do the work yourself. Because planting beds and lawn don't compete well with tractors and graders, it's best to install hardscape first or plan ahead and move choice plants out of harm's way before installation begins.

Early in the planning process, be sure to consult local building and zoning codes. Hardscaping often requires a building permit and many times falls under local as well as neighborhood codes and restrictions on setback, materials, and stormwater handling. The percentages of permeable and impermeable surfaces on your property may also be regulated, because of their affect on the

ORDERING MATERIALS

TO ORDER GRAVEL AND SAND for underlaying hardscaping, first take the depth of the layer you'd like to add (in inches) and divide by 12 to convert it to feet.

For example, a 3-inch layer is .25 feet (3 ÷ 12).

Then multiply that times the surface area of the terrace (length × width) and divide by 27, which is the number of cubic feet in a cubic yard.

For example, a 3-inch-deep layer of sand for a 15 × 15-foot terrace requires about 2 cubic yards: .25 feet × (15 × 15 feet) ÷ 27 = 2.08 cubic yards.

For a circular terrace, multiply the radius (distance from the edge to the center) by itself, then multiply that by pi (3.14) and divide by 27. For example, a circular terrace with a radius of 5 feet requires 2.9 cubic yards of sand: (5 feet × 5 feet) × 3.14 ÷ 27 = 2.9 cubic yards.

For a free-form shape, divide the area into a series of circles and rectangles, then figure out the requirement for each area, add them together, and round up. (In any situation, it's a good idea to round up when ordering to allow for spillage.)

Subtle textural contrast makes this hardscape combination interesting. Smooth bluestone pavers are set against rougher Belgian block edging, which has been planted with low-growing thyme (*Thymus serpyllum* 'Elfin').

Permeable paving makes it possible to grow grass or ground covers on sites where vehicles occasionally park. The pavers protect plant crowns and let water percolate into the soil.

map to experiment with shapes. A variety of landscape design programs that run on a computer are another option.

While a map makes it easier to work out the design on paper, many gardeners skip this step and experiment with shapes right in the garden. If you are this kind of planner — or once you have a pleasing design on your scale drawing — mark it out right in the garden. Use stakes and string for geometric shapes, or a garden hose to experiment with free-form designs. Then experiment with the shape you are considering. Stand on the "terrace" and arrange chairs in the space. Is the area large enough?

In general, terraces, walkways, and other outdoor living spaces need to be larger than corresponding indoor spaces, since they're measured visually against the spaces in the larger landscape. A 12-by-12-foot terrace may seem large on paper, but if it's set against a large lawn or shaded by a 75-foot-tall tree, it will look puny. Also consider the space furniture requires: A square table for two needs a 6-by-8-foot space, while a large table for eight requires at least 8 by 12 feet. Add people, a grill, and other furniture, and you'll quickly realize that larger is better when it comes to outdoor spaces. Even if you can't install a terrace that's the perfect size now, plan for one in your design. There are ways to cut costs and/or install hardscaping over several years to spread out the cost and time commitment. See Selecting Materials on page 61 for more on phasing in a project.

The stakes-and-string technique works well for laying out a walkway or work area as well. If visitors are to be able to walk side by side, a walkway should be 5 to 6 feet wide. For smaller garden paths, 3½ to 4 feet is a minimum if a garden cart is the work vehicle of choice. Wheelbarrows need less space — a minimum of about 1½ or 2 feet. If the site will be an outdoor work area used by car-crazy mechanics, make sure there is adequate space for cars, tools, and people. Whatever the planned activity, if the new space isn't large enough, you'll just be moving your gardening problems, not solving them.

amount of water that runs off into storm drains. This would affect the choice between permeable gravel and impermeable concrete, for example.

Start your plan by drawing a map to scale. Draw the entire landscape, or at least the area where you are planning the installation. Be sure to locate buried cables, pipes, and other features on your drawing that may be affected by the installation. The easiest way to experiment with designs is to draw your scale map on graph paper, and then use tracing paper overlays on top of that

Selecting Materials

Try to match the type of material to the style of the house and garden. Look for materials that will blend: a brick terrace with a brick house, or a free-form concrete terrace set with pebbles for a more informal house. Durability is important as well; otherwise hardscaping will not be worth the expense. Finally, compare the cost of various materials, including installation. Hardscaping materials such as flagstone, precast pavers, and bricks are available new at garden centers, big-box stores, and stone retailers. You can also recycle materials from building sites and buy used materials — bricks, for example — from some retailers. Finally, don't overlook combining materials. If a brick patio is too expensive, or not the style you are looking for, consider poured concrete with brick edging. Or combine flagstone with raked gravel.

If price is a concern, there are various ways to cut costs on hardscaping. Installation often is a significant part of the cost: you can do all of the work yourself, or do some of the work. Installing over several years is another option. With a brick terrace, for example, have a contractor grade the site, install edging, and spread the underlying sand and pack it down; then install the bricks yourself on your own schedule. With a concrete terrace, you could grade and frame the site yourself, spread the underlying gravel, and then have a professional deliver and pour the concrete.

Whether you do all the work or just some of it, keep in mind that saving physical labor is important. A cubic yard of sand (used to set brick) weighs about 10 tons, so getting it delivered as close as possible to the work site really pays. Also investigate rental equipment that will make the job easier. It's possible to rent trailers to haul materials as well as cement mixers, tampers, and more at big-box stores or local equipment rental suppliers.

It's best not to cut costs on the drainage layers under hardscaping, because they can have a significant effect on the durability and life of whatever you install. A standard recommendation is 3 inches of packed gravel topped by 1 inch of sand, but consult local experts or your Cooperative Extension Service for recommendations in your area because the depth varies according to how cold it is in winter (frost heaving is a major destroyer of hardscaping). Mortared terraces and walkways are typically set on top of concrete to prevent heaving and cracking; however, a thick, well-packed gravel bed can provide a footing that is durable enough. In poorly drained sites use an extra-thick layer of gravel to prevent damage.

Set walkways and terraces slightly aboveground so that water drains off the surface quickly and won't pool on top of them. Also construct them with a slight crown in the center to keep water draining away quickly. For example, for a 5- or 6-foot-wide walkway, make the center 1 inch taller than the sides.

Simple details can make hardscape installations especially appealing. Here, ajuga (*Ajuga reptans* 'Burgundy Glow') and lawn grass soften the edges between courses of brick.

The various hardscaping materials all have pluses and minuses. Before deciding on which ones to use, consider not only cost but also how easy they are to work with and the finished look.

CONCRETE. Versatile and inexpensive, concrete is a mix of portland cement, water, and an aggregate such as sand or gravel. Whether you want to cast a few stepping-stones or an entire patio, well-mixed ingredients are essential for success. Bags of premixed concrete are fine for small projects such as pouring stepping-stones, but for larger projects it pays to purchase the ingredients separately and mix them yourself. You also can prepare the site and frame it yourself and either rent a mixer or purchase premixed, ready-to-pour concrete and have it delivered.

Adequate drying time is also essential. That's because concrete owes its strength and durability to a chemical reaction that binds the ingredients together. If it dries out too quickly, the reaction stops and the concrete never attains its proper strength. Covering damp concrete with plastic is one way to keep it damp enough so it has enough time to cure properly. To find other options, consult a book on garden construction or consult the Internet. The basic rule: the slower concrete dries, the stronger it is.

If you don't like the idea of an expanse of plain white concrete in your backyard — or already have one you don't enjoy looking at — consider coloring it. You can buy pigments to incorporate when mixing the concrete or other products to stain concrete that is already cured. You can also stamp or texture concrete while it is still wet. For example, push pebbles into poured concrete, spray it with a hose, and use a stiff-bristled push broom to expose them. You can buy patterns for stamping concrete, or you can make your own pattern simply by drawing a broom over the surface of the concrete while it's still wet. You can also rehabilitate an old concrete terrace or walkway by resurfacing it.

Concrete terraces and other installations usually are poured all at one time, but with a simple design modification, they can be installed gradually on your own schedule. Frame a shallow box, either rectangular or square, with rot-resistant wood, fill it with concrete, and let it cure. Leave the framing in place once the concrete dries — it becomes a decorative element. You can frame the entire terrace at one time, or construct forms and pour sections of concrete as time allows.

DECKING. For replacing lawn or covering another site where compacted soil makes gardening difficult, a deck that is only a couple of inches off the ground makes a fine choice. One big advantage of a deck is that, unlike a flagstone or brick terrace, it can be installed almost anywhere, regardless of

how level the ground is. A ground-level deck is set on footers, just like a conventional deck, and is constructed of wood or recycled plastic wood. If the deck is truly right on the ground, handrails are probably optional, but consult local zoning and building requirements. Decks can be designed and installed around trees too. To avoid damaging the tree, modify the design to accommodate the roots and trunk by adjusting the position of the footers and stringers. If you are using a contractor, be sure to hire one who has experience building decks around trees without harming them.

Modular decking squares are another option. They are less expensive than a conventional deck but don't last as long. For the longest life, set the decking squares on a 2- or 3-inch-thick bed of packed sand and gravel to keep moisture away from the wood. Be aware that any kind of wood decking in shady, moist areas may have more problems with rot and algae, and moss will grow on the wood and make it slippery.

FLAGSTONES AND PAVERS. Bluestone, limestone, granite, sandstone, and shale are the main types of natural rock used for terraces, walkways, and other hardscape elements. The most popular material varies from region to region and generally depends on local availability. If limestone is mined in your area, it will be a more popular and less expensive choice than granite, for example. It's

also wise to consider stone types based on their surface texture. Some kinds of stone — slate, for instance — become slippery when wet.

Flagstones are sold in random, free-form sizes or sawed into squares or rectangles. If you like jigsaw puzzles, consider using random sizes; otherwise buy flagstones that have been cut into regular shapes. Another option is to create a pattern with some large flagstones combined with smaller ones for added texture and interest. The stones can be cut with curved or square edges to create a terrace or walkway of nearly any shape.

Although flagstones can be laid directly on soil, a layer of sand makes it easier to level them and helps water drain away. For a permanent, long-lasting installation, a full drainage layer of gravel and sand is best. Buy flagstones that are at least 1½ to 2 inches thick. Thinner ones will crack unless they are bedded in concrete.

Concrete and precast pavers, which cost less than natural stone, are extremely popular too; many new types and colors are widely available today. In areas with mild winters, terra-cotta and ceramic tiles also make handsome, long-lasting hardscape ground coverings.

It's easy to combine plants with flagstones or pavers: Just intersperse beds into the pattern by leaving out pavers. Once the hardscape installation is finished, improve the soil in the beds and put in the ground cover plants.

(Left) Consider using different types of surfaces to create pathways. In this garden, the main path is constructed of wood slats, while a mulched path edged with brick offers access across the garden.

(Right) This area covered by paving squares interplanted with thyme (*Thymus* sp.) could serve as a pathway, a terrace that gets only occasional foot traffic, or simply a low-maintenance garden accent.

Walkways, Terraces & Play Areas

Mulch and gravel are two popular materials for covering the ground along walkways and for creating informal terraces.

The best way to install gravel as a garden flooring is to start by framing the area. This keeps the gravel in place and discourages grass from migrating into the area. Use brick, wood, or a specially made framing system. For a really firm footing, cover the area with 3 inches of pulverized stone and pack it down with a roller to make an underlayment. Top the pulverized stone with 1 to 2 inches of larger gravel. Another option is to spread a 4- to 6-inch-deep layer of larger stone, compact it, and cover the larger stone with smaller gravel. Either way, compact the final layer.

For a walkway or informal terrace that is mulched with shredded bark or wood chips, plan on replenishing the mulch annually. If desired, use edging strips to keep the mulch in place, as recommended for gravel. If the site is damp, remove the sod (if you're building in a lawn) along with the top inch or so of topsoil, then spread an inch or two of gravel over the site and cover the gravel with mulch. This keeps the area drier and helps wood mulch last longer. For added weed protection, after removing the sod and topsoil, add either a thick layer of newspaper or a layer of cardboard before spreading the gravel. Or use plastic sheeting, with holes punched through the plastic every few inches to allow rainwater to drain away, under the gravel.

Mulch is a better option than grass under children's play equipment. As well as making mowing and trimming unnecessary, a thick (up to 12-inch) layer of mulch softens the ground to help cushion falls. Shredded bark and pea gravel are popular choices, or consider the new rubber mulches, which are made from recycled tires. Be sure to buy a rubber mulch labeled for playground use. Rubber mats also are available. (Note that although rubber mulch may be marketed as a long-lasting substitute for bark mulch, it isn't a good choice for planting beds: It is inorganic and adds no organic matter to the soil. It also won't biodegrade, as mulch will, so if you change your mind about where it has been spread, you'll have to remove it. For these reasons, an organic mulch is a superior choice for beds of ground covers.)

If you want to add interest to an expanse of gravel, consider setting in pavers, using more than one color or size of gravel, or getting creative! This stepping-stone is a circle of chain set in gravel.

PERMEABLE OR GRID PAVERS. Also called perforated pavers, these are an excellent option for covering sites that are occasionally used by vehicles. Since the pavers are permeable and water percolates down through them, they also are a good choice for managing storm water and reducing water runoff. Grid pavers are made of concrete or recycled plastic, which is especially useful on uneven sites. Use them for driveways, overflow parking areas, work areas, places where vehicles or boats are stored, golf cart paths, pool decks, and any spots that are driven on occasionally. The pavers are set in a layer of sand, and the perforations can be filled with gravel or a mix of soil and sand and planted with grass or a ground cover. Areas covered with permeable pavers can be mowed with a conventional lawn mower or cut with a string trimmer.

BRICK. Elegant and classic, brick is also very adaptable. It is easy to use as an edging or to construct a straight walkway or a rectangular or square terrace. With a little ingenuity, you can use bricks to form handsome arcs, curves, and circles, as well as a variety of different patterns. The various types of bricks have different textures and come in a few colors. Paving-grade bricks are best for areas where frost heaving is a fact of life. Recycled bricks — either purchased or gleaned from a building site or other installation — are another popular option. In frost-free climates, bricks can be laid directly on the ground, but they usually wear better and are easier to lay in a flat, uniform surface if they are set on a layer of sand at least 2 inches deep. Use 3 or 4 inches of crushed gravel under the sand if the site is damp or the drainage poor. Bricks can be dry laid (without mortar) or set in mortar.

Bricks vary in size, so measure your site carefully and plan accordingly. If you want a running pattern, with bricks set end to end, brick length won't matter much, but length does matter if you decide on a basket weave or a herringbone pattern. In that case, the width of the bricks must be exactly half their length or the pattern won't work out properly.

Whether used to create a walkway, terrace, or driveway, brick is an elegant paving option. Here, a planting of mountain laurel (*Kalmia latifolia*) combined with perennials softens the edge of the brick and a timber holds the bricks in place.

HARDSCAPING UNDER TREES

SINCE BRICK and many other types of hardscaping require several inches of drainage material for proper installation, they are not good choices for covering the ground under trees, because installing them will damage roots. Raked gravel is one option for hardscaping under a tree, since it allows water to penetrate and provides excellent drainage but doesn't require mowing, although it will eventually need weeding. Gravel is also a superb choice for flooring in an informal sitting area, especially since lawn chairs or other furniture can stay put all summer. On the lawn, they'd have to be moved with every mowing.

Ground-level decks are another option for creating hardscape without damaging trees. See Decking on page 62 for more information.

DECIDING EXACTLY WHICH plant — or plants — to grow in a particular site is one of the biggest challenges in selecting ground covers. Matching the plants to the site conditions is the best place to start. Once you know how much sun or shade a site receives, and what kind of soil it has, you can select ground covers that will thrive there. Matching plant to site is especially important for low-maintenance plantings like ground covers. That's because plants well suited to a site will grow well in the soil as it is and will thrive in the exposure and moisture that's naturally available — all without extra effort from you.

In this section of the book, you'll find lists of ground covers with particular traits or for particular sites, as well as those adapted to certain growing conditions. Keep in mind that most

Also, remember to consult local gardeners and visit nearby gardens, both public and private. Looking at local gardens helps you determine which ground covers grow best in your area and the types of sites they need. You'll also see interesting new ways to use ground covers, including ideas for combining different ones in a single planting. Plus, you'll be able to determine which species are thuglike spreaders in your area, which can be managed with a bit of extra attention, which are perfectly well behaved, and which struggle to survive. The descriptions in this section indicate how fast each species spreads, but the rate varies depending on the site and the climate, so local information is invaluable. (Those marked with a "Think Twice" icon can be seriously aggressive or even invasive in some areas, so it's particularly important to

Matching plant to site is especially important for low-maintenance plantings like ground covers.

plants are much more flexible and adaptable than plant lists would indicate. Experiment with a plant or two of each species you would like to grow and see if it thrives in a particular site before investing in enough plants to cover the site. Or buy a few plants and start propagating your own to cover a site with a minimal investment. You'll find propagation suggestions for each species and directions for each technique in Growing Your Own, beginning on page 203.

do further research if you're considering adding any of them to your garden.)

These plant descriptions also indicate whether a species is native to some part of North America. Sticking with species that are native to your area is a good way to ensure that ground covers will thrive in the conditions naturally available in your garden. See Native Carpets on page 47 for more on selecting plants native to your area.

Perfect Plants for Every Site
2

Active Spreaders
for Sun & Shade

Ground covers that fill spaces in the garden with a thick, lush blanket of foliage and flowers are invaluable for covering all manner of sites, for crowding out weeds, and for reducing garden maintenance.

The best ground covers live to spread, and the plants on these pages are no exception. All are vigorous and adaptable and will cover the ground with a thick, handsome blanket of foliage. While their roots may cruise out to occupy unconquered areas, physical barriers such as walkways, along with stretches of mown lawn, generally keep them in check. Most are fairly easy to dig and either move or discard, unlike more rampant species, which can be tough to eradicate once established.

Be aware that some of these active spreaders can escape and invade wild areas (particularly those with the "Think Twice" designation). After all, they're ground covers, and spreading is what they do best. So, don't plant them along the edges of woods or other uncultivated areas. Also avoid discarding plants or plant parts that are still alive in compost piles. Instead, put them in the trash or leave them in the sun until thoroughly dry and dead before turning them into compost.

1. *Fragaria* 'Pink Panda'
   Strawberry

2. *Leymus arenarius*
   Blue lyme grass

3. *Rubus rolfei* 'Emerald Carpet'
   Creeping bramble

4. *Hosta* 'Francee'
   Hosta

5. *Galium odoratum*
   Sweet woodruff

6. *Convallaria majalis*
   Lily-of-the-valley

7. *Lamium galeobdolon*
   'Hermann's Pride'
   Yellow archangel

8. *Pleioblastus auricomus*
   Reed bamboo

9. *Viola odorata*
   Sweet violet

10. *Indigofera kirilowii*
    Kirilow indigo

Ceratostigma plumbaginoides
Plumbago, leadwort

EXPOSURE: Full sun to partial shade
HEIGHT: 6 to 10 inches
SPREAD: Indefinite

Tough, long lived, and vigorous, plumbago is a handsome, underused, woody-based perennial ground cover. Plants produce mounds of rounded, bright green leaves topped with brilliant gentian blue, five-petaled flowers from midsummer to fall. The foliage is semievergreen, and new leaves emerge late in spring. The red fall foliage is simply outstanding. Plants are adaptable and grow in any well-drained soil. Use plumbago for filling in under trees and shrubs in island beds, as an edging plant, or even in parking lot islands. This species can be an aggressive spreader, so keep it away from less vigorous perennials. Dig plants on the edges of the clump in spring or fall to propagate. Zones 5 or 6 to 9.

Convallaria majalis ▼
Lily-of-the-valley

EXPOSURE: Full sun to full shade
HEIGHT: 9 to 12 inches
SPREAD: Indefinite

Beloved for its fragrant blooms, this tough, wide-spreading perennial produces pairs of deciduous, 6- to 8-inch-long, ovate leaves. Arching clusters of tiny, pendent, bell-shaped, white flowers are produced in spring and are followed by poisonous red berries. Plants spread via branching rhizomes, often called pips. They grow in most soils but spread fastest in rich, moist conditions. They also survive drought but need water in dry weather or the leaves turn brown. This species is an aggressive spreader in colder zones but grows much more slowly in the South (Zones 7 and 8), where the plants require partial shade and moist soil to survive the heat. 'Fortin's Giant' is a vigorous selection with broad leaves that reaches a foot tall. To propagate lily-of-the-valley, divide plants in fall. Zones 2 to 8.

Fragaria spp.
Strawberries

EXPOSURE: Full sun to light shade
HEIGHT: 4 to 12 inches
SPREAD: Indefinite

Several strawberries make fine ground covers and are especially effective combined with other low-growing plants to fill in areas along pathways or to cover ground as a lawn substitute. Plants bear three-leaflet leaves and spread indefinitely by stolons. Although they are able to withstand some drought, they prefer rich, moist, well-drained soil with a neutral to somewhat alkaline pH. Propagate by potting up plantlets that appear at the end of stolons.

F. 'Pink Panda'. This vigorous, 4- to 6-inch-tall cultivar is primarily grown for its bright pink flowers, which appear from late spring through mid autumn. Plants seldom produce fruit. 'Pink Panda' is an aggressive spreader. 'Red Ruby' is a similar but newer selection with deep rose-pink flowers and small edible fruit. Zones 5 to 9.

F. vesca. ▼ European or woodland strawberry. This species is about 6 to 8 inches tall and bears clusters of small white flowers with five petals in late spring. Flowers are followed by edible red fruit. 'Albacarpa' bears white fruit. Zones 5 to 9.

F. virginiana. Wild or Virginia strawberry. Native to eastern North America, this wide-spreading perennial also makes an attractive ground cover. Plants are 4 to 12 inches tall and bear clusters of white flowers in early spring and summer. The flowers are followed by tasty red fruit. Zones 5 to 9.

Ceratostigma plumbaginoides

▼ May be considered invasive in some regions.

Galium odoratum
Sweet woodruff, bedstraw

EXPOSURE: Partial to full shade
HEIGHT: 6 to 10 inches
SPREAD: Indefinite

This rhizomatous perennial bears whorls of narrow, rich green leaves topped by clusters of tiny, starry white flowers that are lightly fragrant. Sweet woodruff brings a lovely, delicate fern-like texture to the shade garden, but its constitution is far from delicate. Plants spread vigorously and indefinitely and can cover medium to large areas even in dense shade. They will engulf less vigorous perennial bed companions but are handsome filling in under large perennials as well as trees and shrubs. Plant sweet woodruff in evenly moist soil. In hot, humid summer weather, plantings tend to die back: shear or mow them down if they become unattractive. Propagate by dividing plants in spring or fall. Zones 4 to 8.

Hosta hybrids
Hostas

EXPOSURE: Partial to full shade
HEIGHT: 2 inches to 3 feet
SPREAD: 6 inches to 4 feet or more

Most hostas are clump forming, although a few species do spread by rhizomes. Nevertheless, vigorous cultivars spread fairly quickly and warrant a place on this list. 'Francee', with dark green, white-edged leaves and pale lavender flowers in summer is one fast-spreading cultivar; established clumps can be 3 feet across, and the foliage mound ranges from 1½ to 2 feet tall. See page 152 for a list of cultivars that can be used as ground covers. Use hostas as edgings or for filling in under trees and shrubs, alone or combined with other moderate

Galium odoratum with *Betula jacquemontii* and irises

spreaders. To build your hosta collection quickly, look for overcrowded pots and divide clumps at planting time, spacing out individual crowns, which will fill in. Hostas thrive in rich, well-drained soil but grow in nearly any soil and also tolerate constantly wet conditions, provided the crowns are set above water level. They can tolerate drought, especially if kept mulched, but the foliage suffers in very dry weather. Divide clumps in spring or fall to propagate. Zones 3 to 8.

Hosta 'Francee'

Hypericum calycinum
Creeping St. John's wort

EXPOSURE: Full sun to partial shade
HEIGHT: 1 to 1½ feet
SPREAD: Indefinite

Also commonly called Aaron's beard, rose-of-Sharon, and gold flower, this is a dwarf, semievergreen or evergreen shrub that spreads widely and vigorously by underground runners. It has rounded, dark green leaves and from midsummer into fall produces showy, 3- to 4-inch-wide, five-petaled flowers featuring a large boss of golden stamens in the center. Shear plants every few years to keep them looking neat. Top growth may be killed back in winter in Zone 6, and the foliage can be damaged by summer heat and drought. In warmer climates, plants are best in partial shade. Use this species in large dramatic drifts, as an edging in contained areas, or to hold soil on slopes. Divide clumps in spring or fall to propagate or take cuttings in spring or summer. Zones 6 to 10.

Indigofera kirilowii
Kirilow indigo

EXPOSURE: Full sun
HEIGHT: 1½ to 3 feet
SPREAD: 3 to 4 feet

A suckering shrub or subshrub, this species forms a dense clump of soft-textured, pinnate foliage, with leaflets arranged in a fernlike fashion. It bears dense, 5-inch-long racemes of small, rose-pink, pealike flowers from early to midsummer. Use this species as a ground cover for large areas. Plants thrive in rich, well-drained, loamy soil, from acid to slightly alkaline, although they grow in any slightly moist soil. They do not tolerate drought well. Plants benefit from light shade in the South. Cut back to live wood in late winter, or simply mow down plantings at that time to keep them neat looking. In the North, plants may be killed to the ground in winter, but flowers are produced on new wood, so pruning or

dieback does not eliminate them. Propagate by cuttings in spring or summer. Zones 6 to 9. The closely related *I. tinctoria* 'Rose Carpet', hardy in Zones 5 to 8, bears pealike rose-pink flowers in midsummer. Plants reach 2 feet and spread as far.

Juniperus spp.
Junipers

EXPOSURE: Full sun
HEIGHT: 1 to 60 feet or more
SPREAD: 1 to 20 feet

Most ground-covering junipers have spreading horizontal stems, although some selections are low-growing, mounded forms of full-size trees. Tough and adaptable, junipers provide valuable evergreen cover for sunny, dry sites. Use them to clothe slopes or flat areas. They grow in any well-drained soil and are fairly easy to keep in bounds by pruning. Plants withstand drought but need good air circulation in areas with hot,

humid, rainy summers. Several species are native to North America. See page 140 for more on these hardworking ground covers. They are best purchased as container-grown plants rather than propagated. Zones 2 to 9.

Lamium galeobdolon ▼
Yellow archangel

EXPOSURE: Partial to full shade
HEIGHT: 1 to 1½ feet
SPREAD: Indefinite

Formerly *Lamiastrum galeobdolon,* this herbaceous perennial spreads quickly by both rhizomes and stolons. It has toothed green leaves and small clusters of two-lipped yellow flowers in summer. Yellow archangel tolerates most soils but spreads quickest in rich, moist loam; it is not drought tolerant. It can be an aggressive spreader but may be useful for covering the ground in dense shade. 'Hermann's Pride', which features silver-streaked leaves and yellow flowers, is a clump-forming selection and is less vigorous than the species. 'Compactum' also is smaller and less rampant than the species. Keep yellow archangel away from other, less vigorous plants, which it will smother, and avoid planting it along wooded areas or on other sites where it can escape the garden. To propagate, divide clumps in spring or fall, or take cuttings any time during the growing season. Zones 4 to 8.

Leymus arenarius
Blue lyme grass

EXPOSURE: Full sun to light shade
HEIGHT: 1 to 1½ feet
SPREAD: Indefinite

This fast-spreading grass boasts arching, evergreen leaves that are gray-green. Plants range from 3 to 4 feet in bloom,

Indigofera kirilowii

▼ May be considered invasive in some regions.

but the foliage mound is generally much shorter. Blue lyme grass spreads by rhizomes, and where unrestrained, it can become an aggressive spreader. Use it only on sites with barriers that will contain the wandering roots, such as islands in parking lots, the space between street and sidewalk, or beds along foundations. Plants grow in sandy soil — they are ideal for holding slopes, including dunes — and are fairly salt tolerant. They also can be substituted for lawn grass and tolerate mowing and some foot traffic. Plants also tolerate heat, poor soil, and drought. Because this is a cool-season grass, growth slows in summer. Mow plantings back after flowering to keep them neat. Propagate by dividing the clumps any time from spring through fall. Zones 4 to 9.

Pachysandra terminalis ▼
Japanese pachysandra

EXPOSURE: Light to full shade
HEIGHT: 6 to 12 inches
SPREAD: Indefinite

This popular evergreen ground cover spreads quickly via underground stems to form a thick mat of glossy, coarsely toothed leaves. Small clusters of tiny white flowers appear in early summer. Consider Japanese pachysandra for medium to large shady sites — the species grows in light to dense shade, but morning sun and afternoon shade are fine as well. Plants grow in nearly any well-drained soil, are fairly drought tolerant, and can cover the ground under trees and shrubs or hold the soil on shady slopes. These vigorous to aggressive spreaders can be combined with robust perennials such as large hostas and ferns, but avoid locations where they may creep into nearby natural areas.

Pachysandra terminalis 'Variegata'

'Variegata', with white-edged leaves, is much slower growing than the species and can be used with other perennials or as a ground cover in a smaller area. Compact 'Green Carpet' spreads more slowly than the species and has darker, shinier green leaves. 'Green Sheen', also a slower spreader, is more drought tolerant than the species and has waxy, very glossy dark green leaves. To propagate all forms, divide plants in spring or fall or take cuttings any time. Zones 4 to 8.

Pleioblastus spp.
Reed bamboos

EXPOSURE: Full sun to partial shade
HEIGHT: 6 inches to 3 feet
SPREAD: Indefinite

Bamboos are notorious spreaders, and while the members of this genus spread by rhizomes and travel fairly widely, the various species listed here are not as invasive as some bamboos. Nevertheless, you need to keep them in check by planting them where physical barriers, such as broad expanses of paving or mowed turf, will control their spread. (Some dedicated bamboo growers dig around their plants annually or every couple of years to keep them under control.) All are more invasive in warmer climates — Zones 9 to 11 — than they are

Pleioblastus auricomus

in the North. You may consider them for large areas where they can be put to work holding soil. They also can be planted around ponds or along streams, but the roots rot in wet soil, so site them above water line in rich, moist, well-drained conditions. Variegated forms require full sun, while green-leaved plants can be grown in partial shade. To propagate, divide clumps in spring, and keep the divisions constantly moist until they are established. Take rhizome cuttings in fall, cover them with 3 inches of soil, and keep them moist and warm until small plantlets appear.

Among the dwarf species that can make fine ground covers is golden-striped bamboo (*P. viridistriatus*), with yellow leaves striped with green; it averages 1½ to 2½ feet tall and is hardy in Zones 6 to 11. *Pleioblastus humilis*, sometimes called dwarf bamboo, is a green-leaved, 2½-foot-tall species. *Pleioblastus humilis* var. *pumilus* is more vigorous than the species and reaches about 2 feet tall. Both are hardy in Zones 8 to 11. *Pleioblastus pygmaeus* is green leaved, 6 to 10 inches tall, and hardy in Zones 5 to 11. Finally, white-striped bamboo (*P. variegatus*) reaches 3 feet and features leaves striped with dark green and white; it is hardy in Zones 6 to 11.

Vigorous Natives

Species native to North America are a great choice for covering large stretches of ground in any garden.

If you need vigorous native plants for ground cover here are three to consider. Many more native plants are included in the lists throughout this book.

Artemisia ludoviciana. White sage, western mugwort. This herbaceous perennial, native to the Midwest and western North America, is grown for its gray leaves rather than its insignificant flowers. It has wide-spreading rhizomes and tolerates heat, drought, and poor soil, plus acid to alkaline pH. Plants quickly form drifts more than 3 feet across. This species should be watered during severe droughts, but it does not tolerate wet feet or heavy, wet, clay soil. Root and crown rots can be a problem in very wet, humid weather. Cut any plant that becomes ragged looking to the ground to encourage fresh new growth. Zones 4 to 9. Cultivars include silver-leaved 'Silver King', which is hardier (to Zone 3) and can be very invasive where happy, as well as 'Silver Queen', which has wide, silver leaves. 'Latiloba', at 1 to 2 feet tall, is perhaps the best ground cover; it has white, woolly leaves but is not very heat-tolerant and is best in Zones 4 to 7. With all forms, divide the clumps every few years in spring or fall for propagation or if they die out in the center and need to be rejuvenated.

Dennstaedtia punctiloba. Hayscented fern. Sometimes called boulder fern, and also listed as *D. punctilo-bata* and *D. punctilobula,* this native of eastern North America spreads quickly by creeping rhizomes. The yellow-green fronds, which are fragrant when handled or brushed against, are brittle, and drifts of the plant can be ragged looking by the end of the season. Still, this is a useful species for informal areas under trees and shrubs, to fill in around rocks or other obstacles on sites where it is difficult to maneuver a lawn mower, or to cover slopes. Plants spread too quickly for small gardens. Although happiest in partial shade to full shade, they tolerate light shade and full sun, and they survive a fair amount of drought as well. Plants grow in poor, acid soil and are native to dry woodlands in partial shade and open meadows. Divide clumps in spring to propagate. Zones 3 to 8.

Rhus aromatica. Fragrant sumac. Also called lemon sumac, sweet-scented sumac, and polecat bush, this deciduous shrub is native from Ontario to Minnesota and south to Florida and Texas. Plants spread aggressively by suckers and will overcome smaller shrubs and perennials. They have pinnate leaves, with leaflets arranged in a featherlike fashion, and bear clusters of tiny yellow flowers in spring followed by edible red berries. Fall color is spectacular: leaves turn orange to red-purple. Use fragrant sumac for holding soil on slopes, for filling parking lot islands, or as a tall ground cover in front of trees. Plants grow in any well-drained soil but are happiest in poor, acid conditions; they are quite tolerant of salt and drought. 'Gro-low' is 2 to 2½ feet tall and spreads to 6 or 8 feet. To propagate, dig suckers when plants are dormant, take cuttings in summer, or take root cuttings in winter. Zones 3 to 9.

Rubus rolfei 'Emerald Carpet'

Rubus rolfei 'Emerald Carpet'
Creeping bramble

EXPOSURE: Full sun to partial shade
HEIGHT: 2 to 4 inches
SPREAD: 5 feet

Also listed as *R. calycinoides* 'Emerald Carpet', *R. pentalobus* 'Emerald Carpet', and *R.* 'Formosan Carpet', this charming trailing woody plant makes a fine ground cover. Plants produce lobed, ivy-like semievergreen to evergreen leaves that have the texture of sandpaper. Small insignificant saucer-shaped flowers appear in summer and are followed by red fruit. The foliage turns rich red in fall. The trailing shoots root as they touch the ground and mingle nicely with other ground covers when planted under shrubs and large perennials. This species also can be used to cover midsize or even large areas, and can be planted around the base of trees or shrubs. Plants grow in most well-drained soils and tolerate some drought, although they're happiest in evenly moist soil. Propagate by taking cuttings or by severing and digging rooted portions of stems during early summer. Zones 6 to 8.

Sasa veitchii
Sasa bamboo, Kuma bamboo

EXPOSURE: Full sun to full shade
HEIGHT: 2 to 5 feet
SPREAD: Indefinite

This moderate- to fast-spreading bamboo bears lance-shaped dark green leaves that develop a white edge in fall and winter. (The white edge is actually dead tissue, but is quite attractive.) The species spreads by dense, woody roots to form thick colonies. Plants are taller in shade than sun, but they can be sheared or cut back to the ground in spring. Use sasa bamboo to fill in under large shrubs as well as cover and hold soil on shady slopes. Select sites with physical boundaries on all sides or regularly mow around clumps to keep them contained. Established plants are fairly drought tolerant and also survive soil that is temporarily waterlogged. Divide clumps in spring, or take cuttings of young rhizomes in late winter. Keep divisions and cuttings evenly moist while they become established. Zones 6 to 10.

Veronica spp.
Speedwells

EXPOSURE: Full sun to light shade
HEIGHT: 4 to 18 inches
SPREAD: Indefinite

These fast-spreading perennials are excellent substitutes for lawn grass. Or plant them along paths, in rock gardens, or between pavers. They're also suitable for scrambling around rocks. They can be difficult to contain, as their common name suggests. Plants need well-drained soil and will not survive in damp or wet conditions. They thrive in fairly rich soil but also tolerate poor soil. Because of their shallow roots, the plants are not drought tolerant. Shear or mow them after flowering to keep them neat and vigorous. Propagate by dividing the clumps in spring or fall.

V. chamaedrys. Germander speedwell. Also called bird's eyes or angel's eyes, this 12- to 18-inch-tall species is native to Europe but has naturalized in North America. Plants spread indefinitely and bear rounded semi-evergreen leaves. Clusters of small saucer-shaped blue flowers with white eyes bloom from summer to fall. Zones 3 to 7.

V. prostrata. Prostrate speedwell. This 6- to 10-inch-tall species spreads to 2 feet or more and forms a dense mat of foliage. Spikelike clusters of blue flowers appear in early summer. 'Alba' bears white flowers. 'Heavenly Blue' is 2 to 4 inches tall. Zones 5 to 8.

V. repens. Creeping speedwell. A 4-inch-tall species that spreads indefinitely, creeping speedwell bears spikelike clusters of pale blue flowers in late summer. Zones 5 to 8.

Viola odorata
Sweet violet

EXPOSURE: Partial to full shade
HEIGHT: 8 inches
SPREAD: 1 foot or more

Also called English violet, this species bears heart-shaped evergreen or semi-evergreen leaves and, from late winter into early spring, fragrant blue or white flowers. Plants spread quickly by rhizomes and also self-sow enthusiastically. A fine choice for underplanting larger perennials such as hostas as well as shrubs, sweet violets thrive in rich, moist, well-drained soil. Propagate by dividing plants in spring or fall or by sowing seed in spring. Zones 6 to 8.

Sun Lovers
for a Patterned Garden

Well-behaved ground covers are easy to contain and maintain, and they also are ideal for combining to cover all manner of garden sites.

In the long run, plants that spread moderately, including the species in this section, are often easier to manage than vigorous spreaders. Use them to cover a small patch of ground, space out specimens of a single species to blanket a medium-size area, or combine several species to create a patchwork quilt of color. All of the plants listed on these pages are fairly well-behaved ground covers that make fine edging plants, and they also can be used alone or in combination with other plants to replace lawn grass over large areas. Spacing them out over a rocky or uneven site is another option. (In general, space plants somewhat closer than their spread at maturity so they will cover the site fairly quickly.) If your objective is a rock garden effect, with drifts of several species covering an area instead of a thick blanket of one type of plant over the whole site, moderate spreaders like these may be a good choice. They will cover a bit less thickly than more vigorous ground covers and will fill in around rocks, eliminating the need to trim. They won't blanket the site so densely that they will swallow up all the rocks as more aggressive ground covers would.

1. *Sedum* 'Vera Jameson'
   Sedum

2. *Stachys byzantina* 'Countess Helen von Stein'
   Lamb's ears

3. *Sedum spurium* 'Tricolor'
   Sedum

4. *Arabis alpina* subsp. *caucasica*
   Wall rock cress

5. *Geranium* 'Ann Folkard'
   Hardy geranium

6. *Artemisia abrotanum*
   Artemisia

7. *Geranium* × *magnificum*
   Hardy geranium

8. *Artemisia* 'Powis Castle'
   Artemisia

9. *Artemisia ludoviciana* 'Valerie Finnis'
   Artemisia

10. *Euphorbia polychroma*
    Euphorbia

11. *Veronica peduncularis*
    Speedwell

12. *Coreopsis rosea*
    Coreopsis

Anagallis monellii
Monell's pimpernel

EXPOSURE: Full sun
HEIGHT: 4 to 8 inches
SPREAD: 1½ to 3 feet

This low-growing tender perennial produces a carpet of saucer-shaped, ½-inch-wide flowers borne in summer above rounded, 1-inch leaves. The flowers usually are deep blue, but cultivars with pink or red flowers also are available. Plants require moist, well-drained soil, although they tolerate short periods of drought. The stems rot in wet conditions. Propagate by sowing seeds or dividing plants in spring. Zones 7 to 9.

Anagallis monellii

Arabis alpina subsp. *caucasica*
Wall rock cress

EXPOSURE: Full sun
HEIGHT: 6 to 12 inches
SPREAD: 1½ feet

A perennial with gray-green leaves that are semievergreen or evergreen, wall rock cress bears fragrant, four-petaled white flowers in spring. Also listed as *A. caucasica,* it is effective on well-drained rocky sites, including slopes, and also can be planted along the top of garden walls. Best used as a small-scale ground cover, it is handsome combined with other rock garden type ground covers such as the smaller sedums (*Sedum* spp.) as well as candytuft (*Iberis sempervirens*) and pinks (*Dianthus* spp.). Plants are fairly drought tolerant and prefer well-drained sandy or silty soil. Propagate by sowing seeds in fall, taking cuttings in summer, or potting up rosettes in fall. Zones 4 to 10.

Artemisia spp. ▼
Artemisias

EXPOSURE: Full sun
HEIGHT: 6 inches to 3 feet
SPREAD: 1 to 3 feet

Although artemisias are well known as vigorous spreaders, not all species are that pushy. Use the plants listed here to cover ground on sites with full sun and rich, well-drained soil. They suffer in poorly drained conditions. Their silver leaves are handsome when combined with pinks (*Dianthus* spp.), lavenders (*Lavandula* spp.), catmints (*Nepeta* spp.), and sedums (*Sedum* spp.). Propagate by dividing plants in spring or fall or by taking regular cuttings or heel cuttings in early summer. The feathery texture of the foliage also provides a pleasing contrast for plants with bold leaves.

A. abrotanum. Southernwood, lad's love. Deciduous or semievergreen, this species makes a mound of lacy, deeply cut, gray-green leaves 3 feet high and wide. Remove the insignificant flowers and cut back plants in spring or summer to reduce their height and encourage bushy, dense growth. Zones 4 to 8.

A. absinthium. Wormwood, absinthe. This 3-foot-tall, woody-based perennial produces deeply cut, silver-gray leaves and insignificant grayish yellow flowers in late summer. 'Lambrook Silver' is 2½ feet tall and has deeply cut silver leaves. Both the species and 'Lambrook Silver' form 2-foot-wide clumps. They can be sheared to reduce their height and encourage dense growth. Zones 4 to 8.

A. ludoviciana 'Valerie Finnis'. A moderate spreader (unlike the species or its cousins 'Silver King' and 'Silver Queen') with silver-gray leaves, this artemisia grows 2 feet tall and spreads to about 2 feet. Zones 4 to 9.

A. 'Powis Castle'. Also a woody-based perennial, this hybrid forms fluffy mounds of lacy, deeply cut silver leaves. Plants reach 2 to 3 feet tall and spread to 3 or more feet. Cut back plants in spring and shear them in summer to maintain dense growth. Zones 6 to 8 or 9.

A. schmidtiana. Silvermound artemisia. This species produces soft, lacy clumps of finely cut silver-gray leaves on 1-foot-tall plants that spread to 1½ feet. Its cultivar 'Nana' is 3 or 4 inches tall. Zones 5 to 8.

A. stelleriana. Beach wormwood. More commonly grown than the 2-foot tall species, 'Boughton Silver' has lobed silver leaves on 12-inch-tall plants that spread to about 1½ feet. Zones 3 to 7.

▼ May be considered invasive in some regions.

Dianthus collection flanking a walkway.

Coreopsis verticillata
Thread-leaf coreopsis, thread-leaf tickseed

EXPOSURE: Full sun to light shade
HEIGHT: 1½ to 2 feet
SPREAD: 1½ to 2 feet

This popular, long-blooming perennial is native to the Southeastern United States. Plants produce mounds of narrow, threadlike leaves that are covered with 2-inch-wide, daisylike flowers in summer. Shear back the clumps after they have mostly stopped blooming, and they will produce a second flush of flowers in fall. Plants thrive in rich, well-drained soil, and established clumps tolerate dry soil and drought. They spread by short rhizomes. 'Moonbeam', with soft yellow blooms, is very popular. 'Zagreb' bears deep, golden yellow flowers on 12-inch-tall plants. Propagate all forms by dividing clumps in spring or by taking cuttings from the base of the plant in early spring. Zones 3 to 9.

Pink coreopsis (*C. rosea*) is a similar-looking species — 1 foot tall and spreading to 2 feet — that can be used as a ground cover. Native to the northeastern United States and Canada, it bears pink flowers in summer. This species grows naturally in sandy, wet, acid soils but also thrives in rich, moist, well-drained conditions. Zones 4 to 8.

Dianthus spp.
Pinks

EXPOSURE: Full sun to partial shade
HEIGHT: 6 to 18 inches
SPREAD: 1 to 2 feet

Pinks form low mats or mounds of linear- to lance-shaped leaves topped by pretty single, semidouble, or double flowers in spring or early summer. Flowers may be fragrant. The plants are not suitable for covering the ground over a large area but are quite effective in a small space or when combined with other ground covers. Pinks prefer well-drained, neutral to alkaline soil, although they tolerate slightly acid soil. They are shallow rooted and thus not very drought tolerant, and their roots rot in damp or wet soil. (Keep mulch, which holds moisture, away from the crowns of the plants.) If in doubt about drainage, work some coarse sand or gravel, or both, into the soil at planting time. Use pinks in raised beds, in rock gardens, in terraced beds, on gentle slopes, and as edgings in beds and borders. Dig and divide plants as necessary to keep the centers of the clump from dying out. Propagate pinks by taking cuttings of nonflowering shoots in summer.

D. Allwoodii Group. Modern border pinks. This group of plants offers good choices for use as ground covers. Look for cultivars such as 'Doris' or 'Helen', both with fragrant, double, salmon pink flowers, and 'Ian', with fragrant, double, red blooms. Plants are 12 to 15 inches tall in bloom. Zones 4 to 8.

D. deltoides. Maiden pinks. This species grows 4 to 8 inches tall and spreads to 15 inches. The single blooms are white, pink, or red, often with a darker eye. Cultivars to look for include 'Albus' (white), 'Fanal' (red), 'Microchip' (reds, pinks, and white), 'Samos' (red), and 'Zing Rose' (red). Zones 3 to 9.

D. gratianopolitanus. Cheddar pinks. Growing 6 to 8 inches tall and spreading to a foot or more, this species has single rose-pink to pink flowers that usually are very fragrant. 'Tiny Rubies' bears double, dark pink flowers on 4-inch plants, while 'Bath's Pink' is 10 inches tall and bears single, fringed, soft pink flowers. Zones 3 to 9.

Herbs for Covering

Great garden plants in their own right, many herbs also make handsome ground covers.

All of the plants listed here have herbal uses — either historic or present day — and also feature aromatic foliage or flowers. Be aware that they spread at different rates: Mints (*Mentha* spp.) are fast spreaders, while other herbs on this list form mounds but don't root-and-run the way mints do.

Calamintha nepeta. **Calamint.** Self-sowing herbaceous perennial with fresh, minty-smelling leaves and white flowers. Grows 12 to 18 inches tall, spreading 20 to 36 inches. Full sun to partial shade; moist to somewhat dry, well-drained soil. Zones 5 to 9.

Chamaemelum nobile. **Roman chamomile.** See page 90.

Comptonia peregrina. **Sweet fern, meadow fern.** See page 114.

Convallaria majalis. **Lily-of-the-valley.** See page 70.

Galium odoratum. **Sweet woodruff.** See page 71.

Geranium maculatum. **Wild geranium.** See page 160.

Lavandula angustifolia. **English lavender.** Subshrub with fragrant foliage and flowers. Grows 1½ to 2½ feet tall, spreading from 3 to 4 feet or more. Full sun; average, well-drained soil. 'Hidcote' is 2 feet tall and spreads to nearly 3 feet, while 'Munstead' is 18 inches tall and spreads to 2 feet. Zones 5 to 9.

Mahonia aquifolium. **Oregon grape holly.** See page 000.

Mentha spp. **Mints.** See page 000.

Origanum vulgare. **Oregano.** Rhizomatous herbaceous perennial with aromatic leaves. Grows 12 inches tall, spreading to 1½ or 2 feet. Shear after flowering to prevent self-sowing. Full sun. Zones 5 to 9.

Rosmarinus officinalis. **Rosemary.** Evergreen, aromatic shrub. Grows 2 to 4 feet tall, spreading to 4 feet. Cultivars are the best choices for ground cover. 'Prostratus' is usually 6 to 12 inches tall, spreading from 2 to 3 or more feet. 'Collingwood Ingram' is 1 to 2 feet tall by 4 feet wide. 'Lockwood de Forest', 2 feet tall, spreading to 5 or more feet. Zones 8 to 10. 'Arp' is 2 to 5 feet, spreading to 3 feet; hardy to Zone 7. Full sun; poor to average, well-drained soil.

Salvia officinalis. **Garden sage.** Shrubby evergreen or semievergreen perennial with aromatic foliage. Grows 1½ to 2½ feet tall, spreading to 2 to 3 feet. Heat and drought tolerant. Full sun; average, well-drained sandy soil. Zones 6 to 9.

Stachys byzantina. **Lamb's ears.** See page 87.

Tanacetum parthenium. **Feverfew.** Perennial with deeply cut deciduous or semievergreen leaves. Grows 1 to 2½ feet tall, spreading to 2 feet. 'Aureum' and 'Golden Moss', both 1½ feet tall, have yellow new foliage. Full sun; moist, well-drained soil. Zones 6 to 8.

Teucrium chamaedrys. **Germander.** See page 103.

Thymus spp. **Thymes.** See page 94.

A combination of various thymes makes for a colorful, aromatic, and drought-tolerant ground cover.

Euphorbia spp.
Euphorbias, spurges

EXPOSURE: Full sun to partial shade
HEIGHT: 4 to 18 inches
SPREAD: 1 to 3 feet

The two species of euphorbia described here are mound forming and make handsome additions to mixed plantings of ground covers. These euphorbias tolerate a range of soils but are happiest in loose, well-drained soil that is sandy or gravelly. While both of these species tolerate drought, they grow best in evenly moist soil. Propagate by dividing clumps in spring or by taking cuttings from the base of the plant in spring or early summer. Dip cuttings in warm water to prevent the flow of milky white sap. Another option is to dig up and relocate self-sown seedlings.

E. polychroma (formerly *E. epithymoides*). Cushion spurge. This herbaceous species forms 10- to 18-inch-tall mounds that spread to 3 feet. Plants produce rounded clusters of yellow flowers in spring. They are best for gardens located in areas with cool summers. In areas with warm summers south of Zone 5, give plants a site with shade during the hottest part of the day. Zones 4 to 8; farther south in areas with cool summers.

E. myrsinites. Myrtle euphorbia. A nearly prostrate species that grows 4 to 8 inches tall, myrtle euphorbia spreads from 1 to 2 or more feet. This evergreen species produces yellow flowers in spring. Originally native to the Mediterranean, they tolerate heat and can withstand summer humidity even in the Southeast. They are determined spreaders that need to be watched carefully. Zones 5 to 8; farther south in areas with cool summers.

Gazania spp.
Gazanias

EXPOSURE: Full sun
HEIGHT: 8 inches
SPREAD: 10 to 12 inches

Although grown as annuals in northern climates, gazanias are tough, useful perennials in warmer areas. They produce rosettes of attractive evergreen leaves that are gray-green and in summer are topped by showy daisylike flowers. Many hybrids are available, and these bear 3- to 4-inch-wide blooms in shades of red, pink, bronze, orange, yellow, and white. Many gazanias produce two-tone flowers. Typically the flowers close at night and in cloudy weather, but newer cultivars, including the Daybreak series, produce blooms that remain open during cloudy weather. Give gazanias sandy, well-drained soil, and use them as edging plants, along foundation plantings, and in beds with other sun-loving ground covers. Propagate by sowing seed in late winter or spring or by taking cuttings from shoots that arise at the base of the plant in late summer. Zones 8 to 10.

Geranium spp.
Hardy geraniums, cranesbills

EXPOSURE: Full sun to partial shade
HEIGHT: 12 to 15 inches
SPREAD: 1 to 3 feet or more

Hardy geraniums forming low mounds that are broader than tall make fine flowering ground covers, especially when mixed with other perennials to cover a large area. Use them to plant around trees and shrubs, in rock gardens, and as ground covers around and under foundation plantings. Also consider them for edging walkways or flower beds and borders. All bear five-lobed flowers and palmately lobed leaves (with lobes arranged like fingers on a hand). Hardy geraniums thrive in rich, moist, well-drained soil that is acid to slightly alkaline. They are not very drought tolerant and require watering during dry weather. Plants bloom best in full sun in cooler areas, but a site with afternoon shade is better in warmer zones. Cut them back hard after the main flush of flowers has faded to encourage dense, bushy growth, to control the height of taller plants, and to encourage a second

Euphorbia myrsinites

flush of flowers. Propagate by dividing the clumps in spring or by taking cuttings from shoots at the base of the plant in spring or early summer. Cuttings root best with bottom heat.

Geranium hybrids include 'Ann Folkard', with chartreuse leaves and magenta pink flowers from midsummer to fall on 18-inch-tall plants that sprawl to 2 or 3 feet. This cultivar doesn't form a very dense ground cover but is handsome mixing with other perennials. Zones 5 to 9. 'Johnson's Blue', another popular hybrid, is 1 to 1½ feet tall and spreads to form a 2- to 2½-foot-wide clump. Plants bear spectacular blue flowers in summer. Zones 4 to 8.

The following *Geranium* species are superb choices:

G. × cantabrigiense. This compact evergreen is a foot tall, slowly spreading by runners to form a 2-foot-wide mound. Plants have aromatic leaves and produce dense clusters of pink or white flowers from early to midsummer. 'Biokovo' is 9 inches tall and makes an especially fine ground cover. Zones 5 to 8.

G. cinereum. An evergreen species that is 6 inches tall and spreads a foot wide, this hardy geranium is especially suitable for raised beds, since plants require very well-drained soil. Clusters of white or pale pink flowers appear in late spring and early summer. 'Ballerina' sports deeper pink blooms with dark eyes and veins. Zones 5 to 8.

G. clarkei. Clark's geranium. This vigorous species ranges from 18 to 20 inches tall and can spread indefinitely by rhizomes. Plants produce loose clusters of violet-purple or mauve-pink flowers all summer. 'Kashmir Purple', sporting lilac-blue flowers with red veins, is a very fast spreader. 'Kashmir White', with white flowers, is somewhat less vigorous. Zones 5 to 8.

G. dalmaticum. Dalmatian cranesbill. Growing 4 to 6 inches tall and spreading 18 to 20 inches by rhizomes, this species bears aromatic foliage that is evergreen in areas with mild winters. Plants produce clusters of pink flowers in summer. Zones 5 to 7.

G. endressii. This 18-inch-tall evergreen species spreads to 2 feet by rhizomes. Plants bear dense clusters of bright pink flowers from early summer to early fall. Zones 5 to 8.

G. himalayense. A 12- to 18-inch-tall plant that spreads by rhizomes to form a 2-foot-wide mound, this species produces loose clusters of showy violet-blue flowers with white centers. The main flush of flowers comes in early summer, then blooms appear sporadically until fall. The plant also boasts good red fall foliage. Zones 4 to 8.

G. × magnificum. A vigorous grower, this species reaches 1½ to 2 feet tall and forms a 2-foot-wide mound covered with clusters of violet-purple flowers with darker veins in midsummer. The plant exhibits good red fall foliage color. Zones 4 to 8.

G. × oxonianum. Another vigorous, clump-forming hardy geranium, this species bears evergreen leaves. Plants are 2 to 2½ feet tall and spread to 2 feet. They bear loose clusters of pink flowers from late spring to fall. 'Claridge Druce', with rose-pink blooms, is one of many cultivars that make fine ground covers. It forms dense clumps and also self-sows. Zones 5 to 8.

G. procurrens. An 18-inch-tall species, this is a vigorous spreader with stems that root at the nodes. Plants form 3-foot-wide mounds and bear loose clusters of starry, purple-pink flowers from midsummer to fall. They tolerate dry soil and can be used to fill in under hedges and shrub borders. Zones 7 to 9.

G. sanguineum. Bloody cranesbill. This species has deeply cut leaves and in summer bears loose clusters of magenta-pink flowers with darker veins. The foliage turns red in fall. Plants are 1 foot tall and spread to 1½ feet. The many cultivars include 3-inch-tall 'John Elsley', with rose-pink flowers all summer; 1-foot-tall 'Elsbeth', with pink flowers; 8-inch tall 'Max Frei', with magenta flowers; and 'New Hampshire Purple', which is 8 inches tall and spreads to 2 feet with wine red flowers. Zones 4 to 8.

G. wallichianum. Growing 4 to 12 inches tall and spreading to 3 or 4 feet, this species bears loose clusters of lilac or pinkish purple flowers with a white center and darker veins from midsummer to fall. Zones 4 to 8.

Geranium × magnificum

Liriope muscari 'Big Blue'

Hypericum spp.
St. John's worts

EXPOSURE: Full sun to partial shade
HEIGHT: 1 to 1½ feet
SPREAD: 1 to 2 feet

Several species of St. John's wort are moderate spreaders that make fine ground covers. An ideal site is one with rich, acid soil that is moist but well drained, although the plants tolerate a range of soils. Although fine during short spells of dry weather, they are not particularly drought tolerant and require watering to survive drought. The plants bloom best in sun. Propagate by taking cuttings in summer or by dividing them in spring or fall.

H. buckleyi. Blue Ridge St. John's wort. A native plant from the Appalachian Mountains, this species reaches a foot in height and spreads to about 2 feet. Plants bear small, gray-green leaves and 1-inch-wide, yellow summer flowers, which are carried on wood from the previous year. They spread at a moderate pace and tolerate summer heat and humidity. This species is effective for rock gardens and for combining with other low-growing ground covers. Zones 5 to 8.

H. cerastioides. Native to Greece and Turkey, this species is 6 inches tall and spreads to about 16 inches. Plants bear gray-green leaves accented by yellow flowers from late spring to early summer. Zones 6 to 9.

H. ellipticum. Pale St. John's wort. This species, native to the northeastern United States and southeastern Canada, grows a foot tall and spreads by rhizomes to form a 2- or 3-foot-wide clump. Plants bear semievergreen leaves and mid- to late-summer yellow flowers. Zones 4 to 7 or 8.

H. suffruticosum. Trailing St. John's wort. Native to the southeastern pinelands, this species is especially suited for sandy soil. The plants are only 2 to 6 inches tall and spread to 1 or 2 feet. They bear narrow, oval leaves and pale yellow flowers from spring to early summer. Zones 7 to 9.

Iberis sempervirens
Candytuft

EXPOSURE: Full sun to light shade
HEIGHT: 1 foot
SPREAD: 3 to 4 feet

This popular evergreen subshrub makes a handsome edging plant along walkways, in front of shrubs, or in drifts with other sun-loving ground covers. Plants form clumps of glossy, narrow, very dark green leaves. They are covered by flat-topped clusters of brilliant white flowers from late spring to early summer. 'Purity' produces its flowers over a longer season than the species. 'Little Gem', also sold as 'Weisser Zwerg', is about 5 inches tall by 10 inches wide and makes a nice addition to smaller ground cover plantings. 'Autumn Beauty', 'Autumn Snow', and 'Christmas Snow' produce a second flush of flowers in fall. All forms of candytuft grow in any well-drained soil. Although they're fairly drought tolerant, plants appreciate regular watering during dry weather. They bloom best in full sun. Propagate by taking cuttings in late spring or summer. Zones 5 to 7.

Liriope spp.
Lilyturfs, liriopes

EXPOSURE: Full sun to full shade
HEIGHT: 8 to 24 inches
SPREAD: 1½ to 2 feet

Handsome ground covers for edging walkways or driveways, liriopes also are excellent plants for filling in under foundation shrubs, planting around trees, edging beds and borders, or growing along the front of shrub borders. Liriopes also can be used as lawn grass substitutes, either alone or planted in drifts with other ground covers. Their fleshy roots make them drought tolerant, and they grow in any well-drained soil. Plants spread more slowly in heavy shade than in sun. When using lilyturfs as a lawn grass substitute, space plants on 8-inch centers. Propagate by dividing the clumps in spring.

L. muscari. Big blue lilyturf. A popular ground cover, this species makes clumps of evergreen, strap-shaped,

Ophiopogon japonicus 'Nanus'

Nepeta × faassenii

flowers. 'Monroe White' has white blooms and is slower to spread than the species. Variegated forms, including 'John Burch', with leaves edged in gold, and 'Silver Dragon', with silver-and-green striped leaves, also spread more slowly. Zones 6 to 9.

L. spicata. Creeping lilyturf. This species bears narrower leaves — to about ¼ inch wide — that are semievergreen. Plants are 10 inches tall and spread fairly rapidly by rhizomes to 1½ feet. Zones 4 or 5 to 10.

Ophiopogon species are similar and are commonly called mondo grass or lilyturf. All bear linear leaves and racemes of pinkish flowers in summer.

O. japonicus. Mondo grass. This species grows 8 to 12 inches tall and spreads to 1 foot. 'Compactus', a dense grower, is only 2 inches tall; 'Nanus' reaches 3 to 6 inches tall. Zones 7 to 10.

O. planiscapus. Growing to 8 inches tall, this species also spreads to 1 foot. 'Nigrescens' bears maroon-black leaves. Zones 6 to 10.

Nepeta × faassenii
Catmint

EXPOSURE: Full sun
HEIGHT: 1 to 2 feet
SPREAD: 1½ to 3 feet

A popular hardy perennial, catmint is a mounding, somewhat sprawling plant that can be used to cover the ground. Plants bear aromatic, gray-green leaves and spikelike clusters of small, two-lipped flowers from early summer to early fall. They are drought tolerant and grow in any well-drained soil, from sandy to clayey. Shear them back after the first flush of flowers are about finished to encourage branching, denser growth, and additional bloom. 'Walker's

Low' produces a sprawling, 10-inch-tall mound of gray-green leaves and pale lavender-blue flowers. 'Blue Wonder' is compact and reaches about 15 inches tall. 'Snowflake' bears white flowers and also is compact, to about 15 inches tall. Propagate by dividing the clumps in spring or fall or by taking cuttings in early summer. Zones 4 to 8.

Sedum spp.
Sedums, stonecrops

EXPOSURE: Full sun
HEIGHT: 1 to 10 inches
SPREAD: 2 to 3 or more feet

These low-growing, fast-spreading, fleshy-leaved perennials make excellent ground covers and also require minimal maintenance. The plants are extremely tolerant to drought and heat. They grow in nearly any well-drained site and tolerate poor soil, including rocky and gravelly conditions. Use the species described as vigorous spreaders to create drifts on hot, dry sites and to fill in around larger ground covers — most will overwhelm smaller, more delicate perennials. Sites that contain these enthusiastic spreaders naturally are often best, because stems root wherever they touch the soil and even leaves can root and grow into full-size plants. Vigorous sedums will cover slopes, but they are fairly shallow rooted and not the best choice for holding soil in place if the grade is steep. Species described as moderate spreaders can be used to edge walkways and fill in around larger perennials. They are also ideal for rock gardens. Propagate by dividing the clumps in spring or by taking cuttings of nonflowering shoots in summer. Pieces of stem that fall on the soil generally root and grow as well.

1- to 1½-inch-wide leaves and bears spikes of lilac purple flowers in late summer to fall. Plants grow 1 foot tall and spread to about 1½ feet. They tolerate heat and humidity as well as drought. 'Big Blue' reaches 10 inches tall and produces violet-blue

S. acre. Goldmoss stonecrop. A vigorous spreader, this evergreen species bears tiny triangular leaves and flat-topped clusters of starry yellow flowers in summer. Plants are 1 to 2 inches tall. They spread quickly and vigorously to several feet and also tolerate some foot traffic. Zones 3 to 8.

S. album 'Chloroticum'. White stonecrop. This diminutive moderate spreader is 1 to 2 inches tall and spreads to 1 foot or more. Plants bear white flowers in summer and tiny fleshy evergreen leaves that resemble baby tears (*Soleirolia soleirolii*). They grow in partial shade as well as full sun and tolerate light foot traffic. Zones 4 to 9.

S. humifusum. Tiny and compact, this moderate spreader is ½ inch tall and spreads from 6 to 12 inches. Plants produce tight rosettes of fleshy evergreen leaves that turn bronzy in fall. Starry yellow flowers appear in early summer. Zones 4 to 9.

S. kamtschaticum. Kamchatka stonecrop. A moderate semievergreen spreader, this species is 3 to 4 inches tall and spreads to about 1½ feet. Plants bear spoon-shaped leaves and flat-topped clusters of small starry flowers in summer. 'Variegatum' has white-edged leaves. Zones 4 to 9.

S. lydium. Lydian stonecrop. This diminutive 2-inch-tall species is a moderate spreader producing tight rosettes of tiny, cylindrical evergreen leaves that are green and tipped with red. Plants spread about 8 or 10 inches and bear small clusters of tiny white flowers in summer. Zones 5 to 8.

S. middendorfianum. Middendorf stonecrop. Another moderate spreader, this species bears evergreen leaves that are linear and grooved in the middle. Plants are about 12 inches tall and spread to 18 inches. They produce clusters of small yellow flowers in summer. Zones 3 to 9.

S. 'Ruby Glow'. This handsome hybrid is 9 or 10 inches tall and spreads to 18 inches. It bears rounded, purple-green leaves and showy, rounded clusters of star-shaped, ruby red flowers from midsummer to early fall. Zones 5 to 9.

S. rupestre. Stone orpine. Also listed as *S. reflexum*, this vigorous spreader is an evergreen with cylindrical, spruce-like, gray-green leaves and clusters of small starry yellow flowers in summer. Plants are about 4 inches tall and easily spread to 2 feet or more. They are fine in the heat and humidity of the Southeast and also grow in partial shade. Zones 6 to 9.

S. spathulifolium. A slow to moderate evergreen spreader native to the Pacific Northwest, this species reaches 4 inches and spreads to about 2 feet. Plants produce brittle rosettes of spoon-shaped, green or blue-green leaves topped by small clusters of starry yellow flowers in summer. They do not tolerate heat and humidity but will grow in partial shade. 'Cape Blanco' has leaves powdered with white bloom. Zones 5 to 9.

S. spurium. Two-row sedum. This vigorous, fast-spreading species is 2 to 6 inches tall and forms dense mats from 2 to 3 feet or more in diameter. Plants bear rounded evergreen leaves topped by rounded clusters of starry pink or white flowers in late summer. A number of cultivars are available, including 'Dragon's Blood', also listed as 'Schorbuser Blut', with purple-tinted green leaves and deep pink flowers. 'Tricolor', also listed as 'Variegatum', features leaves striped with green, pink, and white. 'John Creech' is 2 inches tall and bears pink flowers. Zones 4 to 9.

S. 'Vera Jameson'. A handsome clump former, this hybrid bears arching stems with rounded, toothed, deciduous green leaves flushed with bronze-purple. Plants are 9 to 12 inches tall and spread to 1½ feet. They are topped with showy, rounded clusters of mauve-pink flowers in late summer and early fall. Zones 4 to 9.

Sedum spurium 'Tricolor'

Grasses for Massing

A variety of clump-forming ornamental grasses can be used very effectively as ground covers, provided they are mass planted.

Ornamental grasses add an interesting and dramatic textural contrast to plantings. One advantage of planting clumpers instead of species that spread aggressively by rhizomes is a control issue: you won't have to fight to keep them from taking over the rest of the flower bed where they've been put. Use the grasses listed here to replace lawn, form tall edgings, or combine with other perennials — just match the size of the grass with the sizes of the other perennials in the planting. For solid, fairly quick cover, space plants densely.

Calamagrostis × acutiflora. **Feather reed grass.** Grows 2 to 6 feet tall, spreading to 4 feet. Full sun; rich, moist soil is best but tolerates poor soil. Zones 5 to 9.

Carex spp. **Sedges.** See page 149.

Chasmanthium latifolium (formerly *Uniola latifolia*). **Wild oats.** Native to the eastern United States and northern Mexico. Grows 3 feet tall and spreads to 2 to 3 feet. A clumping plant that self-sows. Full sun to partial shade; tolerates a range of soils, and established plants tolerate drought. Zones 5 to 9.

Deschampsia cespitosa. **Tufted hair grass.** See page 174.

Festuca glauca. **Blue fescue.** Grows 10 to 12 inches tall, spreading to 12 inches. Rich silver-blue 'Elijah Blue' grows 8 inches tall. Full sun; poor to average, well-drained soil. Zones 4 to 8.

Helictotrichon sempervirens. **Blue oat grass.** Grows 4½ feet tall in bloom (foliage to 3 feet high), spreading to 2 feet or more. Full sun; poor to average, well-drained soil. Zones 4 to 9.

Pennisetum alopecuroides. **Fountain grass.** Grows 2 to 5 feet tall, spreading to 4 feet. Both it and the cultivar 'Moudry' are vigorous self-sowers. Dwarf cultivars include 'Hameln', 3 feet tall, spreading to 4 feet; 'Little Bunny', 1½ feet tall, spreading to 1½ feet; and 'Little Honey', to 1 foot tall and wide. Full sun; rich, well-drained soil. Zones 6 to 9.

Sporobolus heterolepis. **Prairie dropseed.** Native to eastern and central North America. Grows 18 to 24 inches tall, spreading to 2 feet. Full sun; any well-drained soil. Zones 3 to 9.

A massed planting of panic grass (*Panicum* sp.), tufted hair grass (*Deschampsia cespitosa*), feather reed grass (*Calamagrostis × acutiflora*), and Mexican feather grass (*Stipa tenuissima*).

Stachys byzantina
Lamb's ears

EXPOSURE: Full sun to light shade
HEIGHT: 4 to 18 inches
SPREAD: 2 to 3 feet

Grown more for its softly textured, silvery foliage than its flowers, lamb's ears bears thick, woolly, lance-shaped leaves topped by woolly spikes of small, two-lipped, pinkish purple flowers from early summer to fall. The leaves alone form a 4- to 6-inch-tall carpet, and many gardeners remove the 12- to 18-inch-tall flower spikes altogether. 'Helen von Stein', also sold as 'Big Ears', has 10-inch-long leaves. 'Primrose Heron' has yellowish gray leaves. 'Silver Carpet' produces grayish white leaves and does not flower. Grow lamb's ears in any well-drained soil, although plants are happiest in rich, moist conditions. They tolerate some drought. Propagate by dividing clumps or potting up rooted plantlets in spring. Zones 4 to 8.

Veronica spp.
Speedwells

EXPOSURE: Full sun
HEIGHT: 3 to 6 inches
SPREAD: 1½ to 3 feet or more

The moderate- to fast-spreading veronicas listed here all make nice ground covers. All require well-drained soil and can be combined in drifts with other ground covers to replace lawn grass. Use them to fill in around rocks, or plant them along sidewalks and walkways. They also can be planted between stepping-stones, but they do not tolerate foot traffic. Look for sites with physical boundaries such as paved pathways, walls, or curbs to keep them in bounds. Propagate veronicas by dividing the clumps in spring or fall.

Lamb's ears (*Stachys byzantina*) with stonecrop (*Sedum* 'Angelina') and blue fescue (*Festuca glauca*).

V. pectinata. This evergreen, 3-inch-tall species spreads to about 8 inches and has rounded, toothed, gray leaves and short racemes of saucer-shaped blue flowers with white eyes. Plants bloom in summer. They tolerate somewhat drier soil than the other species of veronica and also will grow in partial shade. Zones 3 to 7.

V. peduncularis. A mat-forming, 4-inch-tall grower, this species spreads to 2 feet. Plants bear lance-shaped leaves flushed with purple. From spring to summer they produce racemes of saucer-shaped blue flowers with small white eyes. Zones 6 to 8.

V. prostrata. Prostrate speedwell. See page 75.

Ground Huggers
for Paths & Stepping-Stones

Compact, low-growing plants make a charming carpet for pathways, whether used as an edging, planted around stepping-stones, or allowed to pop up in walkway cracks or in gravel.

All of these plants are ideal for planting between stepping-stones, too, and all will withstand some foot traffic. In informal designs, low plants like these also are commonly allowed to billow over the edges of pathways, and whether planted alone or in combination, they can make pathways as interesting to look at as flower beds. Bringing plants into — plus planting them alongside — a pathway softens it and helps link the hardscape element (in this case the brick, stone, concrete, or gravel pathway) to the rest of the garden. Stepping-stones help protect the plants by keeping the brunt of the traffic off the soil and away from the plant crowns.

Keep in mind that while all of these plants tolerate light foot traffic — perhaps once or twice a week — they are happiest when walked on as little as possible, or not at all. None of these plants are good choices for really high-traffic areas. Lawn grass withstands foot traffic far better than any other ground cover, and even it doesn't survive regular pounding by countless feet. See Covering Ground with Hardscape on page 57 for more on dealing with high-traffic areas. If foot traffic isn't an issue, consider combining any of these plants with low-growing species that do not tolerate foot traffic (see Small-Scale Spreaders on page 97 for a list). Also, the species that thrive in partial shade are good candidates for growing around and under shrubs and over tree roots; see Creating Planting Pockets on page 198 for tips on getting them started.

1. *Holcus mollis* 'Albovariegatus'
   Variegated velvet grass

2. *Sagina subulata*
   Corsican pearlwort

3. *Waldsteinia lobata*
   Mock strawberry

4. *Lavandula* sp., *Thymus* sp., and *Lobularia maritima*
   Lavender, thyme, and sweet alyssum

5. *Ajuga reptans* 'Rainbow'
   Creeping bugleweed

6. *Mazus reptans*
   Creeping mazus

7. *Thymus serpyllum* 'Coccineus'
   Thyme

8. *Sagina subulata*
   Corsican pearlwort

9. *Herniaria glabra*
   Rupturewort

Ajuga reptans ▽
Creeping bugleweed, carpet bugleweed

EXPOSURE: Partial shade
HEIGHT: 3 to 4 inches
SPREAD: Indefinite

This fast-spreading to invasive species travels by both stolons and rhizomes. It also can self-sow and will invade lawn areas and outcompete more polite perennials. Plants are evergreen and produce rosettes of dark green, spoon-shaped leaves topped by spikelike clusters of small blue flowers in late spring and early summer. The foliage is 3 to 4 inches tall, but plants reach about 6 inches in bloom. Bugleweed tolerates foot traffic and can grow through a stone path, and plantings can be mowed after bloom to keep them neat. Plants scorch in full sun, and crown rot can kill entire

Ajuga reptans 'Rainbow'

plantings in moist, cool weather. 'Catlin's Giant' is a large, vigorous cultivar that reaches 8 inches or more in bloom. Variegated cultivars are much less vigorous than the species. 'Multicolor', also listed as 'Rainbow', boasts green, pink, burgundy, and cream leaves. 'Chocolate Chip' is a dwarf hybrid growing 3 to 6 inches tall with small leaves and clusters of purple-blue flowers. Propagate bugleweed by potting up rooted rosettes or by rooting cuttings in early summer. Zones 3 to 9.

Chamaemelum nobile
Roman chamomile

EXPOSURE: Full sun or light shade
HEIGHT: 6 to 12 inches
SPREAD: 1½ feet

Although this fast-spreading herb can be substituted for lawn grass, it works more as a visual than a practical substitute, since it doesn't form as dense a ground cover as grass and withstands only very limited foot traffic. The species can spread aggressively, though. To keep plantings neat and short, mow in spring and again after the plants produce their small white daisylike flowers in summer. Plants bear aromatic leaves divided into threadlike leaflets. They thrive in sandy, well-drained soil and are deep rooted and drought tolerant. 'Treneague' is less vigorous than the species, does not flower, and is 4 inches tall. Propagate Roman chamomile by sowing seeds where the plants are to grow or by dividing plants in spring. Zones 6 to 9.

Dichondra micrantha
Dichondra

EXPOSURE: Full sun to partial shade
HEIGHT: 3 inches
SPREAD: Indefinite

In the warmest zones, dichondra is a popular lawn substitute that can withstand considerable foot traffic. The species bears spoon-shaped leaves and spreads by runners that travel across the soil surface and root wherever they touch. Tiny flowers — in white, green, or yellow-green — appear from summer to fall. In the North, this species can be used as an annual in containers or as an edging plant. Give plants average to rich, well-drained soil. When used as a lawn substitute, dichondra needs to be mowed, watered, and fed regularly. Propagate by sowing seed in spring where the plants are to grow or by severing and rooting the runners in spring or summer. Zones 10 to 11.

Herniaria glabra
Rupturewort, burstwort

EXPOSURE: Full sun to light shade
HEIGHT: 2 to 3 inches
SPREAD: 1 foot

This humble, low-growing species with a somewhat mosslike appearance has tiny, rounded, evergreen leaves that turn bronzy in winter. The greenish flowers are insignificant. Rupturewort forms a dense ground cover that excludes weeds and tolerates light foot traffic. Plants grow in any well-drained, neutral to slightly acid soil, although they are not deep rooted and thus not drought tolerant. Propagate by dividing the plants in spring, by sowing seed in spring or fall, or by taking cuttings in early summer. Zones 5 to 10.

Holcus mollis 'Albovariegatus' ▽
Variegated velvet grass

EXPOSURE: Full sun or partial shade
HEIGHT: 6 to 8 inches
SPREAD: 1½ feet

While the green-leaved species is too aggressive for cultivation (it has been listed as invasive in some states), 'Albovariegatus' makes a fine ornamental grass for covering ground. Plants spread by rhizomes to produce dense mats of blue-green leaves with white margins,

▽   May be considered invasive in some regions.

Mazus reptans

Mentha pulegium

and they bear only a few, wispy flowers in mid- to late-summer. They tolerate occasional foot traffic. As cool-season growers, plants are most attractive during cool weather in spring and fall. Give them a spot in full sun in northern climates, but site them in partial shade from about Zone 7 southward. Shear in midsummer to remove flower heads and keep plantings neat. Rogue out any all-green seedlings that appear. Propagate by dividing the clumps in spring. Zones 5 to 9.

Mazus reptans
Creeping mazus

EXPOSURE: Full sun to partial shade
HEIGHT: 1 to 2 inches
SPREAD: 2 feet or more

This ground-hugging perennial forms a thick mound of rounded, coarsely toothed green leaves topped by small, pale purple-blue flowers with large showy lips. 'Albus' bears white flowers. In addition to being a fine choice for use as an edging or between pavers,

creeping mazus thrives under trees and shrubs and also can be grown around ponds and water gardens. Plants need rich, evenly moist, well-drained soil and are not drought tolerant. Propagate by dividing plants in spring. Zones 4 to 9.

Mentha spp.
Mints

EXPOSURE: Full sun to partial shade
HEIGHT: 1 to 3 inches
SPREAD: Indefinite

In addition to well-known species like spearmint (*M. spicata*) that grow to 3 feet tall, this genus of fast-spreading perennials contains some mat-forming species that make excellent paving or edging plants. Also consider these low-growing vigorous species for smaller beds with edging strips or other physical barriers, or use them to fill in around larger ground covers, vigorous perennials, and shrubs. They can even be allowed to trail over rocky sites, provided the soil is rich and remains evenly moist. Both species described here tolerate some foot traffic. Propagate the plants by dividing them in spring or fall, or by rooting pieces of rhizome any time during the growing season.

M. pulegium. ▼ Pennyroyal. This mat-forming species bears rounded, aromatic leaves and spreads by creeping rhizomes. Plants are topped by small whorls of tiny two-lipped lilac flowers in summer. The pungent leaves are used medicinally and in potpourris but are not recommended for use in teas. Plants spread to 2 feet or more and grow in full sun to light shade. Zones 7 to 9.

M. requienii. Corsican mint. Another mat former that spreads by creeping rhizomes, this species is ½ to

1½ inches tall. Plants produce small round or heart-shaped leaves that are strongly peppermint scented (they have been used as flavorings, including crème de menthe). Where happy, with rich, moist soil, plants spread indefinitely. Give them a site in partial to full shade. Zones 6 to 10.

Potentilla spp.
Potentillas, cinquefoils

EXPOSURE: Full sun to light shade
HEIGHT: 3 to 12 inches
SPREAD: 1 to 2 feet

While the best-known potentillas are summer-blooming shrubs, this genus also contains low-growing species that make ideal ground covers. The species listed here can withstand occasional foot traffic and make fine lawn substitutes or plants for decorating a path. (See page 133 for shrubby cinquefoils.) They thrive in most well-drained soils, from poor and sandy to loamy. Plants also are fairly drought tolerant but benefit from watering during dry weather.

More Plants for Paving

Pathways planted with ground-hugging species are always charming, and plants help crowd out weeds that would otherwise fill in the cracks.

Instead of just using a single species to fill pathway spaces, why not combine several different ground covers to create a colorful patchwork? The plants listed here also tolerate light foot traffic and can also be used along the edge of a pathway. Unless otherwise noted, all grow in full sun to part shade and thrive in average to rich well-drained soil.

Anthemis carpatica. Grows 3 to 6 inches tall, spreading to 6 inches. Zones 6 to 10.

Arabis × sturii. Mountain rockcress. Grows 4 to 8 inches tall, spreading to 8 inches. Zones 4 to 8.

Arenaria spp. Sandworts. Corsican sandwort (*A. balearica*) grows ½ inch tall, spreading to 1 foot; Zones 7 to 10. Moss sandwort (*A. verna*, also listed as *Minuartia verna*) grows 1½ to 2 inches tall, spreading 8 to 12 inches; Zones 3 to 9. Both need sandy to loamy well-drained soil.

Azorella trifurcata (also listed as *A. nivalis*). Grows 4 inches tall, spreading 8 to 10 inches. Zones 6 to 7.

Cerastium alpinum. Alpine mouse-ear chickweed. Grows 3 to 6 inches tall, spreading 6 to 8 inches. Zones 6 to 10.

Erysimum kotschyanum. Dwarf yellow wallflower. Grows 2 to 4 inches tall, spreading to 8 inches. Zones 6 to 8.

Leptinella squalida (formerly *Cotula squalida*). Grows 6 inches tall, spreading indefinitely. Zones 4 to 7.

Lysimachia japonica var. *minutissima*. Dwarf creeping Jenny. Grows 1 inch tall, spreading to 12 inches. Zones 6 to 10.

Petrorhagia saxifraga (formerly *Tunica saxifraga*). Grows 3 to 6 inches tall, spreading to 8 inches. Zones 5 to 7.

Persicaria affinis. Himalayan fleeceflower. See page 100.

Scleranthus uniflorus. Grows 1 to 2 inches, spreading to 8 inches. Zones 6 to 10.

Sedum spp. Sedums, stonecrops. Including *S. album* 'Chloroticum', *S. humifusum*, and *S. spurium* 'John Creech'. See page 84.

Silene acaulis. Moss campion. Grows 2 inches tall, spreading to 8 inches. Zones 3 to 5.

Soleirolia soleirolii. Baby's tears. Grows 1 to 2 inches tall, spreading indefinitely. Zones 9 to 11.

Leptinella squalida 'Platt's Black'

All the species listed here bear showy, five-petaled flowers and palmate leaves (with leaflets arranged like the fingers on a hand). To propagate these species, divide the clumps in spring or fall.

P. alba. This low-growing mat-former is only 3 inches tall and spreads to 1 foot. Plants bear five-leaflet leaves and loose clusters of white, saucer-shaped flowers from late spring to early summer. Zones 5 to 8.

P. cinerea (formerly *P. tommasiniana*). Rusty cinquefoil. This low grower reaches 2 to 4 inches tall and spreads to 1 foot or more. Plants bear gray-green, five-leaflet leaves and are topped by yellow, saucer-shaped flowers in spring. Zones 3 to 9.

P. neumanniana (formerly *P. verna* and *P. tabernaemontani*). This is a 3- to 6-inch-tall species that spreads fairly quickly to form 1- to 2-foot-wide mats of semievergreen palmate leaves with five to seven lance-shaped leaflets. Plants bear loose clusters of saucer-shaped yellow flowers in spring and early summer. 'Nana' is 3 inches tall. Zones 4 to 9.

P. reptans. This fast-growing perennial is 3 to 6 inches tall, and plants quickly spread to form 1- to 2-foot-wide mounds that will blanket rocks and rough ground easily. Plants produce yellow flowers with heart-shaped petals in early summer and palmate leaves with five to seven leaflets. Zones 4 to 10.

P. tridentata. Native from Greenland to the United States as far west as Wisconsin and south to Georgia, this species has three-leaflet, evergreen leaves. Plants are woody at the base, grow 4 to 12 inches tall, and spread slowly to form 1-foot-wide mats. They bear

Sagina subulata

loose clusters of small white flowers in early summer. Plants are drought tolerant and especially suited for acid soils on dry slopes and rocky outcroppings. Zones 2 to 8.

Pratia pedunculata
Blue star creeper

EXPOSURE: Full sun to partial shade
HEIGHT: 2 to 5 inches
SPREAD: Indefinite

This vigorous, herbaceous perennial forms a ground-hugging mat of rounded leaves. Where happy, plants spread vigorously by stolons and rhizomes. They are topped by small star-shaped pale blue flowers in summer. Closely related to lobelia, and formerly listed as *Lobelia pedunculata*, this is a great choice for attractive filling in between stepping-stones or covering a small area. Give plants full sun toward the northern limits of their hardiness range, along with gritty soil that remains moist but is very well drained, since perfect drainage helps with winter survival. Farther south, give them partial shade and rich, moist, sandy or gritty soil. Plants don't grow well in areas with long, hot summers. Water regularly in warm weather, because they are not drought tolerant. Zones 5 to 7.

Sagina subulata
Corsican pearlwort

EXPOSURE: Full sun to light shade
HEIGHT: 2 to 4 inches
SPREAD: Indefinite

Also called Irish moss and Scotch moss, this low-growing species has evergreen linear leaves and forms a mosslike mat of foliage topped by small white flowers in summer. (The common name Irish moss is a confusing one that emphasizes the importance of using botanical names. It is also used to refer to two tender species — baby's tears, *Soleirolia soleirolii,* as well as trailing spikemoss, *Selaginella kraussiana* 'Brownii', which is also sometimes listed as Scotch moss. *Minuartia verna* subsp. *caespitosa* is also sold as Irish moss, but plants sold under this name probably are *Sagina subulata* 'Aurea'.)

Sagina subulata is handsome growing between stepping-stones and also can be used to cover the ground alongside paths, among rocks, or in other small spaces. Plants tolerate occasional foot traffic and can be used as a substitute for lawn grass. Give them a spot with rich, acid to neutral soil that is well drained. Loamy or sandy soils are ideal, but crown rot can be a problem in clay soil. Plants are not drought resistant, so water regularly in dry weather. 'Aurea' features chartreuse leaves, but plants self-sow and seedlings usually are green. Mow plantings before the flowers fade to reduce self-sowing. The mounds created by established plants can become lumpy. Dig up mounded portions, discard some of the older growth, and press down the remaining plants to smooth out the surface of the planting. Zones 5 to 9 or 10.

Satureja douglasii
Yerba buena, savory

EXPOSURE: Full sun to partial shade
HEIGHT: 2 inches
SPREAD: 3 feet

Native from British Columbia to southern California, this drought-tolerant species is a fine ground cover for decorating pathways, and its evergreen leaves are aromatic, a feature that adds appeal when plantings are occasionally stepped upon. The trailing stems bear small oval leaves with rounded teeth, along with white to purple flowers from spring to late summer. Give plants rich, moist, well-drained soil. They grow best in full sun in areas with humid summers but should be planted in partial shade elsewhere. Mow plantings in spring to keep them low and neat. Zones 5 to 10.

Satureja glabella, native from Kentucky to Arkansas, is another good ground cover that forms a somewhat taller cover, from 1 to 2 feet tall. Plants produce pale purple flowers in summer. Zones 6 to 9.

Thymus spp.
Thymes

EXPOSURE: Full sun to light shade
HEIGHT: 1 to 6 inches
SPREAD: 1 to 2 feet

Low-growing thymes are ideal for covering the ground in spots where plants may receive light foot traffic. Use them around stepping-stones, along pathways, or to fill in around rocks or boulders, or combine several cultivars and species to create a thyme lawn. All of the species listed here feature aromatic evergreen leaves and are quite low growing. For information on taller thymes, see page 103. All thymes require excellent drainage and are happiest in loose, poor, somewhat dry, sandy soil. They will grow in rich or clayey soil, provided it is very well drained. Thymes also are quite drought tolerant. Propagate them by dividing plants in spring, by potting up sections of rooted stems in spring or summer, or by taking cuttings in early or midsummer.

T. caespititius. This ¾- to 2-inch-tall subshrub forms a dense mat of small dark green leaves. Plants spread to about 1 foot and are topped from late spring to early summer with rounded clusters of tiny pink, lilac, or white flowers. Zones 4 to 9.

T. herba-barona. Caraway thyme. Ranging from 2 to 4 inches tall, this subshrub forms a mat of dark green, caraway-scented leaves topped by rounded clusters of pink flowers in summer. Plants spread to about 8 inches. Zones 6 to 9.

T. polytrichus. Formerly known as *T. praecox,* this 2-inch-tall subshrub forms a dense, 2-foot-wide mat of dark green leaves. Plants bear rounded clusters of pale to dark purple flowers in summer and tolerate light foot traffic. 'Bressingham' has bright pink flowers. Zones 5 to 9.

Thymus serpyllum 'Coccineus'

Waldsteinia lobata

T. pseudolanuginosus. Woolly thyme. This 1- to 2-inch-tall species spreads to about 1 foot and is perhaps the best choice for a spot that receives occasional foot traffic. Plants have hairy, rounded, gray leaves and pale pink summer flowers, although they do not bloom as much as other thymes. They require perfect drainage and are best used in rock gardens, in raised beds, or on sites with gravelly or sandy soil — especially where hot, humid, rainy summer weather keeps the soil moist. Zones 5 to 8.

T. serpyllum. Creeping thyme, wild thyme, mother-of-thyme. This mat-forming, subshrub normally ranges from 1 to 4 inches, although some forms are taller. Plants bear trailing stems, tiny, aromatic leaves, and rounded clusters of flowers in summer. A number of different forms are available, including supercompact 'Elfin' and 'Minimus', both of which are 1 to 2 inches tall and spread to about 4 or 6 inches. 'Aureus' bears golden leaves. 'Annie Hall' features pink flowers. 'Pink Chintz' has gray-green leaves and produces pink flowers. 'Snowdrift' displays white blooms. 'Coccineus', also listed as a cultivar of *T. polytrichus,* has reddish pink flowers. Plants tolerate very light foot traffic. Zones 4 to 9.

Trifolium repens 'Purpurascens Quadrifolium'
Purple-leaved clover

EXPOSURE: Full sun
HEIGHT: 4 inches
SPREAD: Indefinite

Despite its small size, this species is a vigorous spreader that forms a thick carpet of maroon-purple leaves edged in green; each leaf has four rounded leaflets. Clusters of small white flowers appear in summer. Plants tolerate light foot traffic and are vigorous enough to replace lawn on small- to medium-size sites. Give them rich, moist, well-drained soil. The green-leaved species has been classified as invasive in several states. Zones 4 to 8.

Waldsteinia spp.
Mock strawberries

EXPOSURE: Full sun to partial shade
HEIGHT: 4 to 8 inches
SPREAD: 2 feet or more

These mat-forming herbaceous perennials spread by rhizomes and feature handsome, glossy leaves and saucer-shaped, five-petaled flowers. They make fine lawn grass substitutes and also will happily fill in under shrubs and trees or around large clumps of perennials. Plants tolerate very light foot traffic. Propagate by dividing the clumps in early spring.

W. fragarioides. Barren strawberry. Native to the Southeastern United States, this species is 4 to 8 inches tall and spreads to 2 feet or more. Plants bear glossy evergreen leaves that are divided into three rounded, scalloped leaflets. Five-petaled yellow flowers appear in spring and summer. Plants thrive in any well-drained soil, are somewhat drought tolerant, and spread fastest in rich soil. Zones 4 to 7.

W. lobata. Lobed barren strawberry. This species is not popular in commerce but may be available from native plant specialists. Plants bear glossy evergreen leaves that are lobed and have smaller flowers than *W. fragarioides.* They are 4 to 8 inches tall and spread to 2 feet or more. The species is native from North Carolina south to Georgia, and plants easily tolerate heat and humidity, making this a good native ground cover for the Southeast. Plants grow in full sun provided the soil is evenly moist, but otherwise they require partial shade. Zones 7 to 9.

W. ternata. Dry strawberry. Native to Siberia, this species is 4 inches tall and spreads by both rhizomes and stolons to form a dense cover that can range from 2 to many feet across. Plants bear semievergreen, three-part leaves that are shallowly lobed and toothed and are topped by loose clusters of bright yellow flowers in late spring and early summer. They tolerate dry sites in partial shade. Zones 3 to 8.

Small-Scale
Spreaders

Low-growing species that spread nicely, but not too vigorously, offer a handsome option for edging paths or covering small spaces anywhere in the garden.

Ground covers that spread politely are useful for carpeting all sorts of sites in the garden. Most of the species listed here do not tolerate foot traffic and so are best alongside paths and walkways, but not in between stepping-stones. They are all ideal for replacing areas of lawn to reduce landscape maintenance. Plant them alone, or combine several species to create a colorful carpet of flowers and foliage.

There are two options for arranging plants when covering ground with a combination of several different species. To highlight the textures and colors of the foliage and flowers of each species, arrange the plants in drifts with several specimens of each species planted together. In an informal design, create free-form drifts, and don't worry about planting the same number of plants in each drift. For a garden with a formal design, stick to geometric shapes and let the elements of the design help determine how large each block of plants is.

Yet another planting option is to interplant several species and simply let them grow together to create a carpet with colors and textures created by the mix of plants, rather than by drifts of individual species.

1. *Phlox subulata*
   Moss phlox

2. *Corydalis ochroleuca*
   Corydalis

3. *Sempervivum* sp.
   Hens-and-chicks

4. *Thymus × citriodorus* 'Aureus'
   Lemon thyme

5. *Armeria maritima* 'Splendens'
   Common thrift

6. *Prunella grandiflora*
   Selfheal

7. *Sempervivum tectorum*
   Hens-and-chicks

8. *Armeria maritima, Sedum* sp.,
   Saxifraga sp.
   Common thrift, sedum, saxifrage

9. *Phlox subulata*
   Moss phlox

10. *Persicaria affinis* 'Donald Lowndes'
    Himalayan fleeceflower

11. *Corydalis lutea*
    Corydalis

Achillea tomentosa
Woolly yarrow

EXPOSURE: Full sun
HEIGHT: 6 to 14 inches
SPREAD: 1½ feet

Named for its densely woolly, gray-green foliage, this species forms a low mat of deeply cut leaves topped by flat-topped clusters of yellow flowers from early summer to fall. Plants thrive in hot, dry, sunny spots and poor, sandy soil. Use them in rock gardens and raised beds where they will get the absolutely perfect drainage they require. Plants languish in hot, humid, rainy conditions. Zones 3 to 7.

Antennaria dioica
Common pussytoes

EXPOSURE: Full sun to light shade
HEIGHT: 2 to 12 inches
SPREAD: 1½ to 2 feet

This ground-hugging perennial bears semievergreen, spoon-shaped leaves that are gray-green. The foliage is quite low to the ground — perhaps 2 inches — and white or pale pink flowers are borne in small clusters above the foliage in early summer. The plants tolerate light foot traffic as well as drought and make nice additions to raised beds with rich, well-drained soil. Plants grow well in sandy conditions too, and they are handsome around low shrubs, perennials, or herbs. This species also is an excellent choice for a rock garden. Zones 3 to 9. While common pussytoes is native to Europe, northern Asia, and North America, several species are native strictly to North America and make nice ground covers as well. At native plant specialists, look for ladies' tobacco (*A. plantaginifolia*), solitary pussytoes (*A. solitaria*), *A. alpina*, *A. parlinii,* and *A. virginica.*

Armeria maritima
Common thrift

EXPOSURE: Full sun to light shade
HEIGHT: 8 inches
SPREAD: 1 foot

A low-growing perennial producing clumps of grasslike leaves, common thrift spreads slowly but nevertheless makes a nice ground cover for a small area. Plants produce round clusters of pink or white flowers from late spring into summer. They require well-drained soil and won't survive in heavy clay. For best results, give them light afternoon shade in the South. More compact cultivars include 'Alba' with white flowers, 'Dusseldorf Pride' with rose-pink blooms, and 'Vindictive' with pink flowers. These cultivars and the species are hardy in Zones 3 to 9. Popular 'Bees' Ruby', a hybrid, bears bright pink flowers on 1½-foot stalks and is hardy only in Zones 6 and 7. Propagate all forms by dividing clumps in early spring or by rooting cuttings taken from the base of the plant in summer. *A. juniperifolia* is smaller than *A. maritima*; it reaches 2 to 3 inches tall and spreads to perhaps 6 inches. Flowers come in white as well as pale to dark pink. Zones 5 to 7.

Bergenia spp.
Bergenias

EXPOSURE: Full sun to partial shade
HEIGHT: 1 foot
SPREAD: 2 feet

This low-growing ground cover is also called pigsqueak, a common name that refers to the sound made when you rub the large leathery leaves between your fingers. The leaves are 3 inches to as much as 10 inches long, rounded, and usually evergreen or semievergreen, although they are fairly tattered looking

Armeria maritima, Sedum sp., Saxifraga sp.

by late winter. Plants produce clusters of small pinkish purple or white flowers in late winter or early spring. Many cultivars are available, quite a few of which develop rich bronze-purple foliage in winter. Give bergenias any rich, moist, well-drained soil. They grow in full sun to light shade in cooler regions but need light to partial shade in the warmer areas. Plants spread slowly by fleshy rhizomes and are somewhat drought tolerant. Divide clumps that begin to die out in the middle. Propagate by division in spring or fall or by rooting sections of rhizomes. Zones 4 to 8.

Coreopsis auriculata
Dwarf-eared tickseed

EXPOSURE: Full sun to light shade
HEIGHT: 1 to 2 feet
SPREAD: 2 feet

Also called mouse-eared coreopsis, this native of the southeastern United States spreads by stolons and forms a handsome cover of rounded leaves topped by 2-inch-wide, golden yellow flower heads from early to midsummer. 'Nana' is the best choice for ground cover use, as it is only 8 inches tall. 'Superba', to 18 inches tall, produces showy, 2- to 3-inch-wide blooms that are orange-yellow marked with maroon at the center. For the best results, give plants rich, evenly moist, well-drained soil. The foliage deteriorates if they are subjected to drought. Propagate in spring by dividing clumps or by taking cuttings from shoots at the base of the plant. Zones 4 to 9.

Corydalis spp.
Corydalis

EXPOSURE: Full sun to partial shade
HEIGHT: 1 to 1½ feet
SPREAD: 1 foot

These handsome perennials do not creep to cover the ground, but they do self-sow. They fill in around other plants and make fine additions to ground cover gardens. All bear fernlike, deeply cut leaves and racemes of small, tubular flowers. Use corydalis as edging plants, and combine them with other perennial ground covers of similar stature. The species listed here thrive in rich, well-drained soil. Propagate by sowing seed as soon as it is ripe or moving self-sown seedlings while they are still small.

C. cheilanthifolia. This evergreen species forms dense rosettes of fine-textured, very fernlike leaves. Clusters of yellow flowers appear from spring to summer. Plants self-sow very freely. Zones 5 to 7.

C. lutea. A mound-forming perennial, this species spreads by short rhizomes as well as self-sown seeds. Plants produce handsome clumps of fernlike, semievergreen or evergreen leaves and showy yellow flowers from spring to early fall. Plants grow in average, fast-draining soil as well as rich, moist conditions. Zones 5 to 8

C. ochroleuca. This clump-forming species produces mounds of fernlike leaves that are evergreen or semievergreen. Plants bear clusters of white flowers from late spring to summer. Zones 6 to 8.

Corydalis ochroleuca

Cymbalaria muralis
Kenilworth ivy

EXPOSURE: Partial to full shade
HEIGHT: 1 to 2 inches
SPREAD: 3 feet or more

Also called Coliseum ivy and ivy-leaved toadflax, this species creeps as well as climbs, and it can scale walls provided it finds enough moisture for its roots. The plants can climb to 3 feet, and they produce lobed, kidney-shaped leaves and lilac summer flowers. 'Alba Compacta' spreads to 12 inches. Give plants a site with well-drained soil that is constantly moist. They do not tolerate heat or drought. Use Kenilworth ivy for filling in around rocks or covering the cracks in a wall. Zones 4 to 8.

Gypsophila repens
Creeping baby's breath

EXPOSURE: Full sun
HEIGHT: 8 inches
SPREAD: 1½ to 2 feet

A mat-forming baby's breath, *G. repens* bears linear, blue-green leaves that are semievergreen. Plants creep slowly to form a dense ground cover and are topped by small clusters of ½-inch star-shaped white or pink flowers in summer. 'Alba' bears white flowers and is 4 inches tall. 'Dorothy Teacher' is only 2 inches tall and bears pink flowers. A spot with light sandy or gravelly soil that is very well drained is best. Unlike other baby's breaths, this species grows in acid as well as alkaline soil. Plants are resistant to drought but grow best when watered deeply during dry summer weather. Zones 3 to 8.

Jovibarba spp.
Houseleeks

EXPOSURE: Full sun to light shade
HEIGHT: 6 inches
SPREAD: 1 foot

The plants in this genus very much resemble hens-and-chicks, and in fact were once classified in *Sempervivum.* Whatever the name, these are drought-tolerant plants that rarely need watering. They produce evergreen rosettes of fleshy, pointed leaves topped by clusters of small, bell-shaped flowers. They spread by stolons and form a dense cover. Grow them in poor soil that is gritty or sandy and has perfect drainage. Give the plants full sun, or find a spot that offers full morning sun and light afternoon shade. Since they will not bloom again, pull up rosettes that have flowered to make room for new growth. Propagate by potting up offsets in spring or early summer.

J. hirta (formerly *S. hirtum*). This species produces rosettes of olive-green leaves tipped with brown, purple, or red, and rosettes are only 1 to 3 inches wide. Plants produce clusters of yellow-brown flowers on 6-inch stalks in summer. Zones 5 to 8.

J. sobolifera (formerly *S. soboliferum*). The foliage rosettes of this species are 1 to 2 inches wide and consist of bright green leaves with fringed edges that

GROUND-HUGGING SHRUBS

IF THEY ARE COMPACT ENOUGH, dwarf shrubs can be used as edgings alongside paths. The following are all under a foot tall and generally don't spread beyond 1½ or 2 feet.

Arctostaphylos uva-ursi. **Bearberry, kinnikinick. See page 114.**

Cotoneaster adpressus. **Creeping cotoneaster. See page 130.**

Cotoneaster dammeri. **Bearberry cotoneaster. Especially 'Moner' (sold as Canadian, 'Eichholz', 'Lowfast', and 'Streib's Findling'. See page139.**

Cotoneaster perpusillus. **See page 131.**

Hypericum olympicum. **Olympic St. John's wort. See page 115.**

Juniperus spp. **Junipers. See page 72, 140.**

Salix uva-ursi. **Bearberry willow. See page 134.**

flush with red as they age. Plants produce greenish yellow flowers in summer. Zones 5 to 8.

Nierembergia repens
White cup flower

EXPOSURE: Full sun to partial shade
HEIGHT: 2 to 6 inches
SPREAD: 1 to 2 feet

This tender species bears spoon-shaped leaves and 2-inch-wide flowers that are white with yellow centers and resemble morning glories. Plants produce mats of creeping stems that root where they touch the soil. Give them a site with rich, moist, well-drained soil. They prefer full sun toward the northern limits of their range and light to partial shade farther south. Propagate by sowing seed in fall, by dividing clumps in spring, or by digging up rooted tips of stems anytime. Zones 7 to 10.

Persicaria affinis
Himalayan fleeceflower

EXPOSURE: Full sun to partial shade
HEIGHT: 6 to 10 inches
SPREAD: 2 to 3 feet or more

Also called Himalayan knotweed, and formerly classified as *Polygonum affine*, this is a mat-forming evergreen that makes a good general ground cover and tolerates very infrequent foot traffic. The plants produce rounded to lance-shaped leaves that turn maroon to brown in autumn. They produce cylindrical spikes tightly packed with tiny, pale pink flowers from midsummer to midfall. Himalayan fleeceflowers require rich, evenly moist soil and don't tolerate heat well. Use them under trees or as a skirt around the edges of shrubs. They are also a good choice for planting along the south or west side of ever-

Persicaria affinis

greens, where plants will get some light. 'Darjeeling Red' bears large leaves and pink flowers that age to red. 'Superba' features pale pink flowers that turn reddish along with handsome brown fall foliage. Zones 3 to 8.

Phlox subulata
Moss phlox, moss pink

EXPOSURE: Full sun to light shade
HEIGHT: 4 to 6 inches
SPREAD: 2 feet

This phlox, native to the eastern and central United States, bears evergreen, needlelike leaves that form dense, prickly, soil-hugging mounds. Moss phlox plantings are covered with showy five-petaled flowers in late spring. The blooms come in shades of purple, pink, reddish pink, and white, and plants produce a thick carpet of flowers that are held just above the foliage, nearly obscuring the leaves. Many cultivars are available. This species is a fine alternative to lawn grass, although the plants don't withstand foot traffic. Plants grow in any well-drained soil, are fine in sandy conditions, and also withstand some drought. Use them to edge pathways, combine them with low-growing shrubs as part of a foundation planting, or plant them on rocky sites and let them fill in to eliminate trimming. Another phlox suitable for covering ground in sun is *P. × procumbens*, commonly called hybrid or trailing phlox. It is the result of crossing *P. subulata* with *P. stolonifera*, another native species. Plants are semievergreen, come in similar colors, and bloom in early summer. Propagate by dividing the plants in spring. Both types of phlox are hardy in Zones 3 to 8.

Prunella grandiflora
Selfheal, prunella

EXPOSURE: Full sun to partial shade
HEIGHT: 6 to 12 inches
SPREAD: 1½ to 3 feet

Also called carpenter weed, this semievergreen perennial spreads as stems root wherever the leaf nodes touch the soil. Plants produce clumps of rounded leaves topped by spikelike clusters of two-lipped flowers that are pale lavender with darker purple lips. Cultivars with white, pink, violet-blue, and pinkish red flowers are available. All perform best in rich, well-drained soil and need evenly moist conditions in summer, since they are not particularly drought tolerant. Selfheal can seed freely and has naturalized in some areas. Use it with other ground covers for covering rough ground or as an edging under larger perennials. Mow plantings when the flowers fade to prevent self-sowing, since cultivars do not come true from seed. Propagate by dividing clumps in spring or fall. Zones 5 to 8.

Saponaria ocymoides
Rock soapwort

EXPOSURE: Full sun
HEIGHT: 4 to 8 inches
SPREAD: 1½ to 3 feet

Although not a thick, densely rooting ground cover, rock soapwort is handsome when used to edge a pathway where it can billow over the edges. It's also suitable for planting along the top of walls, on gentle slopes, and on rocky sites. Plants bear lance-shaped leaves and masses of five-petaled pink flowers in summer. They grow in most well-drained soils, including sandy ones, and also tolerate drought. Shear or mow plantings immediately after flowering to keep them neat and to encourage thick growth. Several cultivars with white and pale to deep pink flowers are available. Zones 4 to 8. *Saponaria × lempergii*, a hybrid, is another nice soapwort for covering the ground that grows in much the same conditions as *S. ocymoides*. Plants are 12 inches tall, spread to about 18 inches, and produce magenta flowers in mid- to late summer. 'Max Frei' bears pale pink flowers from early to midsummer. Zones 5 to 8.

Sempervivum spp.
Hens-and-chicks

EXPOSURE: Full sun to light shade
HEIGHT: 2 to 6 inches
SPREAD: 1 to 2 feet

These tough, fleshy-leaved perennials produce rosettes of fleshy leaves, somewhat like pinecones, topped in summer by clusters of relatively insignificant starry flowers. Plants spread when the large rosette in the center (the "hen") produces offsets at the end of runners (the "chicks"). The rosettes, which can vary from 1 to 4 inches across, can be green, green flushed with red, or covered with cobweblike hairs. Use houseleeks in broad drifts, or plant a collection of cultivars with different colors to create a tapestry-like pattern. They are supremely tolerant of drought and heat and grow in poor to average soil provided it is very well drained. (Dig in grit or coarse sand at planting time to ensure perfect drainage.) These plants also can be used to fill small cracks between pavers but won't take foot traffic because the leaves and stems are brittle. The rosettes, or "hens", die after flowering: pull them up and toss them on the compost pile to make more room for the offsets. Propagate by potting up offsets in spring or early summer. Zones 4 or 5 to 8, depending on the species.

Sempervivum calcareum 'Mrs. Giuseppi'

Bulbs for Adding Color

Drifts of ground-hugging plants offer a perfect opportunity for adding an extra tier of spring color to your garden.

Underplant low-growing ground covers with drifts of the so-called little bulbs, which will happily bloom just above the foliage of low-growing ground covers. To ensure years of bloom, be sure to let the bulb foliage ripen; don't clip it off until after it has turned yellow. As for bulbs that mice and voles relish — like crocuses — plan on replanting every few years. After all, the little bulbs listed here are inexpensive and very easy to stick into the soil. To plant them, simply use a trowel to make room between ground covers and set the bulbs about 3 or 4 inches deep.

Anemone blanda. Grecian windflower. Zones 4 to 8.

Chionodoxa spp. Glory-of-the-snow. Zones 3 to 9 for most species.

Crocus spp. Crocuses. Especially snow crocus (*C. chrysanthus*), Scotch crocus (*C. biflorus*), Dutch crocus (*C. vernus*), and *C. tommasinianus.* Zones 3 to 8.

Eranthis hyemalis. Winter aconite. Zones 4 to 9.

Galanthus nivalis. Common snowdrop. Zones 3 to 9.

Hyacinthoides hispanica. Spanish bluebells. Zones 4 to 9.

Iris reticulata. Reticulated iris. Zones 5 to 8.

Leucojum aestivum. Summer snowflake. Zones 4 to 9.

Muscari spp. Grape hyacinths. Zones 3 or 4 to 9, depending on the species.

Narcissus spp. Daffodils and narcissus. Especially compact cultivars such as 'Baby Moon', 'Chit Chat', 'Hawera' 'Jumblie', 'Little Gem', and 'Minnow', along with species selections such as *N. bulbocodium conspicuus*, commonly called hoop-petticoat daffodil. Zones 4 to 9.

Puschkinia scilloides. Striped squill. Zones 3 to 9.

Scilla spp. Squills. Zones 3, 4, or 5 to 8, depending on the species.

Tulipa spp. Tulips. Especially selections of species such as *T. bakeri, T. batalinii,* and *T. humilis,* as well as Kaufmanniana tulips such as 'Heart's Delight', 'Scarlet Baby', and 'Stresa'. Zones 3 to 8.

Finally, don't forget fall-blooming bulbs, which often are too short to plant with full-size perennials. For fall bloom, consider *Crocus cartwrightianus, C. goulimyi, C. kotschyanus, C. longiflorus, C. medius, C. niveus, C. ochroleucus, C. pulchellus, C. sativus,* and *C. speciosus.* Autumn crocuses (*Colchicum* spp.) also provide spectacular bloom, but be aware that they produce large clumps of leaves in spring and the leaves can be quite unsightly while they are ripening. Use these plants in informal beds where the yellowing leaves won't detract from the rest of your spring display. Winter daffodil (*Sternbergia lutea*) is another excellent bulb for adding yellow, somewhat crocuslike flowers in fall.

Siberian squill (*Scilla sibirica*) adds a dose of color to early spring lawns.

Teucrium chamaedrys
Germander

EXPOSURE: Full sun to light shade
HEIGHT: 8 to 18 inches
SPREAD: 1 to 2 feet

Also called wall or ground germander, this is a semievergreen subshrub with small, rounded, glossy dark green leaves. Plants bear loose clusters of pale pink or purplish, two-lipped flowers from summer to early fall. They are somewhat slow spreaders and are especially effective edging paths, combined in drifts with other ground covers such as candytuft (*Iberis sempervirens*), or planted around sculptures, rocks, or other garden highlights. Plants can be kept clipped for use as a low hedge. Give germander any well-drained soil. Although plants are fairly drought tolerant once established, they perform best when the soil remains evenly moist. Propagate by taking cuttings in early or midsummer. Zones 5 to 9.

Thymus spp.
Thymes

EXPOSURE: Full sun to light shade
HEIGHT: 1 foot
SPREAD: 1 to 2 feet

Whether used as lawn substitutes, ground covers for small areas, or edging plants, thymes contribute aromatic foliage and dainty flowers to the garden. For information on low-growing species, see Ground Huggers for Paths and Stepping-Stones on page 89. The species covered here are evergreen shrubs or subshrubs, and their woody stems do not tolerate any foot traffic. All need excellent drainage, are drought tolerant, and grow best in somewhat dry soil. Wet soil in winter is fatal. While the plants will grow in light shade, they are happiest in full sun. Propagate them by potting up sections of rooted stems in spring or summer, by taking cuttings in early summer, or by mound layering (see Mound Layering on page 209).

T. × citriodorus. Lemon thyme. A mounding shrub, lemon thyme is usually 4 to 8 inches tall but can reach 1 foot tall. Plants spread to form fairly broad, 1- or 2-foot-wide mounds covered with small, lemon-scented leaves. They bear clusters of tiny, lavender-pink flowers in summer. Zones 6 to 9.

T. vulgaris. Common thyme. Growing 6 to 12 inches tall, this species spreads 1½ or 2 feet. Plants bear rounded, dark green leaves that are richly fragrant and produce clusters of white or rosy purple flowers in late spring or early summer. Zones 4 to 9.

Verbena spp.
Verbenas, vervains

EXPOSURE: Full sun
HEIGHT: 3 to 12 inches
SPREAD: 1 to 2 feet

Perennial verbenas used as ground covers have trailing stems and showy clusters of flowers that are very attractive to butterflies. Use them to cover a small area, or combine them with other ground covers. They also can be grown along the top of a rock wall or allowed to trail down a gentle slope. Verbenas grow in a range of well-drained soils, including poor and sandy ones. They are also are fairly drought tolerant, although they bloom and grow best when watered during dry weather. Shear or deadhead the plants after they flower to keep them neat and to encourage branching. Propagate by taking cuttings in spring or summer or by dividing clumps in spring or fall.

Verbena 'Homestead Purple'

V. bipinnatifida. Dakota verbena. A species native from the Dakotas south to Alabama, this verbena bears deeply cut leaves on prostrate stems that reach 3 inches tall and sprawl to 1½ or 2 feet. Dense clusters of trumpet-shaped, pale purple flowers appear from late spring through frost. Zones 4 to 7.

V. canadensis. Rose verbena, rose vervain, creeping vervain. Native to the southeastern United States, this species is 4 to 6 inches tall and spreads to 2 feet. Plants grow naturally in sandy and rocky soils and are ideal for similar sites with poor soil in gardens. They bear deeply cut leaves and dense, rounded clusters of rose-pink flowers in summer. 'Homestead Purple' has purple flowers and is mildew resistant. Zones 4 to 7.

V. peruviana. Peruvian verbena. A tender evergreen perennial with toothed, lance-shaped leaves, this species is 4 to 6 inches tall and spreads to 3 feet. Plants produce dense, flat-topped clusters of brilliant red flowers from summer to fall. Zone 8 to 10.

Perennials
for Bold Cover in Sun

Sometimes a vigorous constitution — without rapidly advancing rhizomes — is all it takes for a plant to be a good ground cover.

In addition to vigorous growth, the plants on this list all bring colorful flowers and attractive foliage to the garden. Cover an area with drifts of several different species to create a ground cover planting that resembles a flower bed. But to ensure quick coverage, space plants more closely than you might for a typical perennial garden.

Other showy species you may want to consider for a bold-color ground cover garden include daylilies (*Hemerocallis* spp.), orange coneflowers (*Rudbeckia fulgida*), taller sedums (*Sedum* spp.) such as the popular 'Autumn Joy' (also sold as 'Herbstfreude'), sundrops (*Oenothera* spp.), the many salvias (*Salvia* spp.), and veronicas (*Veronica* spp.) such as 'Goodness Grows' and 'Sunny Border Blue'. Admittedly, these plants are taller than traditional ground covers, but there's absolutely no hard-and-fast rule that says ground covers have to hug the ground.

But don't stop here. New cultivars are being introduced all the time, and dwarf selections are especially popular. There even are ground-covering New England asters (*Aster novae-angliae*): 'Purple Dome' is only 1½ feet tall and spreads to 3 feet, although the species ranges from 4 to 5 feet tall and spreads nearly as wide.

1. *Caryopteris × clandonensis* 'Longwood Blue' Bluebeard
2. *Iris ensata* Japanese iris
3. *Centranthus ruber* Jupiter's beard
4. *Iris tectorum* Japanese roof iris
5. *Yucca filamentosa* 'Golden Sword' Adam's needle
6. *Callirhoe involucrata* Poppy mallow
7. *Campanula poscharskyana* Bellflower
8. *Sedum spectabile* 'Brilliant' Sedum
9. *Paeonia suffruticosa* Peony

Callirhoe involucrata
Poppy mallow

EXPOSURE: Full sun to light shade
HEIGHT: 3 to 10 inches
SPREAD: 4 to 5 feet

This prairie plant, native from the Midwest to Texas, is a is a tap-rooted perennial that bears magenta flowers from late spring to midsummer. Plants form sprawling clumps and are effective combined with other perennials that need good drainage. They grow in any well-drained soil, including alkaline ones, and tolerate drought and heat. Avoid sites that are wet in winter. Zones 4 to 7.

Campanula spp.
Bellflowers

EXPOSURE: Full sun to light shade
HEIGHT: 4 to 12 inches
SPREAD: 1 to 2 feet or more

Although not heat tolerant, rhizomatous bellflowers can be used to cover the ground and decorate it with their blue, purple, or white flowers. Most bear larger, often heart-shaped leaves at the base of the plant and have smaller leaves along the stems. While bellflowers don't produce the dense foliage blanket that more conventional ground covers do, they can make satisfactory and very showy additions to plantings. Give them average to rich, moist but well-drained soil. They need full sun to light shade in the northern part of their range; light shade is best in the southern part. Propagate by sowing seed in spring, by dividing plants in spring or fall, or by taking cuttings from shoots at the base of the plant in spring.

C. carpatica. Carpathian harebell. This 8- to 12-inch-tall species spreads to 2 feet. Plants bear solitary, upturned, bell-shaped flowers for several months in summer in shades of blue, violet-purple, or white. Zones 3 to 8.

C. garganica. Gargano bellflower. This species bears showy racemes of starry blue to lilac flowers in summer. Plants grow 5 to 6 inches tall and spread to 1 foot or more. Zones 4 to 7.

C. portenschlagiana. Dalmatian bellflower. This species grows 4 to 6 inches tall and spreads to form 2-foot-wide mounds. From mid to late summer, plants bear loosely branched panicles of deep purple, tubular to funnel-shaped flowers Zones 4 to 8.

C. poscharskyana. Serbian bellflower. This vigorous bellflower grows from 6 to 12 inches tall. Plants spread by underground runners to 2 feet or more. From summer to early fall they bear panicles of pale lavender, star-shaped flowers. Zones 3 to 7.

C. rapunculoides.▼ Creeping bellflower. Despite the common name, this 2- to 4-foot-tall perennial isn't a creeper, it's an extremely aggressive species that is best avoided. Plants spread widely both by stolons and by self-sowing. They bear racemes of nodding, blue to violet flowers that are funnel- to bell-shaped. Zones 3 to 7.

Caryopteris × *clandonensis*
Bluebeard

EXPOSURE: Full sun
HEIGHT: 2 to 3 feet
SPREAD: 5 feet

A woody-based perennial, bluebeard bears gray-green leaves and clusters of tiny purple-blue flowers from late summer to fall. Plants need well-drained

Callirhoe involucrata

Caryopteris × *clandonensis* 'Longwood Blue' with *Phormium tenax* 'Atropurpureum'

▼ May be considered invasive in some regions.

soil, ideally somewhat sandy or light textured, and tolerate some drought. This species is shrubby in the South, but in Zones 4 to 6, plants die to the ground like herbaceous perennials. Either way, cut them back in late winter. Zones 4 to 9.

Centranthus ruber ▼
Jupiter's beard, red valerian

EXPOSURE: Full sun to light shade
HEIGHT: 3 feet
SPREAD: 3 feet or more

This species bears showy, loose clusters of small, fragrant, funnel-shaped flowers from late spring to late summer in shades of pink, pinkish red, or white. Plants are clump-forming, and they spread as the clumps expand as well as by self-sowing. (In a few western states, the plants self-sow freely enough to be classified as invasive.) They are ideal for sites with somewhat dry soil, are drought tolerant, and require well-drained conditions. Use them on rocky slopes or to help hold soil on steep banks. Zones 5 to 8.

Chrysanthemum × morifolium
Chrysanthemum, hardy mum

EXPOSURE: Full sun
HEIGHT: 2 to 3 feet
SPREAD: 3 to 4 feet

The typical mums sold everywhere in fall often don't generally perform as perennials and can't be used to cover much ground, but some hardy, garden-proven mums do make great ground covers. 'Sheffield Pink', with pink daisies in fall, is one. Others that can be used as ground covers include 'Mei-kyo' (small, lavender, button-type flowers), 'Penelope Pease' (white daisies), and 'Venus' (pale pink), as well as mums developed by the University of Minnesota's breeding program. Give them rich, well-drained soil. Zones 4 or 5 to 9.

Gold and silver chrysanthemum (*Ajania pacifica*, formerly *Chrysanthemum pacificum*) is a chrysanthemum relative that can be used to cover ground as well. Plants are 1 foot tall and spread to 3 feet. They bear green leaves edged in silver accented by clusters of small gold flowers in fall. Zones 5 to 9.

Iris spp.
Irises

EXPOSURE: Full sun to light shade
HEIGHT: 2 to 3 feet tall
SPREAD: 2 feet or more

Popular bearded irises are rhizomatous and will cover ground, but they need to be divided every couple of years, plus borers are a problem. For gorgeous flowers without all the work, consider these species.

I. ensata. Japanese iris. This species produces clumps of grassy leaves that are topped by flowers in shades of purple, lilac, white, pink, blue, and purple-red in early summer. Plants grow 2 to 3 feet tall and spread 2 feet or more with time. Give them rich, acid soil and steady moisture in spring and summer, with drier conditions in fall and winter. Zones 4 to 9.

I. sibirica. Siberian iris. Grown for their showy purple, violet-blue, lavender, white, or yellow flowers, which are borne in early summer, Siberian irises also produce handsome clumps of grassy foliage. Plants reach 2 to 3 feet tall and spread 2 feet or more with time. Give them rich, moist soil or boggy conditions. Zones 3 to 9.

I. tectorum. Japanese roof iris. This species bears strappy leaves and lilac or

Iris sibirica

Iris ensata

Edging in Style

PLANTINGS THAT EDGE WALKWAYS are typically subdued, all-green affairs. Here, large drifts of flowering perennials edge a walkway, creating a garden space that overflows with color and style. When using ground covers in your own garden, keep in mind that you get to make the rules. Let your own taste and garden style determine what works. You may end up with a solid green mat, a mix of plants with subtly variegated leaves, a blanket of bold perennials, or some other style of planting that suits you best.

1. Coreopsis
   (*Coreopsis grandiflora*)
2. Catmint
   (*Nepeta* 'Six Hills Giant')
3. California poppy
   (*Eschscholzia californica*)
4. Iris foliage
   (*Iris* sp.)
5. Orange Asiatic lily
   (*Lilium asiaticum*)

white early-summer flowers. Plants grow 10 to 16 inches tall and spread to several feet with time, forming a durable ground cover. Zones 4 to 8.

Paeonia spp.
Peonies

EXPOSURE: Full sun to partial shade
HEIGHT: 1½ to 3 feet or more
SPREAD: 3 to 4 feet

These herbaceous perennials are never sold as ground covers, but plant an area with clumps spaced fairly closely and that's what you have. Space peonies to be used as ground covers — or even low hedges — on 2½- or 3-foot centers, or farther apart to avoid overcrowding down the line. Plants will cover the ground with 2½-foot-tall mounds of handsome leaves, topped by spectacular flowers in shades of pink, rose, or white from late spring to early summer. Some species even have attractive seedheads. Give peonies rich, well-drained soil. Zones 3 to 8.

Sedum spp.
Sedums, stonecrops

EXPOSURE: Full sun
HEIGHT: 1½ to 2 feet
SPREAD: 2 feet or more

Even though taller sedums such as the popular 'Autumn Joy', also sold as 'Herbstfreude', aren't rhizomatous, they can be massed to make very effective ground covers. Clumps expand steadily, and if plants are spaced fairly closely (perhaps on 1½-foot centers, depending on the size of the plants) they will form a dense, weed-suppressing blanket in a season or two. 'Autumn Joy' produces clumps of fleshy leaves and flower clusters that emerge green in summer and look something like broccoli. Flowers turn from green to pink in early fall and finally deepen to bronze-pink. Spent flowerheads also add winter interest in the garden. *S. spectabile* and its cultivars are also suitable for massing as ground covers. 'Brilliant' bears bright

pink blooms, 'Carmen' darker mauve-pink ones. Give sedums any average, well-drained soil. Zones 3 to 9.

Yucca filamentosa
Adam's needle, yucca

EXPOSURE: Full sun
HEIGHT: 2½ feet
SPREAD: 5 feet

Grown more for foliage than flowers, this species is native from New Jersey to Florida. Plants produce clumps of strap-shaped, evergreen leaves topped by 5- to 6-foot-tall panicles of 2-inch-long bell-shaped white flowers in mid-summer. For extra color, plant variegated cultivars: 'Bright Edge' bears green leaves edged with yellow, while 'Golden Sword' has yellow leaves with green edges. When massed, yuccas can be used to cover a large area. Or combine them with other drought-tolerant perennials or shrubs. Zones 5 to 10.

Paeonia suffruticosa

Sedum spectabile 'Brilliant'

Yucca filamentosa 'Golden Sword'

Ground Covers for Seaside Sites

Stiff breezes, windborne salt, and sandy soil are just some of the challenges of gardening near the coast.

All of the plants listed here tolerate the conditions inherent in a seaside garden. They'll also grow well in sandy soil that's far from the ocean, so try them in other types of sandy or salty sites as well, including along sidewalks and roads where road salt is a problem.

Perennials

Ajuga spp. Ajugas, bugleweeds. See page 148.
Armeria maritima. Common thrift. See page 98.
Artemisia stelleriana. Beach wormwood. See page 78.
Callirhoe involucrata. Poppy mallow. See page 106.
Chrysanthemum × morifolium. Chrysanthemum, hardy mum. See page 107.
Dianthus spp. Pinks. See page 79.
Festuca glauca. Blue fescue. See page 86.
Gypsophila repens. Creeping baby's breath. See page 99.

Hemerocallis spp. Daylilies. See page 118.
Hosta spp. and hybrids. Hostas. See pages 71, 152 and 161.
Iberis sempervirens. Candytuft. See page 83.
Leymus arenarius. Blue lyme grass. See page 72.
Liriope spicata. Lilyturf. See page 83.
Ophiopogon spp. Ophiopogons. See page 84.
Pachysandra terminalis. Japanese pachysandra. See page 73.
Paeonia spp. Peonies. See page 109.
Phlox subulata. Moss phlox, moss pink. See page 100
Potentilla spp. Potentillas, cinquefoils. See page 91.
Sedum spp. Sedums, stonecrops. See pages 84 and 109.
Sempervivum spp. Houseleeks, hens-and-chicks. See page 101.
Stachys byzantina. Lamb's ears. See page 87.
Thymus serpyllum. Creeping thyme, wild thyme, mother-of-thyme. See page 95.
Veronica prostrata. Prostrate speedwell. See page 75.

Shrubs

Arctostaphylos pumila. Dune manzanita. See page 138.
Arctostaphylos uva-ursi. Bearberry, kinnikinick. See page 114.
Carissa macrocarpa. Natal plum. See page 138.
Chaenomeles japonica. Japanese flowering quince. See page 130.
Clethra alnifolia. Summersweet. See page 136.
Comptonia peregrina. Sweet fern, meadow fern. See page 114.
Coprosma × kirkii. Creeping coprosma. See page 114.
Cotoneaster spp. Cotoneasters. See pages 130 and 139.
Cytisus spp. Brooms. See page 114.

Thyme (*Thymus serpyllum*) and Mexican feather grass (*Stipa tenuissima*) tolerate the tough conditions on this California beach.

Hydrangea macrophylla. Bigleaf hydrangea. See page 136.

Ilex vomitoria. Yaupon holly, cassine holly. See page 140.

Juniperus spp. Junipers. See page 72 and 140.

Lavandula angustifolia. English lavender. See page 80.

Leucothoe axillaris. Fetterbush, coast leucothoe.
See page 161.

Muehlenbeckia axillaries. Creeping wire vine. See page 116.

Myrica pensylvanica. Bayberry. See page 137.

Potentilla spp. Potentillas, cinquefoils. See page 91.

Rhus aromatica. Fragrant sumac. See page 74.

Rosa spp. Roses. See page 133.

Rosmarinus officinalis. Rosemary. See page 80.

Vaccinium vitis-idaea. Cowberry. See page 135.

Vines

Celastrus scandens. American bittersweet. See page 124.

Clematis spp. Clematis. See page 124.

Hydrangea anomala subsp. *petiolaris.* Climbing hydrangea.
See page 125.

Lonicera spp. Honeysuckles. See page 126.

Muehlenbeckia complexa. Complex wire vine. See page 116.

Parthenocissus quinquefolia. Virginia creeper, woodbine.
See page 126.

Schizophragma hydrangeoides. Japanese hydrangea vine.
See page 127.

Catmint (*Nepeta* 'Six Hills Giant') edges a seaside yard in Connecticut.

GROUND COVERS FOR SAND

NOT MANY PLANTS grow in pure sand, but there are a few species suitable for sand dunes, sandy scrub areas, and other spots where pure, or nearly pure, sand is the norm. The plants listed here grow in sand, tolerate salt, and are very drought tolerant. All need full sun and are quite useful for holding sandy soil in place.

Ammophila breviligulata. American beach grass, American dune grass. Native to costal areas from Newfoundland to North Carolina and around the Great Lakes. Grows 3½ feet tall, spreading indefinitely. Zones 5 to 8 or 9.

Calamovilfa longifolia. Sand reed grass. Native to Canada and the northern United States. Grows 2 to 5 feet tall, spreading indefinitely. Sand or sandy loam. Full sun to light shade. Zones 3 to 5 or 6.

Hudsonia tomentosa. Beach heather. Native subshrub from New Brunswick to Minnesota and south to Virginia. Grows 3 to 12 inches tall, spreading to 1½ feet. Grows in open dunes in pure sand as well as in scrub areas with sandy soil. Very drought tolerant. Zones 2 to 8.

Leymus arenarius. Blue lyme grass. See page 72.

Uniola paniculata. Sea oats. Native to coastal areas from Virginia to Florida and Texas as well as eastern Mexico. Grows 4 feet tall, spreading indefinitely. Zones 8 to 10.

Ground Covers
for a Sunny Slope

A thick carpet of ground covers can transform a dangerous-to-mow site into a handsome asset.

When covering a slope with a planting of ground covers, keep in mind that plant selection — in addition to getting the plants established and growing vigorously — is a challenge. The steeper the site, the more difficult the task. Rain tends to run quickly off sloping sites, leaving little time for water to percolate down into the soil. As a result, choosing the right plants for a sloping site is especially important, and the ground covers that are up to this task must be able to cope with dry conditions, whether the underlying soil is sandy, loamy, or clayey. Preventing soil erosion is very important too, since water running down a slope will carry topsoil away with it. The ground covers on this list tolerate both drought and heat, and they also form a dense network of roots that will spread out to bind the soil and hold it in place. Although all are drought tolerant once established, they do need regular watering when first planted as well as when rainfall is scarce during the first season or two. For information on getting these ground covers started — plus tips on slowing down the water that runs across sloping sites so it can sink in where plants can get to it — see Planting on Slopes on page 196.

1. *Cerastium tomentosum*
   Snow-in-summer

2. *Hemerocallis lilioasphodelus*
   Lemon daylily

3. *Arctostaphylos uva-ursi*
   'Massachusetts'
   Bearberry

4. *Achillea* 'Summerwine'
   Yarrow

5. *Comptonia peregrina*
   Sweet fern

6. *Oenothera speciosa*
   Showy evening primrose

7. *Amorpha canescens*
   Lead plant

8. *Oenothera macrocarpa*
   Missouri primrose

9. *Achillea* 'Coronation Gold'
   Yarrow

10. *Delosperma cooperi*
    Hardy ice plant

11. *Cerastium tomentosum*
    Snow-in-summer

Shrubs

Amorpha canescens
Lead plant

EXPOSURE: Full sun or partial shade
HEIGHT: 3 to 4 feet
SPREAD: 5 feet

A legume native to central North America, from Mannitoba to Lousiana, this species is grown for its hairy, gray, pinnate leaves that have leaflets arranged in a featherlike fashion. Spikelike clusters of pea-shaped, violet-blue flowers appear in late summer and early fall. Plants die to the ground in northern areas, where they can be managed like perennials. They grow well in poor soil (as legumes they can take nitrogen from the air and return it to the soil) as well as in acid or alkaline soil. Plants also self-sow. To propagate, move seedlings while they are still small or start from seed in fall; soak the seeds overnight before sowing. Zones 3 to 9.

Amorpha canescens

Arctostaphylos uva-ursi
Bearberry, kinnikinick

EXPOSURE: Full sun to light shade
HEIGHT: 4 to 12 inches
SPREAD 2 TO 4 FEET OR MORE

Another low-growing shrub, this native of North America, Europe, and northern Asia features glossy, rounded, evergreen leaves on spreading stems. Small clusters of flowers from palest pink to white appear in summer and are followed by round red berries. This species is good for tough slopes, including those with sandy or rocky soil, as well as windy sites. Plants are also handsome filling in under shrubs such as blueberries (*Vaccinium* spp.). A number of cultivars are available, including 'Massachusetts' and 'Vancouver Jade'. Bearberry is best on exposed sites with good air movement; plants tolerate salt but they do not withstand poor drainage. To propagate, look for sections of stem that have rooted at the nodes, then sever and pot them up anytime. Another option is to sow seeds in fall. Zones 3 to 7.

Comptonia peregrina
Sweet fern, meadow fern

EXPOSURE: Full sun
HEIGHT: 2 to 4 feet tall
SPREAD: 4 to 8 feet or more

This native species, found from Nova Scotia to Virginia, isn't a fern, as its common name suggests, but a rhizomatous, suckering shrub. Plants bear narrow, aromatic, fernlike leaves and insignificant, yellow-green flowers. They tolerate salt, can fix nitrogen, and grow in any acid soil, from rich to poor and sandy. To propagate, dig rooted suckers or layer shoots in early spring. Zones 2 to 8.

Comptonia peregrina

Coprosma × kirkii
Creeping coprosma

EXPOSURE: Full sun to partial shade
HEIGHT: 3 to 5 feet
SPREAD: 6 feet or more

A tough cover for banks in mild climates, creeping coprosma is grown for its evergreen leaves, which are oblong to narrowly oblong and generally yellow-green. The inconspicuous flowers are followed by bluish fruit in fall. Plants grow in most soils and once established are fairly drought tolerant. They tolerate salt, making them a good choice for seaside gardens. Zones 8 to 10.

Cytisus spp.
Brooms

EXPOSURE: Full sun
HEIGHT: 8 to 30 inches
SPREAD: 1½ to 4 feet

These shrubs bring clusters of showy, pealike flowers plus stellar drought resistance to the garden. Several species are low growing enough to make fine ground covers. All succeed in a range of well-drained soils, from sandy or gravelly to loamy, and are best in soil that is poor to average in fertility. They're also good on windy sites. Use them on slopes, in rock gardens, or any dry and windy spot. Brooms self-sow, and some species (particularly *C. scoparius*) have become invasive in some areas; check local invasive plant lists. Propagate by taking cuttings in mid- or late summer.

C. × beanii. This species is 1 to 2 feet tall and spreads to 3 feet. Plants bear linear leaves and clusters of yellow spring flowers. Zones 7 to 8.

C. decumbens (formerly *Genista decumbens*). Prostrate broom. This small-scale ground cover usually ranges from 4 to 8 inches tall, although plants can reach a foot high. Plants have oblong leaves on wiry stems that spread to 3 feet, and they bear clusters of yellow flowers in late spring and early summer. Zones 6 to 9.

C. × kewensis. A 10- or 12-inch-tall broom, this species spreads to 4 or 5 feet and bears three-leaflet leaves. Plants produce clusters of cream flowers in spring. Zones 6 to 8.

Diervilla lonicera
Dwarf bush honeysuckle

EXPOSURE: Full sun to light shade
HEIGHT: 2 to 4 feet
SPREAD: Indefinite

This is a rhizomatous, suckering shrub, native to the Midwest and Northeast, that has oval leaves. In summer, plants produce sulfur yellow flowers that fade to red. They grow in well-drained, acid to neutral soil, and especially thrive in sandy or gravelly conditions; in fact, one common name is gravel weed. Plants are very drought tolerant. Use this species for massing or naturalizing, as well as for controlling erosion on slopes.

Keep in mind, plants are determined spreaders and require a deep edging to keep them from spreading beyond their bounds. Shear or cut back plants hard to promote dense, compact growth. Propagate by severing and digging up suckers in early spring or by taking cuttings in summer. Zones 3 to 7.

Southern bush honeysuckle (*D. sessifolia*) is a similar, although slightly taller, native species from the Southeast. Plants grow 3 to 5 feet tall and spread to 5 feet or more. Plants bear sulfur yellow flowers as well. Propagate either species by severing and digging up suckers or by taking cuttings in summer. Zones 5 to 8.

Hypericum spp.
St. John's worts

EXPOSURE: Full sun to partial shade
HEIGHT: 1 to 1½ feet
SPREAD: 1 to 3 feet

Several St. John's worts have densely branching roots and rhizomes that are excellent for binding soil on slopes. Propagate by taking cuttings in summer or by dividing the plants in spring or fall. In addition to creeping St. John's wort (*Hypericum calycinum*), covered on page 71, consider these.

H. 'Hidcote'. This hybrid is usually about 3 feet tall, but plants can reach 5 feet tall and spread to about 5 feet. They bear blue-green leaves and showy yellow flowers from midsummer to fall. In Zone 5, where they require extra winter protection, plants die to the ground and resprout each spring. Since they bloom on new wood, flowering isn't interrupted. Zones 5 to 9.

H. olympicum. Olympic St. John's wort. A 10- to 12-inch-tall shrub that spreads from 1 to 3 feet, this species has gray-green leaves. Plants bear golden yellow flowers from spring to midsummer. Zones 6 to 8.

H. patulum. Goldencup St. John's wort. This is 3-foot-tall shrub that spreads to 4 or 5 feet. Plants produce oval green leaves decorated with clusters of showy yellow flowers from summer to early fall. Zones 6 or 7 to 9.

Hypericum olympicum

Diervilla lonicera

Muehlenbeckia spp.
Wire vines

EXPOSURE: Full sun to light shade
HEIGHT: 8 inches to several feet
SPREAD: 3 feet to indefinite

Suitable for gardens in warm climates, wire vines are spreading shrubs or twining climbers that can be used to cover sites with poor soil. Despite the common name, creeping wire vine (*M. axillaris*) is actually a shrub. Plants bear small, rounded green leaves and insignificant yellow-green flowers on sprawling stems that often root where the nodes touch the soil. Plants are about 8 inches tall and spread to 3 feet. They can be used along pathways and around stepping-stones as well, since plants tolerate some foot traffic. They also tolerate annual mowing to keep them close to the ground.

Complex wire vine or maidenhair vine (*M. complexa*) is a vigorous sprawling vine that can be kept to about 1½ feet in height, although its twining stems will quickly climb to 10 feet if offered support, and they can spread indefinitely. Plants bear evergreen to deciduous leaves that are rounded to oval and clusters of tiny, insignificant, yellow-green flowers. Give these species well drained, sandy soil. Established plants tolerate some drought as well as wind, are suitable for rocky sites or rock gardens, and also tolerate salt, making them good choices for seaside sites. Propagate by rooting cuttings in summer. Both are hardy in Zones 8 to 10.

Sorbus reducta
Dwarf Chinese mountain ash

EXPOSURE: Full sun to light shade
HEIGHT: 2½ to 4 feet
SPREAD: 4 feet or more

A suckering, rhizomatous shrub, this species most commonly grows about 2½ feet tall. Plants are coarse textured, with compound leaves that have up to 15 toothed, paired leaflets. Clusters of tiny, fragrant, white flowers appear in spring, followed by berrylike pink fruit. This species is best used on large sites, where it can be massed or allowed to form dense thickets. Plants grow in most soils and tolerate some drought but perform best in evenly moist conditions. To propagate, pot up rooted suckers in spring. Zones 6 to 8.

Sorbus reducta

Symphoricarpos × chenaultii 'Hancock'
Hancock coralberry

EXPOSURE: Full sun to partial shade
HEIGHT: 2 to 6 feet
SPREAD: 12 feet

A hybrid created by crossing coralberry (*S. orbiculatus*), a species native to eastern North America and Mexico, with *S. microphyllus,* which is a Mexican native, this spreading shrub most often stays about 2 feet tall and spreads by suckers to 12 feet. Obviously, it's not a plant for small gardens, but it is quite effective on large sites and can effectively hold a slope to control erosion. 'Hancock' forms broad mounds and has rounded, dark green leaves. Plants bear white or pale pink, late-summer flowers that are followed by pink fruit. Zones 4 to 7. Coralberry (*S. orbiculatus*), one of the parent species of 'Hancock,' has a suckering habit, and plants range from 2 to 5 feet tall and spread to 6 feet. Zones 2 to 7. Both species grow in any soil and are drought tolerant once established.

MORE COVERS FOR SLOPES

THE PLANTS LISTED HERE also can be used to cover slopes. All tolerate drought once established but will need regular watering until they have had time to spread their roots and begin growing actively.

Cotoneaster spp. Cotoneasters. See page 130 for *C. apiculatus* and *C. horizontalis,* and page 139 for *C. dammeri* and *C. salicifolius.*

Juniperus spp. Junipers. See page 72 and 140.

Forsythia 'Arnold Dwarf'. Forsythia. See page 131.

Hypericum calycinum. Creeping St. John's wort. See page 71.

Rhus aromatica. Fragrant sumac. See page 74.

Sedum spp. Sedums, stonecrops. See page 84 and 109.

Keep the soil evenly moist while plants are getting established, and for the best results, water during dry spells. Propagate by digging suckers in fall or by taking cuttings in summer.

Perennials

Achillea spp.
Yarrows

EXPOSURE: Full sun
HEIGHT: 2 to 5 feet
SPREAD: 2 to 5 feet

These fast-spreading plants are grown for their attractive, aromatic foliage and their showy clusters of flowers. They grow in any well-drained soil; poor, sandy conditions are fine. Soil that is too rich causes plants to flop. Good drainage is essential. Use yarrows with larger perennials, since they'll overwhelm smaller plants. They're best for informal gardens and meadow-style ground cover plantings. Plants tolerate drought and are great for sites that are hot and dry. Deadheading encourages repeat bloom. Dig and divide clumps in spring or fall when they begin to die out in the center, to keep them vigorous, or for propagation. Or propagate by cuttings in spring or early summer.

A. filipendulina. Fernleaf yarrow. Deeply cut, fernlike leaves and flat-topped clusters of golden yellow flowers characterize this 3- to 5-foot-tall species. Plants bloom from early summer to early fall. Cultivars include 'Cloth of Gold' and 'Gold Plate'. Zones 3 to 8.

A. hybrids. While many hybrids are available, two of the best are listed here. 'Coronation Gold' bears silver-gray leaves on 2- to 4-foot-tall plants that spread to 3 feet. Blooms are golden yellow and appear from midsummer to fall. Zones 3 to 9. 'Moonshine', from 1 to 2 feet tall and spreading to 2 feet, bears lacy, deeply cut, gray-green foliage and lemon yellow flowers from early summer to fall. Zones 3 to 7.

A. millefolium. Common yarrow. This species is found growing wild in North America, but it is naturalized, not native. Plants, which spread rapidly by rhizomes, are 2 feet tall and easily spread to 5 feet. They bear very deeply cut, fernlike leaves and flat-topped clusters of white or pink flowers from early to late summer. Many cultivars are available, with flowers ranging from pink and white to red, lavender, or orange-red. Cultivars include magenta 'Cerise Queen', red 'Fire King', and orange-red 'Paprika.' Zones 3 to 9.

Cerastium tomentosum
Snow-in-summer

EXPOSURE: Full sun to light shade
HEIGHT: 6 to 12 inches
SPREAD: Indefinite

A handsome, old-fashioned perennial, snow-in-summer is a mat former with evergreen leaves that are woolly and silver or white. Plants bear clusters of starry white flowers in late spring and summer. They grow in any well-drained soil — including pure sand — and are ideal for covering slopes and any other sites that have poor, dry soil. In hot-summer areas a spot in light shade is best, because the centers of the clumps tend to die out in hot, humid weather. Plantings spread most quickly in areas with cool summers. Propagate by dividing the clumps in spring or by taking cuttings in summer. Zones 3 to 7.

Cerastium tomentosum

Delosperma spp.
Hardy ice plants
EXPOSURE: Full sun
HEIGHT: 2 to 6 inches
SPREAD: Indefinite

Fire retardant and extremely tolerant of heat and drought, these fleshy-leaved, succulent perennials produce showy flowers that look like daisies. Use them on flat or sloping ground. Plants thrive in hot, dry conditions and will fill in around rocks or boulders, grow in raised beds, cover the edges of a gravel driveway, or carpet nearly any other site containing well-drained soil, including sloping sites. Also use them to fill in around other drought-tolerant shrubs such as junipers. While a number of species are suitable for warm-climate areas, 2-inch-tall *D. nubigenum*, with orange-red flowers in summer, is the hardiest species, surviving in Zones 5 to 10. *D. cooperi*, with magenta flowers on 6-inch plants, is hardy in Zones 7 to 10. Propagate either species by rooting cuttings in spring or summer.

Hemerocallis spp. ▼
Daylilies
EXPOSURE: Full sun to light shade
HEIGHT: 1½ to 3 feet
SPREAD: 1½ to 3 feet

These popular perennials produce clumps of strap-shaped leaves topped by clusters of trumpet-shaped flowers. The blooms come in shades of yellow, orange, red, pink, maroon, purple, and cream; the majority open for only a day. Most daylilies are clump forming, although some are rhizomatous, including tawny or orange daylily (*H. fulva*), which has naturalized along roadsides in North America, and lemon daylily or lemon lily (*H. lilioasphodelus*). Daylilies grow in any soil but are happiest and bloom best in rich, well-drained conditions. The plants are drought tolerant — and thus can be used on slopes — although dry, poor soil reduces flowering. Literally thousands of cultivars are available. Plant any of them in broad drifts, either alone or combined with other perennials. To propagate, divide clumps in spring or fall. Zones 2 or 3 to 9.

Lathyrus latifolius ▼
Perennial pea
EXPOSURE: Full sun to light shade
HEIGHT: 8 to 12 inches
SPREAD: 5 to 6 feet

Also called everlasting pea and wild sweet pea, this species will climb anything it can wrap its tendrils around, including shrubs, fences, and nearby perennials, so plants can be considerably taller than a foot. They bear rounded blue-green leaves and clusters of pink to magenta-pink flowers from summer to early fall. 'White Pearl' bears white flowers; 'Blushing Bride' has white flowers flushed with pink. If left to sprawl, perennial peas are effective ground covers for preventing erosion and carpeting slopes and banks. Plants easily conceal all manner of evils, including piles of wood, fallen-down fences, and other debris. Grow them in any well-drained soil. They tolerate drought and poor soil. Propagate by sowing seed, since established plants resent being disturbed. Zones 4 to 9.

Oenothera spp.
Evening primroses, sundrops
EXPOSURE: Full sun to light shade
HEIGHT: 1 to 3 feet
SPREAD: 2 to 3 feet

Grown for their saucer- to cup-shaped flowers, several species of native *Oenothera* make fine ground covers. They're best when combined with other vigorous perennials or planted around shrubs. Plants grow in nearly any well-drained soil, although sandy to loamy conditions are ideal. They tolerate some heat and are fairly drought tolerant. Propagate by taking cuttings from shoots that arise at the base of the plant in late spring or early summer or by dividing the clumps in early spring.

Oenothera fruticosa subsp. *glauca*

▼ May be considered invasive in some regions.

COVERING SLOPES IN SHADE

WHILE MANY GROUND COVERS that can hold slopes thrive in light shade, the choice narrows for sites in partial to full shade. The plants listed here all thrive in shade and can be used to cover and hold slopes.

Convallaria majalis. Lily-of-the-valley. See page 70.

Cymbalaria muralis. Kenilworth ivy. See page 99.

Dennstaedtia punctiloba. Hayscented fern. See page 74.

Decumaria barbara. Wood vamp. See page 125.

Hosta spp. and hybrids. Hostas. See pages 71, 152, and 161.

Hydrangea anomala subsp. *petiolaris.* Climbing hydrangea. See page 125.

Pachysandra terminalis. Japanese pachysandra. See page 73.

Partherocissus tricuspidata. Virginia creeper. See page 126.

Sarcococca humilis. Dwarf Himalayan sweet box. See page 161.

Sasa veitchii. Sasa bamboo, kuma bamboo. See page 75.

Vinca minor. Common periwinkle, dwarf periwinkle. See page 55.

O. fruticosa. Common sundrops. A bushy perennial native to eastern North America, this species has red-tinged stems and leaves that turn dull red in fall. Plants are 1½ to 3 feet tall and spread to 2 feet or more. They bear racemes of 1- to 2-inch-wide yellow flowers from late spring to late summer. *O. fruticosa* subsp. *glauca,* formerly listed as *O. tetragona,* contains several excellent cultivars including 'Sonnenwende' (sold as 'Summer Solstice'), with red leaves that turn maroon in fall. 'Youngii' is low growing, to about 18 inches tall. Zones 4 to 8.

O. macrocarpa (formerly *O. missouriensis*). Missouri primrose, Ozark sundrops. This species, native to the central United States, ranges from 8 to about 12 inches tall and spreads by trailing stems from 2 to 2½ feet. From late spring to early fall plants bear showy yellow flowers that can reach 5 inches across. Zones 5 to 8.

O. speciosa. Showy evening primrose. Native in the Southwest and Mex-ico, this fast spreader travels by runners. Plants produce 1- to 2-inch-wide flowers that open white and mature to pink. Plants grow to about 1 foot tall, and in rich soil they spread very quickly. They are better behaved in poor to average soil. 'Rosea', formerly *O. berlandieri* and sometimes called Mexican evening primrose, is less aggressive. 'Siskiyou Pink' bears pink flowers on 8-inch plants. Zones 5 to 8.

Rudbeckia fulgida
Orange coneflower

EXPOSURE: Full sun
HEIGHT: 2 to 2½ feet
SPREAD: 2 to 3 feet or more

A rhizomatous perennial with lance-shaped leaves, this species is a popular border perennial that also makes a handsome ground cover for informal or wild gardens. Plants bear 2½- to 3-inch-wide, orange-yellow, daisylike flowers with brown centers from late summer to mid fall. 'Goldsturm' (a cultivar of *R. fulgida* var. *sullivantii*) is more commonly grown than the species. It is somewhat more compact and bears its large, 3½- to 5-inch-wide flowers on 2-foot-tall stems. Both make good ground covers in any soil, although they're happiest and spread fastest in average to rich, moist, well-drained soil. They are effective when combined with ornamental grasses as well as other perennials with late summer blooms, including Russian sage (*Perovskia atriplicifolia*), yarrows (*Achillea* spp.), and sedums (*Sedum* spp.). Plants tolerate drought but bloom best in soil that remains slightly moist. Propagate by dividing clumps in spring or fall. Plants self-sow. Zones 3 to 9.

Zauschneria californica
California fuchsia

EXPOSURE: Full sun
HEIGHT: 1 to 2 feet
SPREAD: 3 to 5 or more feet

This drought-tolerant California native bears showy, trumpet-shaped, red flowers and lance-shaped (or narrowly so) leaves that are evergreen or semievergreen. It blooms over a long period from late summer to fall, and the flowers are very attractive to hummingbirds. Plants grow in average, well-drained soil, but thrive in light, sandy soil. They spread by rhizomes that root where they touch the soil and can cover a considerable amount of ground with time. Combine them with other drought-tolerant perennials and shrubs, including artemisias (*Artemisia* spp.), lavenders (*Lavandula* spp.), and brooms (*Cytisus* spp.). Cut plants back after flowering to keep them neat looking and encourage bushy growth. Propagate by sowing seed in spring or by rooting cuttings from shoots that arise at the base of the plant in spring. Zones 7 or 8 to 10.

Ground Covers for Alkaline Soil

Sometimes referred to as sweet or chalky soil, alkaline soil — with a pH over 7 — can be a challenge for gardeners.

While there are countless lists available to help gardeners with acid soil, there's less information available for individuals who garden on alkaline soil. Azaleas and other plants that prefer acid soil won't grow there without significant soil amendment. Fortunately, many ground covers, including the ones listed here, will grow in alkaline conditions.

A colorful mixed planting at Denver Botanic Gardens shows what can be grown in alkaline soil.

Perennials

Achillea spp. Yarrows. See page 117.
Alchemilla mollis. Lady's mantle. See page 160.
Arabis alpina subsp. *caucasica*. Wall rock cress. See page 78.
Armeria maritima. Common thrift. See page 98.
Artemisia spp. Artemisias. See page 78.
Bergenia spp. Bergenias. See page 98.
Calamintha nepeta. Calamints. See page 80.
Callirhoe involucrata. Poppy mallow. See page 106.
Centranthus ruber. Jupiter's beard, red valerian. See page 107.
Cerastium tomentosum. Snow-in-summer. See page 117.
Ceratostigma plumbaginoides. Plumbago. See page 70.
Chamaemelum nobile. Roman chamomile. See page 90.
Convallaria majalis. Lily-of-the-valley. See page 70.
Cymbalaria muralis. Kenilworth ivy. See page 99.
Dianthus spp. Pinks. See page 79.
Dicentra spp. Bleeding hearts. See page 160.
Euphorbia spp. Euphorbias, spurges. See page 81.
Fragaria spp. Strawberries. See page 70.
Geranium spp. Hardy geraniums, See page 81.
Gypsophila repens. Creeping baby's breath. See page 99.
Hakonechloa macra. Japanese hakone grass. See page 151.
Helleborus × *hybridus*. Lenten rose, See page 151.
Houttuynia cordata 'Chameleon'. Houttuynia. See page 175.
Iberis sempervirens. Candytuft. See page 83.
Iris cristata. Crested iris. See page 167.
Matteuccia struthiopteris. Ostrich fern. See page 170.
Mazus reptans. Creeping mazus. See page 91.
Mentha spp. Mints. See page 91.

Nepeta × faassenii. Catmints. See page 84.

Oenothera spp. Evening primroses, sundrops. See page 118.

Omphalodes verna. Blue-eyed Mary. See page 154.

Ophiopogon spp. Ophiopogons. See page 84.

Origanum vulgare. Oregano. See page 80.

Persicaria affinis. Himalayan fleeceflower. See page 100.

Phlox subulata. Moss phlox, moss pink. See page 100.

Polystichum acrostichoides. Christmas fern. See page 170.

Pratia pedunculata. Blue star creeper. See page 93.

Pulmonaria spp. Pulmonarias, lungworts. See page 155.

Saponaria ocymoides. Rock soapwort. See page 101.

Sedum spp. Sedums, stonecrops. See pages 84 and 109.

Sempervivum spp. Houseleeks, hens-and-chicks. See page 101.

Stachys byzantina. Lamb's ears. See page 87.

Stylophorum diphyllum. Celandine poppy. See page 169.

Teucrium chamaedrys. Germander. See page 103.

Thymus spp. Thymes. See pages 94 and 103.

Tradescantia hybrids. Spiderworts. See page 163.

Shrubs & Trees

Aesculus parviflora. Bottlebrush buckeye. See page 132.

Amorpha canescens. Lead plant. See page 114.

Cercis canadensis. Redbud. See page 142.

Chaenomeles japonica. Japanese flowering quince. See page 130.

Cotoneaster spp. Cotoneasters. See pages 130 and 139.

Cytisus spp. Brooms. See page 114.

Forsythia spp. Forsythias. See page 131.

Genista spp. Brooms. See page 131.

Indigofera kirilowii. Kirilow indigo. See page 72.

Juniperus spp. Junipers. See page 72 and 140.

Mahonia repens. Creeping mahonia. See page 143.

Potentilla fruticosa. Shrubby cinquefoil, shrubby potentilla. See page 133.

Rubus rolfei 'Emerald Carpet'. Creeping bramble. See page 75.

Salix spp. Willows. See page 134.

Hens-and-chicks (*Sempervivum* spp.) tolerate some of the driest, rockiest conditions.

Sasa veitchii. Sasa bamboo, kuma bamboo. See page 75.

Symphoricarpos × chenaultii 'Hancock'. Hancock coralberry. See page 116.

Taxus spp. Yews. See page 145.

Vines

Akebia quinata. Fiveleaf akebia, chocolate vine. See page 124.

Clematis spp. Clematis. See page 124.

Lonicera spp. Honeysuckles. See page 126.

Parthenocissus quinquefolia. Virginia creeper, woodbine. See page 126.

Vines
for Covering Ground

While vines normally travel vertically — climbing trellises and scrambling up shrubs or trees — they also can be trained to trail over the ground.

When used as ground covers, vines are very effective blanketing large areas. They are especially useful for covering rough ground, including slopes, and will skim over and blanket rocky sites, camouflaging everything from fallen-down fences and yard debris to small buildings.

The vines listed here — both native and nonnative — make handsome ground covers when used in this manner. When grown as ground covers, their ultimate height ranges from about 1 to 3 feet or more, depending on whether you clip plants close to the ground or allow them to billow up. There are selections for both sun and shade. All are vigorous plants that will spread indefinitely, so be prepared to stop them with pruning implements when they've traveled too far. Since vining stems can ramble over walls and other obstacles, physical barriers won't work to contain them. Give established plants an annual "hair cut" — and some species listed will require more than one — to keep them in bounds.

To get vines started, arrange the stems along the ground and pin or peg them in place. U-shaped pieces of wire, such as from cut-up coat hangers, are fine for this purpose. Once the plants are established, redirect them as necessary with a combination of wire pins, pruning shears, and even loppers. Prune back any growth that begins to climb shrubs or trees to keep the vine right on the ground and prevent it from completely covering smaller plants. Keep twining climbers away from all other trees and shrubs, because they can wrap around and constrict trunks and limbs. If you like, let some shoots of flowering ground covers like clematis climb up shrubs to show off their flowers.

1. *Hedera canariensis*
   Canary island ivy

2. *Lonicera × brownii*
   'Dropmore Scarlet'
   Scarlet trumpet honeysuckle

3. *Hydrangea anomala*
   subsp. *petiolaris*
   Climbing hydrangea

4. *Akebia quinata*
   Fiveleaf akebia

5. *Gelsemium sempervirens*
   Carolina jessamine

6. *Schizophragma hydrangeoides*
   Japanese hydrangea vine

7. *Parthenocissus quinquefolia*
   Virginia creeper

8. *Clematis montana* var. *rubens*
   Anemone clematis

9. *Lonicera henryi*
   Henry's honeysuckle

Clematis montana var. *rubens*

Akebia quinata ▼
Fiveleaf akebia, chocolate vine

EXPOSURE: Full sun to partial shade

This vigorous twining climber bears rounded, semievergreen or evergreen, five-leaflet leaves. Clusters of small, spicy-scented, maroon-brown flowers appear in spring and are followed by edible, sausage-shaped fruit. The plant spreads very fast and can twine around and over-whelm everything except large trees. It is useful for erosion control or as ground cover on a large site. Give it average to rich, well-drained soil. The species takes some drought but is best in moist soil. It is evergreen in mild climates. To prop-agate, take cuttings in summer or layer vines in winter. Zones 4 to 8 or 9.

Akebia quinata

Celastrus scandens
American bittersweet

EXPOSURE: Full sun

This fast-spreading twining vine is native to eastern North America and a cousin of Oriental bittersweet (*C. orbic-ulatus*), which is an extremely rampant invasive species that should be avoided at all cost. American bittersweet bears ovate leaves and clusters of tiny yellow-green flowers in summer. Blooms are followed by showy orange-yellow fruit that open to reveal red berries. The fruit is prized for fall decorations. Both male and female plants are required for fruit set. Use American bittersweet to cover rough slopes. Keep it away from shrubs and trees, which its twining stems will strangle. Plants grow in any soil and tol-erate drought. A site in poor soil is best, since plants spread more quickly in rich conditions. Propagate by cuttings taken in summer. Zones 3 to 8.

Clematis spp.
Clematis

EXPOSURE: Full sun to light shade

Several species of clematis are large enough to use as ground covers and can be quite effective when trained to sprawl over the ground. They climb by twin-ing leafstalks around supports. Give plants rich, well-drained soil. They tol-erate sandy to clayey soil and are fairly drought tolerant once established. Ide-ally, put them where their roots are shaded by perennials or a wall. In all of these species, the attractive flowers are followed by handsome, fluffy seed-heads. Prune *C. alpina* and *C. montana* immediately after the plants bloom in early summer. Prune *C. terniflora*, *C. viti-cella*, and *C. virginiana* in early spring before they begin to grow. To propagate clematis, take cuttings in spring or early summer, or layer the vines in winter or early spring.

C. alpina. Alpine clematis. This hand-some species bears an abundance of solitary, bell-shaped blue flowers with white centers from late summer to fall. Zones 6 to 9.

C. montana. Anemone clematis. A late spring- to early summer-blooming species, anemone clematis bears small, 2-inch-wide, white or pink (in *C. m.* var. *rubens*) flowers that are soli-tary or carried in small clusters. Zones 5 or 6 to 9.

C. terniflora. ▼ Sweet autumn clematis. This vigorous-to-rampant species bears clouds of fragrant, starry white flowers from late summer to fall. The individual flowers are about 1 inch wide and are borne in large panicles. Zones 4 to 9.

C. viticella. Italian clematis. This species bears bell-shaped 1½-inch wide flow-ers in shades of purple, purple-blue, or rose-purple from midsummer to fall. Zones 5 to 9.

C. virginiana. Virgin's bower. Also called leather flower and Devil's darning needle, this species is native to east-ern North America and is the best choice for trailing over the ground. Plants bear large panicles of ¼- to ½-inch-long flowers from midsummer to fall that are fragrant and greenish white in color. Zones 4 to 8.

▼ May be considered invasive in some regions.

Decumaria barbara
Wood vamp, decumaria
EXPOSURE: Partial to full shade

Also known as climbing hydrangea, this native of the Southeastern United States climbs via aerial rootlets but also can be trained to cover the ground. Plants bear glossy, ovate leaves and 2- to 3-inch-wide clusters of lightly fragrant white flowers in summer. They are not as large or as vigorous as *Hydrangea anomala* subsp. *petiolaris*. Plants thrive in rich, moist, well-drained soil and also tolerate wet soil. To propagate, take cuttings in late summer or early fall. Zones 5 to 9.

Gelsemium sempervirens
Carolina jessamine
EXPOSURE: Full sun to light shade

Also called Carolina jasmine, this shrubby vine is native from the southeastern United States south to Mexico. It can be grown as a sprawler and reaches 3 feet in height when grown without support. Plants spread to 20 or 30 feet and bear evergreen leaves. Fragrant yellow flowers appear from spring to summer. This species is best for large areas away from shrubs, which it will engulf. Use it to hold slopes or let it sprawl over a wall. Plants tolerate most soils and some drought. Propagate by taking cuttings in summer. Zones 7 or 8 to 10.

Hedera canariensis
Canary Island ivy
EXPOSURE: Partial shade

Also called Algerian ivy, this species bears glossy evergreen 4- to 8-inch-long leaves. Cultivars with variegated leaves are most popular, and are less vigorous than the all-green species, which easily can get out of hand. 'Gloire de Marengo' bears lobed green leaves splashed with gray-green and bordered in cream and white. Plants thrive in a wide range of well-drained soils and are fairly drought tolerant once established. Zones 6 to 10; 7 to 10 for variegated cultivars.

Hydrangea anomala subsp. *petiolaris*
Climbing hydrangea
EXPOSURE: Light to full shade

A woody vine also listed as *H. petiolaris*, this species clings to buildings and other structures via aerial rootlets. Plants feature dark green ovate leaves, large flat-topped clusters of fragrant creamy white flowers in midsummer, and cinnamon-colored exfoliating bark. Give them rich, well-drained, moist soil. Plants thrive in partial to full shade. They can tolerate full sun toward the northern part of their range, although only if they receive adequate soil moisture. Use climbing hydrangea to cover rough, rocky sites or to replace lawn on medium to large sites. Plants are best purchased in containers. They are slow to settle in; water regularly for the first couple of years until they are well established. Plants are difficult to propagate. Try taking cuttings in summer or grow from seed. Zones 4 to 9.

Gelsemium sempervirens

Hedera canariensis

Hydrangea anomala subsp. *petiolaris*

Lonicera × brownii 'Dropmore Scarlet'

Lonicera spp.
Honeysuckles

EXPOSURE: Full sun to partial shade

In addition to some good ground covers, this genus also contains some world-class invasive plants — especially Japanese honeysuckle (*L. japonica*), a seriously invasive weed in many states — so select and site these plants with care. All of them can strangle shrubs and small trees they encounter, so locate the plants — or prune — accordingly. Honeysuckles bear rounded leaves and clusters of tubular flowers that may or may not be fragrant. Whether the flowers are fragrant or not, they are popular with hummingbirds, making the plants a welcome addition to any garden designed to attract winged wildlife.

They grow in most well-drained soils but are happiest in rich, moist, well-drained conditions. The plants tolerate drought, and a site where the soil dries out helps slow their spread. Prune honeysuckles immediately after they flower. Propagate by taking cuttings in summer.

L. × brownii. Scarlet trumpet honeysuckle. This deciduous to semievergreen species bears blue-green leaves and lightly fragrant scarlet flowers in summer. 'Dropmore Scarlet' blooms over a long period. Zones 4 to 9.

L. caprifolium.▼ Sweet honeysuckle or Italian woodbine. A vigorous spreader with gray-green deciduous leaves, this species bears very fragrant white to yellow flowers in summer. Zones 5 or 6 to 9.

L. flava. Yellow-flowered honeysuckle. Native from Oklahoma east to North Carolina, this is a weakly twining species with bright green leaves and fragrant orange-yellow flowers from spring to summer. Zones 5 to 9.

L. × heckrottii. Goldflame honeysuckle. This hybrid bears deciduous or semievergreen leaves that are dark green in color. In summer, plants bear clusters of fragrant flowers that are pink on the outside and yellow-orange on the inside. Zones 5 to 9.

L. henryi. Henry's honeysuckle. This evergreen species bears dark green leaves and purple-red flowers in summer. Zones 5 to 9.

L. sempervirens. Coral or trumpet honeysuckle. A native of the eastern and southern United States, this is a deciduous or evergreen species with dark green leaves and clusters of scarlet flowers from summer to fall. Zones 4 to 9.

Menispermum canadense
Common or Canada moonseed

EXPOSURE: Full sun to partial shade

Also called yellow parilla, this fast-growing native of eastern North America has slender twining stems and also travels by suckers. The species produces heart-shaped leaves and tiny yellow-green flowers that appear in summer and are followed by grapelike fruit on female plants (if there is a male moonseed plants growing nearby). Plants grown as ground covers rarely exceed 1 foot in height. Use moonseed under trees and in shady wildflower gardens. The fruit is poisonous, so keep plants away from sites where children or pets may be tempted. Plants thrive in rich, moist, acid soil but also tolerate some drought. Propagate by division in spring. Zones 5 to 8.

Parthenocissus quinquefolia
Virginia creeper, woodbine

EXPOSURE: Full sun to full shade

This fast-spreading vine native to eastern North America bears palmate leaves (with leaflets arranged like fingers on a hand) and climbs by attaching disklike holdfasts borne at the tips

Parthenocissus quinquefolia

▼ May be considered invasive in some regions.

of tendrils. When allowed to creep along the ground, plants form a low cover that ranges from 4 to 8 inches tall. In fall, the leaves turn brilliant red. Use Virginia creeper to cover shady slopes or rough areas. It also can be used to replace lawn grass on shady sites. Plants grow in any well-drained soil and also tolerate some drought, and although they survive in full sun, they are happiest with light to full shade. Propagate by cuttings taken in early to midsummer. Zones 3 to 9.

Schizophragma hydrangeoides

Schizophragma hydrangeoides
Japanese hydrangea vine
EXPOSURE: Full sun to partial shade

A woody vine that attaches itself to trellises and other supports by aerial rootlets, this species bears oval, toothed, dark green leaves. In midsummer, flat-topped, 10-inch-wide clusters of lightly fragrant, creamy white flowers appear. The flowers are tiny, but clusters are rimmed with showy white bracts. 'Moonlight' has silvery blue-green leaves. Use Japanese hydrangea vine as you would its more vigorous relative *Hydrangea anomala* subsp. *petiolaris*. Zones 5 to 8.

COLLECTING IDEAS

ALTHOUGH PICTURES IN BOOKS are a great source of gardening ideas, they're no substitute for getting out and looking at the real thing. There is a wealth of information out there, and visiting gardens will help you discover ways to use ground covers effectively in your own garden. Take a notebook and jot down the names of plants you like or other notes about design or interesting features you don't want to forget.

Look at ground covers that grow well in the gardens of neighbors and friends — and also notice which ones grow too well and threaten to blanket the garden or escape into nearby woodlands and other wild areas.

Pay attention to plants that thrive in each garden, as well as special uses and ground cover combinations that catch your eye. Also evaluate how much work is involved. If your friend or neighbor is always outside fiddling with ground covers, determine if the person is puttering because he or she likes to or because the plantings need lots of maintenance.

A tour of local private gardens is another opportunity for collecting ideas and talking to individuals who have experience growing plants in your area and dealing with the challenges of your climate. Also visit garden centers and nurseries with display gardens, where you can see the plants in the ground and talk to staff members who care for them. Finally, visit botanic gardens, arboretums, and public parks that have ground cover plantings and, if possible, talk to the staff. Identify which species will grow well in your area, which ones appeal to you, and which ones don't. Also look for combinations you'd like to try in your own garden.

Golden sweet potato vine (*Ipomoea batatas* 'Margarita') is used as a temporary ground cover under cannas (*Canna* sp.), castor bean plants (*Ricinus communis*), and bananas (*Ensete* sp.).

Shrubby Ground Covers
for Sun & Shade

Sometimes the most effective plants for covering a particular patch of ground aren't low growing or diminutive. For tough, permanent cover, it's hard to beat shrubs.

Admittedly, it's more expensive to cover a site with shrubs — especially when planting improved cultivars, which tend to be more expensive than straight species. An established stand of shrubs can be both handsome and practical, however. For an especially effective planting, combine the plants as you would in a shrub border, arranging them in drifts of a single cultivar or species — three shrubs make a nice drift. Single specimens of several different shrubs are fine too, and they're a great option for plant collectors who want to make room for as many plants as possible. Aim for a mix of shrubs that feature foliage colors and textures that complement one another. Also consider mixing deciduous and evergreen species. For best cover, space plants somewhat closer than you would when planting a single specimen: the ultimate objective is plants that grow together to create a thick ground-covering mass of branches.

While many of the species listed here are too tall to use as conventional ground covers, lower-growing cultivars are available and are more suitable for most sites. (Plantings of even good-size shrubs make fine ground covers on large sites, but lower-growing selections are generally best for average-size lots.) Be sure to buy from a reputable nursery to make sure the plants you purchase are correctly labeled. Of course, many of the plants listed here also can be used to create low hedges and edgings.

1. *Chaenomeles japonica*
   Japanese flowering quince

2. *Juniperus chinensis* 'San Jose'
   Chinese juniper

3. *Rhodotypos scandens*
   Black jetbead

4. *Potentilla fruticosa*
   Shrubby cinquefoil

5. *Stephanandra incisa* 'Crispa'
   Dwarf cutleaved stephanandra

6. *Juniperus horizontalis* 'Bar Harbor'
   Creeping juniper

7. *Cotoneaster apiculatus*
   Cranberry cotoneaster

8. *Mahonia repens*
   Mahonias

9. *Microbiota decussata*
   Siberian cypress

10. *Genista hispanica*
    Broom

11. *Cephalotaxus harringtonia*
    Japanese plum yew

12. *Juniperus conferta* 'Blue Pacific'
    Shore juniper

Deciduous Shrubs

Aronia melanocarpa
Black chokeberry

EXPOSURE: Full sun to partial shade
HEIGHT: 1½ to 6 feet
SPREAD: 10 feet

While this is a good-sized suckering shrub native to eastern North America that can reach 5 or 6 feet when planted in rich soil, it normally stays smaller, ranging from 1½ to 3 feet. Plants bear rounded, finely toothed, green leaves and clusters of small, white, five-petaled flowers in late spring and early summer. The flowers are followed by black berries that are attractive to birds. In fall the foliage turns purple-red. Plants tolerate soggy soil for short periods as well as poor, dry conditions, and they need acid to neutral pH. To propagate, dig up suckers in spring. Zones 3 to 7.

Chaenomeles japonica
Japanese flowering quince

EXPOSURE: Full sun to light shade
HEIGHT: 2 to 3 feet
SPREAD: 4 to 6 feet

A thorny shrub with rounded leaves, Japanese flowering quince is grown for its spring display of red or orange-red flowers, which are followed by yellow fruit. Blooms appear on one-year-old wood. Plants grow in average, well-drained soil, and are fine in somewhat alkaline soils. Various low-growing cultivars are available, some of which may be hybrids with the taller *C. speciosa*, which normally reaches 8 feet and spreads to 15 feet. Low-growers include 'Jet Trail', 3 feet tall with white flowers; 'Texas Scarlet', 2 to 3½ feet tall with red flowers; and 'Orange Delight', 2 feet tall with orange-red flowers. To propagate, take root cuttings in summer or layer branches in fall. Zones 5 to 8.

Cotoneaster spp.
Cotoneasters

EXPOSURE: Full sun to light shade
HEIGHT: 4 inches to 3 feet
SPREAD: 4 to 8 feet

There are more than 200 species of cotoneaster, and the spreading, low-growing ones make excellent ground covers. All thrive in rich, light, well-drained soil. They're happiest in loamy conditions but tolerate dry, poor soil that can range from sandy to clayey, provided the drainage is good. Plants tolerate drought, acid or alkaline pH, and windy sites, and also are fairly salt tolerant. Use the low-growing cotoneasters listed here to cover medium-size sites. They're also suitable for blanketing slopes or planting in drifts in front of foundation plantings or larger shrub borders. They're equally attractive trailing over a wall, filling in alongside steps, or smoothing out a rough site. All of the species listed here are deciduous and bear small white flowers tinged with red or pink. Flowers are borne either singly or in pairs. See page 139 for evergreen cotoneasters. Propagate deciduous species by taking cuttings in early summer.

C. adpressus. This species bears rounded dark green leaves that turn red in fall. Blooms appear in summer and are followed by round red berries. Plants grow 4 to 10 inches tall and spread from 4 to 6 feet. Zones 5 to 8.

C. apiculatus. Cranberry cotoneaster. This vigorous species bears glossy green, rounded leaves and summer blooms followed by round red berries. Plants grow 2 to 3 feet tall and spread to 5 or 6 feet. Zones 5 to 7.

C. horizontalis. Rockspray cotoneaster. This 2- or 3-foot-tall species has

Chaenomeles japonica 'Texas Scarlet'

branches that stick out in a fishbone-like arrangement. Plants spread to 5 feet. The glossy dark green, rounded leaves turn red in fall. Blooms appear in late spring and are followed by showy, round, pinkish red berries. Zones 5 to 7.

C. perpusillus (formerly *C. horizontalis* var. *perpusillus*). This is a prostrate, 1-foot-tall species that spreads from 5 to 8 feet. Plants bear rounded leaves that turn red in fall and generally stay on the plant longer than the foliage of *C. horizontalis*. The flowers are borne in summer and are followed by round red fruit. Zones 5 to 9.

Deutzia gracilis 'Nikko'
Dwarf slender deutzia

EXPOSURE: Full sun to partial shade
HEIGHT: 2 to 2½ feet
SPREAD: 5 feet

Also listed as *D. crenata* var. *nakiana* 'Nikko', this compact ground-covering shrub bears lance-shaped green leaves that turn burgundy in fall. Clusters of white flowers appear in spring or early summer. 'Nikko' is a good choice for an edging along taller shrub borders or foundation plantings, or for planting in masses to cover a large area. It also is fairly good at holding soil on slopes. Plants perform best in partial shade in warm climates. Zones 5 to 8.

Forsythia 'Arnold Dwarf'
Forsythia

EXPOSURE: Full sun to light shade
HEIGHT: 2 to 4 feet
SPREAD: 6 to 7 feet

While full-size forsythias are large shrubs, this dwarf cultivar makes a handsome ground cover alongside steps and walkways or for edging shrub

Deutzia gracilis 'Nikko'

borders. 'Arnold Dwarf' bears ovate to lance-shaped leaves and bright yellow spring flowers, although it does not bloom as abundantly as standard-size forsythias. *F. viridissima* 'Bronxensis' is another compact forsythia that reaches 1 foot tall and spreads from 2 to 3 feet. Forsythias tolerate nearly any well-drained soil and also are fairly tolerant of drought. The plants survive in partial to full shade but don't bloom well there. Propagate by cuttings taken in spring or early summer or in late summer. Zones 5 to 8.

Genista spp.
Brooms

EXPOSURE: Full sun to light shade
HEIGHT: 1 to 3 feet
SPREAD: 2 or 3 feet

Also called woadwaxens, the species in this genus are similar to another group of plants also commonly called brooms — *Cytisus* spp. *Genista* species are grown for their showy display of yellow, pealike flowers. Most of them have very small leaves. The genus contains full-size shrubs as well as low-growing species that will create a tough, dense cover for sites with poor sandy or gravelly soil. The plants are drought tolerant and make good lawn grass substitutes, although they do not tolerate foot traffic. Use the species listed here for covering

Genista lydia

rough or boulder-covered slopes, planting in rock gardens, or growing in terraces or raised beds. Propagate by taking cuttings in mid- to late summer.

G. hispanica. Spanish broom. This 1- to 2½-foot-tall species forms 4- to 5-foot-wide mounds of spiny stems. Leaves appear on flowering stems only. Plants produce bright yellow blooms in late spring and early summer. Zones 7 to 9.

G. lydia. Lydian broom. Grown for its clusters of yellow flowers borne in early summer, this is a mounding, 1½-foot tall species that spreads to 3 feet. Plants have gray-green branches with prickles on the tips and linear blue-green leaves. Zones 6 to 9,

G. pilosa. Silky-leaved broom, silky-leaved woadwaxen. This species bears yellow flowers in late spring and early summer atop 1 to 1½-foot-tall plants that spread to 3 feet. 'Vancouver Gold' forms a 1½-foot-tall mound with golden yellow flowers. 'Yellow Spreader', also sold as 'Lemon Spreader', is 1 foot tall and features lemon yellow flowers. Zones 6 to 9.

G. tinctoria. ▼ Dyer's broom. A 2- to 3-foot-tall species, this broom spreads to about 3 feet and bears narrow dark green leaves and clusters of golden yellow flowers from late spring to early summer. Zones 4 to 7.

Mega Ground Covers

Plantings of good-size shrubs and small spreading trees such as the ones listed here can cover a large area very effectively.

For a large yard, consider a central planting of one or more of these wide-spreading species, perhaps surrounded by smaller shrubs. If you like, add an additional edging of even lower-growing ground covers to further link the planting to the surrounding area. The shorter edging helps visually connect the taller plants at the center to surrounding lawn areas or walkways. It also eliminates the problem of tall plants flopping onto walkways, sidewalks, or curbs.

Tall plantings — a hedge or large shrub border, hedgerow, tree lines, or woods edge — can loom over a yard. Drifts of low, spreading trees and shrubs used as ground covers helps face them down, linking them to the landscape and making the taller plantings less imposing. This gives the landscape a finished, restful look.

This mixed border at Farmingdale State University in New York covers the ground with both low, spreading shrubs and giant grasses.

Acer campestre 'Compactum'. Compact hedge maple. Grows 2 to 4 feet tall, spreading 3 to 5 feet. Full sun. Zones 5 to 8.

A. palmatum. Weeping Japanese maple. Full sun to partial shade. See page 142.

Aesculus parviflora. Bottlebrush buckeye. Native to the southeastern United States. Grows 8 to 12 feet tall, spreading to 15 feet or more. Full sun to partial shade. Zones 4 to 8.

Corylopsis spp. Winter hazels. Fragrant winter hazel (*C. glabrescens*) grows 8 to 15 feet tall, spreading as far; its cultivar 'March Jewel' is 1½ feet tall and spreads to 5 feet. Both are hardy in Zones 5 to 8. The hybrid 'Winterthur' grows 5 to 6 feet tall, spreading to 10 or 12 feet; Zones 6 to 9. Buttercup winter hazel (*C. pauciflora*) grows 4 to 5 feet tall, spreading to 8 feet; Zones 6 to 8. Spike winter hazel (*C. spicata*) grows 4 to 6 feet tall, spreading to 10 feet or more; Zones 5 to 8. Full sun to light shade.

Syringa meyeri. Meyer lilac. Grows 4 to 8 feet tall, spreading to 6 to 12 feet. 'Palibin' is 4 to 5 feet tall and spreads to 7 feet. Full sun. Zones 3 to 7.

Syringa pubescens subsp. *patula* 'Miss Kim'. Grows 6 to 8 feet tall, spreading to 10 feet. Full sun. Zones 4 to 7.

Viburnum plicatum f. *tomentosum*. Doublefile viburnum. Grows 10 feet tall, spreading to 12 feet or more. For more compact growth, look for 'Shasta' (6 feet tall, spreading to 10 or 12 feet), 'Summer Snowflake' (5 to 8 feet tall, spreading to 10 or 12 feet), or 'Shoshoni' (5 feet tall, spreading to 8 feet). Full sun to partial shade. Zones 5 to 7.

Weigela florida. Old-fashioned weigela. Grows 6 to 9 feet tall, spreading to 9 to 12 feet or more). Purple-leaved 'Alexandria' (sold as Wine and Roses) is 4 to 5 feet tall and wide; 'Elvera' (sold as Midnight Wine) is 1½ to 2½ feet tall and wide. Full sun. Zones 5 to 8.

Itea virginica 'Henry's Garnet'
Virginia sweetspire

EXPOSURE: Full sun to partial shade
HEIGHT: 3 to 4 feet
SPREAD: 5 to 6 feet

This compact cultivar is much lower growing than the species, which reaches heights of 5 to 10 feet and is native to eastern North America. Low-growing 'Henry's Garnet' makes a fine summer-blooming ground cover. Plants bear narrow, rounded, dark green leaves and 6-inch-long racemes of tiny, fragrant, creamy white flowers in summer. In fall, the foliage turns brilliant red. Use 'Henry's Garnet' in masses along a woodland edge, in front of a large shrub border, or in drifts combined with other shrubs of similar height. Plants thrive in rich, acid, well-drained soil that ranges from fairly wet to moist. They also tolerate some drought and can be used to control erosion. Propagate by digging the suckers in spring or fall or by taking cuttings in spring or summer. Zones 5 to 9.

Potentilla fruticosa
Shrubby cinquefoil

EXPOSURE: Full sun to light shade
HEIGHT: 2 to 4 feet
SPREAD: 2 to 5 feet

Along with its easy-to-please disposition, shrubby cinquefoil brings brightly colored flowers to the garden. Plants bear palmate leaves, with five to seven leaflets arranged like fingers on a hand, and saucer-shaped flowers in shades of red, yellow, orange-red, and white from late spring to fall. Many cultivars are available, and heights vary. For ground cover use, look for lower-growing selections such as 'Yellow Gem', which is 2 feet tall and spreads to 4 feet. 'Longacre'

Itea virginica 'Henry's Garnet'

is 3 feet tall and spreads to 4 feet. Use shrubby cinquefoil to cover slopes, fill terraces, or add a low-maintenance ribbon of color along buildings or hedges. Plants grow in poor to average, well-drained soil and are fine in acid or alkaline pH. They are fairly drought tolerant. Remove older stems annually, or cut plants to within a few inches of the ground each year in late winter. Flowers are borne on the current season's growth. Propagate by taking cuttings in early summer. Zones 3 to 7.

Rhodotypos scandens ▼
Black jetbead

EXPOSURE: Full sun to full shade
HEIGHT: 3 to 6 feet tall
SPREAD: 4 to 8 or 9 feet

This is a very tough species that tolerates urban conditions, crowding, poor soil, root competition, parking lot islands, and any exposure. It produces arching branches with rounded, toothed leaves and white, 1- to 2-inch-wide flowers with four petals in early summer. The blooms are followed by black berries in fall. Use black jetbead to hold slopes, to plant under trees, or to fill any other spot where a less rugged plant will falter. Propagate by taking cuttings in late spring or early summer. Zones 4 to 8.

Rosa hybrids
Roses

EXPOSURE: Full sun
HEIGHT: 1 to 3 feet
SPREAD: 2 to 15 feet

Roses rarely make lists of great ground covers, but they deserve to be planted more often for this use. They bring showy flowers and colorful hips to the garden and can be used alone or combined with other sun-loving shrubs as well as perennials such as English lavender (*Lavandula angustifolia*), catmints (*Nepeta* spp.), and thymes (*Thymus* spp.). Give them average to rich, well-drained soil that is evenly moist. All of the roses listed here are disease resistant. Many new hybrids are released each year. Propagate by rooting cuttings of new shoots in summer. Zones 4 to 9. Note that most roses are sold under trademarked names, which are not set off by single quotes.

Baby Blanket. Lightly fragrant, silvery pink blooms; reaches 3 feet tall and spreads to 5 feet.

'Ballerina'. A hybrid musk rose with slightly fragrant pink-and-white flowers; 3-foot plants spread to 5 feet.

Carefree Beauty and Carefree Delight. Both bear lightly fragrant, pink flowers; hardy and disease resistant; plants reach 3 feet and spread as far.

▼ May be considered invasive in some regions.

Carefree Marvel. Lightly fragrant, deep pink blooms; 2-foot plants spread to 3 feet.

Electric Blanket. Lightly fragrant pink flowers; 1½-foot plants spread to about 2 feet.

Sun Runner. Lightly citrus-scented yellow blooms, on a 1½-foot plant that spreads to 3 feet.

Flower Carpet series. Cultivars with red, pink, and white flowers are available; plants are 2 to 2½ feet tall and spread to 4 feet.

Meidiland series. Several kinds, none fragrant, can be grown as ground covers. Panda Meidiland, with single white flowers, is 2 feet tall and spreads to 4 feet wide. Ice Meidiland, also white flowered, is 1½ feet tall and spreads to 6 feet. Mauve-pink Fuchsia Meidiland and pink Magic Meidiland are 2 feet tall and spread to 5 feet. Red-flowered Scarlet Meidiland is 3 feet tall and spreads to 5 feet.

Rosa 'Scarlet Meidiland'

Salix spp.
Willows

EXPOSURE: Full sun to light shade
HEIGHT: 2 inches to 4 feet
SPREAD: 6 feet

While the best-known willows are trees, the genus includes low-growing shrubs that make fine ground covers. Willows bear their tiny flowers in catkins in spring, often before the leaves emerge. The species listed here require sandy, somewhat poor soil that retains moisture. They tolerate some drought but grow best if the soil remains evenly moist. In rich soil, plants get leggy. Use these willows in moist, well-drained soil along streams and ponds or as accent plants with other ground covers. Propagate by taking cuttings in spring.

S. purpurea 'Nana'. ▼ Dwarf purple osier, dwarf arctic willow. Also sold as 'Gracilis', this willow bears oblong dark green to blue-green leaves. Plants grow from 3 to 4 feet tall and spread to 5 feet. Zones 4 to 7.

S. repens. Creeping willow. This prostrate shrub, growing 2 feet tall and spreading 5 to 8 feet wide, bears gray-green to green leaves. *S. repens* var. *argentea* (formerly *S. arenaria*) is 3 feet tall, spreading to 6 feet. It has upright shoots arched at the tips and gray leaves. 'Boyd's Pendulous' is 6 inches tall and spreads to 2 feet or more. Zones 5 to 7.

S. tristis. Dwarf gray willow. This shrub, which is native to the eastern half of the United States, bears leathery, gray-green leaves and is 1½ to 4 feet tall, spreading to 3 to 4 feet or more. Plants will grow in somewhat drier sites than most willows. Zones 2 to 9.

S. uva-ursi. Bearberry willow. A 2-inch-tall shrub native to northern Zones in North America, this species spreads to 3 feet. Plants bear oval, shiny green leaves. Zones 1 to 5.

Spiraea japonica ▼
Japanese spirea

EXPOSURE: Full sun to light shade
HEIGHT: 1½ to 3 feet
SPREAD: 2 to 3 feet

Although this species reaches 5 to 6 feet in height, a number of dwarf cultivars have been released that make attractive ground covers. Rather than travel by rhizomes or suckers, they form clumps and cover the ground with spreading branches, but cover they will. All bear toothed, rounded- to lance-shaped leaves and showy, lacy-looking clusters of tiny pink or white flowers from mid- to late summer. Use them in drifts to cover small to medium-size sites, group them in foundation plantings, grow them in rock gardens, or use them as specimens among perennials. Grow Japanese spirea in any well-drained,

▼ May be considered invasive in some regions.

acid soil. Once established, plants withstand drought. 'Goldflame' has pink flowers and bronzy new leaves that turn yellow once they emerge; plants are 2 to 3 feet tall and slightly wider at maturity. 'Little Princess' is 1½ feet tall, spreads to 3 feet, and bears clusters of rose-pink flowers. 'Magic Carpet' features orange-red to red-purple new leaves that age to yellow-green; plants grow about 1½ to 2 feet tall and spread to 2 or 3 feet. Propagate all forms by taking cuttings in summer. Zones 4 to 9.

Stephanandra incisa 'Crispa'
Dwarf cutleaved stephanandra

EXPOSURE: Full sun to light shade
HEIGHT: 2 feet
SPREAD: 4 feet

This close relative of spiraea is a low-growing, sprawling shrub that spreads by suckers and has attractive toothed and lobed leaves. Plants bear clusters of tiny greenish white flowers in early summer. They grow in rich, well-drained, acidic soil and are fairly drought tolerant, although they appreciate occasional deep watering during dry spells. Use this species to cover small slopes, in drifts along the front edge of foundation plantings or shrub borders, or as a dwarf hedge or edging. Zones 5 to 8.

Vaccinium spp.
Blueberries

EXPOSURE: Full sun to partial shade
HEIGHT: 6 to 24 inches
SPREAD: 2 to 4 feet

While the best-known blueberries are good-size shrubs, there are low-growing species for use as ground covers. All require acid soil that is moist but well drained; they can grow in sandy to peaty conditions as well. Combine them

Vaccinium vitis-idaea

with low-growing azaleas and rhododendrons (see page 156), use them as accents in moss gardens (see page 182), or plant them as edgings or in gardens designed to attract wildlife and combine them with native, acid-loving wildflowers. All bear urn-shaped flowers followed by edible berries. Propagate by taking cuttings from early to late summer.

V. angustifolium. Low-bush blueberry. This shrub is native to eastern North America. Plants range from 6 to 24 inches tall and spread to 4 feet or more. They bear white flowers and blue-black berries that are as attractive to people as they are to birds and other wildlife. The foliage turns deep red before it drops in fall. Zones 2 to 8.

V. crassifolium. Creeping blueberry. Native to the southern United States, this species is 18 inches tall and spreads to 3 feet or more. Plants are evergreen and bear clusters of white flowers followed by purple-black edible berries. 'Wells Delight', which is best in partial shade, is 8 inches tall and spreads to 2 feet. Zones 6 to 8.

V. vitis-idaea. Cowberry. Also called foxberry and lingonberry, this is a 6- to 12-inch-tall shrub that spreads to 2 feet or more. Plants are evergreen and bear clusters of white to pink flowers followed by acidic but edible berries. Zones 2 to 6.

Xanthorhiza simplicissima
Yellowroot

EXPOSURE: Full sun to partial shade
HEIGHT: 2 to 3 feet
SPREAD: 5 feet

This handsome shrub is native to the eastern United States and spreads by suckers. Established specimens can form dense thickets. Plants bear pinnate, or featherlike, leaves that turn yellow and red-purple in fall. Brownish purple flowers appear in spring. Yellowroot grows naturally along stream banks and ponds. Plants tolerate most soils but prefer moist, well-drained (rather than wet) soil. Established plantings have good drought tolerance. Use yellowroot for covering large-scale areas in partial shade, as an edging, along a foundation, along the edge of a wooded area, or in dappled shade under trees. Propagate by digging up suckers and growing them on. Zones 3 to 9.

Shrubs That Travel

With time, shrubs that spread by producing suckers can form broad thickets that function as ground covers — albeit tall ones.

Give them room to spread, and consider underplanting with lower-growing herbaceous species for a really thick cover that suppresses weeds. Unless otherwise noted, these shrubs all grow well in average, well-drained soil.

Calycanthus floridus. Sweetshrub. Native to the Southeastern United States. Grows 6 to 12 feet tall, spreading from 12 to 15 feet. Full sun to partial shade. Zones 4 to 9.

Cephalanthus occidentalis. Buttonbush. Native to moist sites and along streams throughout North America. Grows 3 to 6 feet tall, spreading to 8 feet. Full sun; moist, well-drained soil. Zones 5 to 10.

Clethra alnifolia. Summersweet, sweet pepperbush. Native from Maine to Florida. Look for 'Anne Bidwell'

Hydrangea arborescens 'Annabelle'

(4 to 6 feet tall, spreading to 5 feet), 'Hummingbird' (2½ to 3½ feet tall, spreading to 3 or 4 feet), and 'Sixteen Candles' (2½ feet tall, spreading to 3½ feet). Partial shade. Zones 5 to 9.

Cornus racemosa. Gray dogwood. Native from Maine to Minnesota and south to Georgia and Oklahoma. Grows 10 to 15 feet tall and wide. Cultivars include 'Hurxam' (3 to 4 feet tall, spreading to 4 feet or more) and 'Slavinii', also listed as 'Slavin's Dwarf' (2 to 3 feet tall, spreading to 3 feet or more). Full sun to full shade. Zones 4 to 8.

Cotoneaster divaricatus. Spreading cotoneaster. Grows 5 to 6 feet tall, spreading to 8 feet. Full sun to light shade. Zones 5 to 7.

Fothergilla spp. Fothergillas. Native to the Southeastern United States. Dwarf fothergilla (*F. gardenii*) grows 2 to 3 feet or taller, slowly spreading to 3 to 4 feet or more. Zones 5 to 9. Large fothergilla (*F. major*) grows 6 to 10 feet tall and slowly spreads to 10 feet wide. Full sun to partial shade. Zones 4 to 8.

Hydrangea arborescens. Smooth hydrangea. Native to the eastern United States. Grows 3 to 5 feet tall, spreading to 5 feet or more. Partial shade. Zones 4 to 9.

Hydrangea macrophylla. Bigleaf hydrangea. Species is 6 feet tall and spreads to 8 feet. Compact cultivars include 'All Summer Beauty' (3 to 4 feet tall, spreading to 4 feet), 'Forever Pink' (3 feet tall, spreading to 3 feet or more), and 'Pia' (2 to 3 feet tall, spreading to 3 feet or more). Full sun to partial shade. Zones 6 to 9.

Hydrangea quercifolia. Oakleaf hydrangea. Native to the southeastern United States. Seedlings and 'Snow Flake' grow 6 feet or taller, spreading to 8 feet. For more compact plants, look for 'Pee Wee' (2 to 3 feet tall,

Physocarpus opulifolius 'Dart's Gold'

Rosa carolina

spreading to 3 feet or more) and 'Sikes Dwarf' (2 to 2½ feet tall, spreading to 4 feet). Full sun to partial shade. Zones 5 to 9.

Hypericum frondosum. **Golden St. John's wort.** Native to the southeastern United States. Grows 2 to 4 feet tall, spreading to 4 feet wide. Full sun to partial shade. Zones 5 to 8.

Ilex verticillata. **Winterberry.** Native to eastern North America. Grows 6 to 10 feet tall, spreading to 10 feet or more, especially in wet soil. Compact cultivars include 'Red Sprite' and 'Nana' (2 to 4 feet tall, spreading to 3 to 5 feet. *I. verticillata* × *I. serrata* hybrids also sucker; choices include 'Harvest Red' (9 feet tall, spreading to 16 feet)' and 'Raritan Chief' (6 feet tall, spreading to 12 feet). Full sun or partial shade. Zones 5 to 7 or 8.

Jasminum nudiflorum. **Hardy or winter jasmine.** Grows 2 to 3 feet tall, spreading to 6 or 7 feet. Full sun to partial shade. Zones 6 to 9.

Myrica pensylvanica. **Bayberry.** Native from Newfoundland to New York, and south to North Carolina. Grows 8 or 9 feet tall, spreading to 9 to 12 feet. Full sun to light shade, with moist to dry soil; salt tolerant. Zones 4 to 7.

Nandina domestica. **Nandina, heavenly bamboo.** Species is 6 to 8 feet tall and slowly spreads to 8 feet or more. Dwarf cultivars include 'Atropurpurea Nana' (2 feet tall, spreading to 2 to 3 feet), 'Harbor Dwarf' (2 to 3 feet tall, spreading to 3 feet or more), and 'Moon Bay' (2½ feet tall, spreading to 3 feet). Full sun to full shade. Zones 6 to 9.

Physocarpus opulifolius. **Ninebark.** Native from Quebec to Virginia and Tennessee. Species is 5 to 10 feet tall, spreading to 15 feet. More compact cultivars include 'Nanus' (2 to 6 feet, spreading to 6 feet or more) and 'Dart's Gold' (4 to 5 feet, spreading to 5 feet or more). 'Snowfall' is 5 to 7 feet tall, spreading to 10 feet. Full sun to partial shade. Zones 3 to 7.

Prunus maritima. **Beach plum.** Native to the eastern seaboard, from Maine to Virginia. Grows 6 to 8 feet tall, and spreads to 12 feet or more. Full sun; salt tolerant. Zones 3 to 6.

Rhododendron atlanticum. **Coast azalea.** Native to the Eastern Seaboard from Delaware to North Carolina. Grows 6 to 8 feet tall, spreading to 8 feet or more. Partial to full shade. Zones 5 to 8.

R. periclymenoides, formerly *R. nudiflorum.* **Pinxterbloom azalea.** Native from Massachusetts to Ohio and south to North Carolina. Grows 4 to 6 feet tall, spreading by stolons to 8 to 10 feet. Partial to full shade. Zones 4 to 8.

Robinia hispida. **Bristly locust.** Native to the southeastern United States. Full sun. Species is 6 to 8 feet tall, spreading to 10 feet or more. Zones 6 to 10.

Rosa **spp.** **Wild roses.** North American native species that spread by suckers to form broad clumps include meadow rose (*R. blanda*), 4 to 5 feet tall, spreading to 5 feet or more (Zones 2 to 6); Carolina or pasture rose (*R. carolina*), 3 to 6 feet tall, spreading to 6 feet or more (Zones 4 to 9); and Virginia rose (*R. virginiana*), 4 to 6 feet tall, spreading to 6 feet or more (Zones 3 to 7). Full sun.

Viburnum acerifolium. **Mapleleaf viburnum.** Native from New Brunswick to Minnesota and south to North Carolina. Grows 4 to 6 feet tall, spreading to 6 feet or more. Partial to full shade. Zones 4 to 8.

Evergreen Shrubs

Arctostaphylos spp.
Manzanitas

EXPOSURE: Full sun to partial shade
HEIGHT: 1 foot
SPREAD: 1½ to 6 or more feet

This genus of shrubs and small trees contains a wealth of good evergreen ground cover plants. Most are only suitable for use in western gardens, and the majority of them are native to the West Coast, especially California. Give the species listed here moist, well-drained soil that is sandy or gritty and has an acid pH. They spread by trailing stems and form a dense cover where happy. All are very drought resistant once established, are salt tolerant, and prefer open sites with good air circulation. They do not tolerate poor drainage, excessive heat, or the summertime heat and humidity characteristic of eastern climates. Propagate by sowing seed or by digging and potting up sections of stems, which root where they touch the soil.

A. edmundsii. Little Sur manzanita. A California native with rounded, gray-green leaves, this species bears pinkish flowers in late winter followed by brown berrylike fruit. Plants are about 1 foot tall and spread to 6 feet or more. Zones 7 to 10.

A. hookeri 'Monterey Carpet'. Hooker or Monterey manzanita. Another California native, this species bears rounded leaves and pinkish white flowers in early summer that are followed by round red fruit. Plants are 8 to 12 inches tall and spread from 3 to 12 feet. Zones 8 to 9.

A. pumila. Dune manzanita. A low-growing California native, this species bears small, dark green leaves that are rounded to spoon shaped and 1½- to 3-inch-long racemes of white flowers in summer. Red-brown fruits follow the flowers.

A. uva-ursi. Bearberry. See page 114.

Berberis candidula
Pale-leaved barberry

EXPOSURE: Full sun to partial shade
HEIGHT: 2 feet
SPREAD: 4 feet

This little-known species bears rounded, spine-tipped, evergreen leaves and spiny stems. Plants are deciduous in areas where winter temperatures drop below –10°F. Bright yellow flowers appear in late spring, although they tend to be hard to see among the leaves. Purplish berries follow the flowers in late summer. Plants spread fairly slowly to form dense mounds, and also send out occasional rhizomes that produce suckers. Use them in rock gardens, in raised beds and planters, or as low ground covers along a walkway. The flowers are most visible from below, so plantings along the top of walls or in taller planters are especially effective. Give plants average to rich soil that is moist but well drained. Once established they tolerate drought. Propagate by digging suckers in spring or summer. Zones 5 or 6 to 9.

Carissa macrocarpa ▼
Natal plum

EXPOSURE: Full sun to partial shade
HEIGHT: 6 to 10 feet
SPREAD: 10 feet

Formerly *C. grandiflora,* this is a vigorous species that bears ovate, glossy dark green leaves that are packed densely on spreading stems. Small clusters of pretty 2-inch-wide, five-petaled white flowers

Carissa macrocarpa

appear in late spring and are followed by rounded fruit that ripens from red to purple-black. Natal plum grows best in full sun and needs fairly rich, well-drained soil. The cultivar 'Tuttlei' is 2 to 3 feet tall and spreads to 6 feet. 'Green Carpet' is 1½ feet tall and spreads to 4 feet or more. Zones 8 to 11.

Ceanothus thyrsiflorus var. repens
Creeping blueblossom

EXPOSURE: Full sun to light shade
HEIGHT: 3 feet
SPREAD: 8 feet

This species, native from Oregon to California, bears glossy evergreen leaves and produces panicles of small flowers in spring that range from pale to dark blue. Give plants well-drained, sandy soil that is acid to neutral. They are drought tolerant once established, and soil that is too wet will cause root rot. Propagate by cuttings taken in early summer. Zones 8 to 10.

Ceanothus griseus var. *horizontalis* 'Yankee Point' is another good choice. It is 2 to 3 feet tall and spreads to 10 feet. Zones 9 to 10.

▼ May be considered invasive in some regions.

Cephalotaxus harringtonia
Japanese plum yew

EXPOSURE: Full sun to partial shade
HEIGHT: 2 to 5 feet
SPREAD: 3 to 6 feet

Although this species can reach as much as 20 or 30 feet in height, low-growing forms make fantastic ground covers that resemble yews (*Taxus* spp.). Also called cowtail pine, this evergreen bears dark green needles. Female plants produce rounded, olive-green fruit in fall provided a male plant is located nearby. For ground cover, purchase dwarf cultivars. 'Duke Gardens' is 2 to 3 feet tall and spreads to 4 or 5 feet. 'Prostrata' is 2 to 3 feet tall and spreads from 3 to 5 feet. 'Nana' reaches 6 feet tall and spreads as far. Give plants well-drained sandy to loamy soil. A site in light shade is best, but plants tolerate full sun. They also tolerate heat and some drought and are excellent yew substitutes for southern gardens. Shear them to keep them compact. Propagate by sowing seed in fall or by taking cuttings from shoot tips in summer or fall. Zones 5 or 6 to 8.

Cotoneaster spp.
Cotoneasters

EXPOSURE: Full sun to light shade
HEIGHT: 2 inches to 6 feet
SPREAD: 4 to 8 feet

Like their deciduous relatives, evergreen cotoneasters make fine ground covers. Use them to fill in along steps, cover rocky sites, or hold soil on slopes. Drifts of cotoneasters also can be used to edge hedges and shrub borders or fill medium to large sites, either alone or combined with other species. All thrive in rich, light, well-drained soil. They're happiest in loamy conditions but tolerate dry, poor soil from sandy to clayey,

provided the drainage is good. Plants tolerate drought, acid or alkaline pH, windy sites, and they also are fairly salt tolerant. Propagate evergreen cotoneasters by taking cuttings in late summer.

C. congestus. Pyrenees or congested cotoneaster. Formerly *C. pyreniacus,* this is a prostrate to mound-forming species with rounded evergreen leaves that may drop in very cold weather. Pinkish white flowers appear in summer followed by round red fruit. Plants are 1 to 2½ feet tall and slowly spread to 3 feet or more. Zones 6 to 8.

C. conspicuus. Wintergreen cotoneaster. While this species can reach 5 to 8 feet in height, the dwarf variety *C. conspicuus* var. *decorus,* commonly called necklace cotoneaster, makes a fine ground cover that ranges from 1 to 2 feet tall and spreads to 2 or 3 feet. Plants bear tiny, glossy, evergreen to semievergreen leaves and white flowers in summer followed by red fruit.

They are susceptible to fireblight, a serious bacterial disease. Zones 6 to 9.

C. dammeri. Bearberry cotoneaster. Popular and easy to grow, this species bears evergreen leaves and clusters of white flowers in early summer. Round red fruit ripens in fall. Plants are evergreen to about −10°F. Their fast growth rate makes them good for covering a site quickly, although they tend to become unattractive with age and should then be replaced. Plants grow 1 to 1½ feet tall, with a spread of 6 feet. Several cultivars are available, including 'Mooncreeper', a very prostrate selection that's about 2 inches tall. 'Streib's Findling', also listed as a cultivar of *C. prostratus,* is 4 to 6 inches tall. Zones 6 to 9.

C. salicifolius. Willow-leaved cotoneaster. While the full-size species reaches 15 feet tall, there are compact cultivars of willow-leaved cotoneaster that are useful as ground covers. All bear evergreen,

Cotoneaster dammeri 'Lowfast'

rounded to lance-shaped leaves, clusters of white flowers in summer, and round red berries in fall. The foliage may turn rich red-purple in winter. 'Repens' is 2 feet tall. 'Herbstfeuer' (sold as 'Autumn Fire') is 1 to 2 feet tall. 'Moner' (sold as Emerald Carpet) is 1 foot tall. 'Gnom', a hybrid cultivar, is 8 to 12 inches tall. All spread from 6 to 8 feet. Zones 6 to 7.

Ilex spp.
Hollies

EXPOSURE: Full sun to light shade
HEIGHT: 3 to 4 feet
SPREAD: 5 to 8 feet

This genus contains shrubs as well as full-size trees, and some very handsome evergreen ground covers in the bunch, including the ones listed here. Hollies bear their flowers singly or in small clusters in late spring or early summer, with male and female flowers on separate plants. The blooms usually are white or cream and are followed by red or black berries. Red berries are very ornamental, and all — black or red — are popular

Ilex vomitoria 'Nana'

with birds and other wildlife. Be aware that in most cases you'll need to plant one compatible male holly for three females. Hollies need a spot with average to rich, acid soil that is well drained. Established plants are fairly drought tolerant. Use hollies in foundation plantings, as edging plants for large-scale shrub borders, or along a woodland edge. To propagate, take cuttings in summer or early fall.

I. crenata. ▼   Japanese holly, box-leaved holly. This species bears small dark green leaves that resemble those of boxwood and black fruit. While the species can reach 10 feet or more, dwarf cultivars make excellent low-growing cushions that cover the ground with densely twiggy growth. The plants also withstand severe pruning. Look for 'Elfin', which is 1 foot tall and spreads to 1½ feet; 'Beehive', 3 to 4 feet tall and spreading to 5 or 6 feet; 'Green Island', 3 feet tall and spreading to 6 feet; and 'Kingsville Green Cushion', which is 8 inches tall and 2½ feet wide. In comparison, the popular 'Helleri' is 4 feet tall and spreads to 5 feet. Hardiness varies depending on the cultivar, so consult local nursery owners for the best plants for your area. Zones 5 or 6 to 8.

I. opaca. American holly. Best known as a 40- or 50-foot tree, this species is native to the eastern and central United States. Plants bear typical spiny holly leaves and round red fruit. 'Maryland Dwarf' reaches only 3 to 5 feet in height and spreads to 6 feet or more. Zones 5 to 9.

I. vomitoria. Yaupon holly, cassine holly. A native of the southeastern United States, this species can reach 20 feet tall and spreads by suckers. Plants

bear small, ½- to 1½-inch-long leaves that are dark green and shallowly toothed. They produce scarlet fruit. 'Nana', also listed as 'Dwarf', is 3 to 5 feet tall and spreads to 8 feet. 'Schillings', also listed as 'Stokes Dwarf' is smaller and slower growing: about 3 to 4 feet tall and wide. Yaupon holly grows in dry or very wet soil and tolerates salt spray. Zones 7 to 10.

Juniperus spp.
Junipers

EXPOSURE: Full sun
HEIGHT: 4 inches to 60 feet or more
SPREAD: 1 to 20 or 30 feet

Premier evergreen ground covers for sunny spots, junipers are so tough and adaptable that there's a place for them in nearly every sunny garden. Plants bear needles or scalelike leaves, and the foliage is often pungently scented. They bear male and female cones, and the female cones develop into small berry-like fruit that is attractive to birds and other wildlife. Ground-covering species spread by sprawling stems that may root when they come in contact with the soil, but junipers are fairly easy to keep in bounds by pruning as necessary. In general, they grow in any well-drained soil, from sandy to clayey and acid to alkaline. They tolerate poor soil and withstand drought. Where summers are hot and humid, it's best to plant them on a site with good air circulation. On the West Coast, where summers are cooler than they are in the East, most junipers can be grown in warmer zones than they will tolerate elsewhere. Several species are native to North America. When selecting junipers, pay close attention to the height at maturity listed on the label; many of the popular ground covers are

▼ May be considered invasive in some regions.

low-growing cultivated forms of species that can reach 40 feet or more.

J. chinensis. Chinese juniper. This species from China is a 50- or 60-foot tree, but low-growing cultivars are suitable ground covers. 'Pfitzeriana Compacta' is a gray-green shrub that reaches 2 to 3 feet tall and spreads to 6 feet. 'San Jose', with sage green foliage, is 1½ feet tall and spreads to 6 or 8 feet. 'Prostrata Variegata' features blue-green foliage variegated with creamy white on a 1½-foot-tall plant that spreads to about 5 feet. Zones 4 to 9.

J. communis. Common juniper. This native of North America and Eurasia grows to about 20 feet tall, but low-growing forms make excellent ground covers. 'Green Carpet' is 4 to 6 inches tall and spreads to 3 feet. 'Depressa Aurea' reaches 2 feet high, spreads to 5 feet, and features yellow spring foliage. 'Prostrata' is 1 foot tall and spreads to 6 feet. 'Repanda' reaches 15 inches tall and spreads to 6 to 8 feet. All withstand wind but are not very heat tolerant. Zones 2 to 6.

J. conferta. Shore juniper. This Japanese native is 1 to 2 feet tall and spreads fairly slowly to 9 feet or more. It is ideal for sandy soil and seaside gardens. Many cultivars are available, including 1-foot-tall 'Blue Pacific', with blue-green foliage, and 'Emerald Sea', a 1-foot-tall selection with green foliage. Zones 5 or 6 to 9.

J. horizontalis. Creeping juniper. A native of Canada and northern tier states from Nova Scotia to Alaska and south to New Jersey and Minnesota, creeping juniper ranges from 1 to 2 feet tall and spreads to 8 feet or more. Many cultivars are available, nearly all

Low-growing junipers combine with bearberry (*Arctostaphylos* sp.), inkberry (*Ilex glabra*), heather (*Calluna* sp.), and euonymus (*Euonymus japonica*).

suitable as ground covers. Consider planting selections with contrasting foliage colors to add interest to a juniper planting. 'Bar Harbor' is 1 foot tall and blue-green, turning to purple in winter. 'Blue Chip' is 10 inches tall and also features blue foliage that turns purplish in winter. 'Blue Mat', another blue-foliaged selection, reaches 6 inches tall. 'Douglasii' is 1 to 1½ feet tall and is silver-blue. 'Emerald Spreader', 7 inches tall, has green foliage. 'Procumbens' is 6 inches tall and has green foliage. 'Wiltonii' is 4 to 6 inches tall and sports silver-blue foliage. All are adaptable and grow in acid to slightly alkaline soil and tolerate heavy clay. They survive heat and drought, withstand salt spray, and even are found growing wild in swampy conditions. Zones 3 to 9.

J. procumbens. Japanese garden juniper. A Japanese native that tolerates a wide range of soils, including alkaline ones, this species is 10 to 12 inches tall and spreads to 10 feet. A number of cultivars are available, including 'Nana', which is 2 to 2½ feet tall and spreads to 10 feet or more at maturity. 'Greenmound' is 8 inches tall and spreads to 6 feet. Zones 4 to 8.

J. sabina. Savin juniper. This species is adaptable to soils that are dry and well drained as well as alkaline. It also tolerates pollution and other urban conditions but is not particularly

WEEPING TREES

TREES WITH PENDULOUS BRANCHING HABITS make dramatic — if large — ground covers. For the best effect, let the pendulous branches grow down to reach the ground and underplant them with lower-growing ground covers. In most cases, the tree's mature height depends on the height of the graft union. Unless otherwise noted, these need full sun.

Acer palmatum. **Weeping Japanese maple.** 'Burgundy Lace', cutleaf burgundy leaves, grows 12 feet tall by 15 feet wide. *A. palmatum* var. *dissectum,* deeply cut green leaves, grows 6 feet tall by 10 feet wide. 'Dissectum Atropurpureum', deeply cut red-purple leaves, grows 6 feet tall by 10 feet wide. 'Filigree', green leaves flecked with cream and gold, grows 6 feet tall by 9 feet wide. 'Ornatum', bronze-red leaves that turn green, grows 6 feet tall by 9 feet wide. 'Sherwood Flame', burgundy leaves, grows 13 feet tall by 16 feet wide. 'Waterfall', deeply cut green leaves, grows 10 feet tall by 14 feet wide. Full sun to partial shade. Zones 6 to 8.

Carpinus betulus 'Pendula'. **Weeping hornbeam.** Grows 8 feet or taller by 12 feet or wider. Zones 4 to 8.

Cedrus atlantica 'Glauca Pendula'. **Weeping blue Atlas cedar.** Grows 10 to 15 feet tall, spreading 10 to 15 feet or wider. Zones 6 to 9.

Cercidiphyllum japonicum f. *pendula.* **Weeping katsura tree.** Grows 15 feet tall, 25 feet wide. Zones 4 to 8.

Cercis canadensis. **Redbud.** 'Covey' (also sold as Lavender Twist), grows 4½ to 5 feet tall by 8 feet or wider. Zones 5 to 9. *C. canadensis* var. *texensis* 'Traveler' grows 5 feet tall and 5 to 12 feet wide. Full sun or light shade. Zones 6 to 9.

Cornus spp. **Dogwoods.** Weeping flowering dogwood (*C. florida* 'Pendula') grows 10 to 15 feet tall and wide. Weeping kousa dogwood (*C. kousa* 'Lustgarten Weeping') grows 2 to 8 feet tall and 10 feet wide. 'Wolf Eyes', with variegated leaves, grows 6 to 10 feet tall and 6 to 20 (or more) feet wide. Full sun or light shade. Zones 5 to 8.

Fagus sylvatica f. *pendula.* **Weeping beech.** Grows 50 to 60 feet tall and 80 feet or wider. 'Purpurea Pendula' grows 10 to 15 feet tall and spreads to 15 feet or wider. Zones 5 to 7.

Malus spp. **Weeping crab apples.** 'Egret' and 'Lullaby' (6 feet tall, spreads to 6 feet or more); 'Jewelberry (8 feet tall, spreads to 12 feet); 'Mary Potter' (10 feet tall, spreads to 15 to 20 feet); 'Sea Foam' (4 to 5 feet tall, spreads to 5 feet or more); 'Tina' (4 feet tall, spreads to 10 feet); and 'White Cascade' (10 to 15 feet tall and wide). Zones 5 to 8.

Prunus × subhirtella. **Weeping Higan cherry.** 'Pendula Rosea', 'Pendula Rubra', 'Pendula Rosea Plena', 'Stellata', 'Snofozam' (sold as Snow Fountains), and 'Yae-shidare-higan' all grow 10 to 40 feet tall and spreading to 15 to 30 feet or more. Zones 6 to 8.

Ulmus glabra 'Camperdownii'. **Scotch or wych elm.** Grows 15 to 25 feet tall and spreads 20 to 25 feet or wider. Zones 5 to 7.

heat tolerant. The species reaches about 6 feet; however, dwarf cultivars are available. These include green-foliaged 'Arcadia', 1 to 1½ feet tall and spreading to 6 or 8 feet, and 'Arcadia Compact Form', which reaches only 1 foot in height. 'Blue Donau' (also sold as 'Blue Danube') has blue-green leaves and is 1½ feet tall by 5 feet wide at maturity. 'Monna' (sold as Calgary Carpet) is 6 to 9 inches tall and spreads to 10 feet. Zones 3 to 7.

J. sargentii. **Sargent juniper.** A low-growing species native to China and Japan, Sargent juniper has blue-green foliage. It reaches about 1 foot tall and spreads to 8 or 10 feet or more. Zones 3 to 9.

J. scopulorum. **Rocky Mountain juniper.** This native tree from British Columbia to Arizona and Texas reaches 40 feet in height, but cultivars suitable for use as ground covers are available. Selections to look for include 'Monam' (sold as Blue Creeper), a 2-foot-tall selection that spreads to 6 or 8 feet, and 'Silver King', a silvery-leafed plant to 2 feet tall and spreading to 6 feet. 'Table Top' is 5 to 6 feet tall and spreads to 8 feet. The plants are very drought tolerant and adaptable, although they don't do well in areas with hot, humid, rainy summers, such as the Southeast. Zones 3 to 7.

J. squamata. **Singleseed juniper.** This Chinese species reaches 30 feet, but dwarf cultivars make excellent ground covers. The plants are adaptable, tolerating dry soil and drought, but they aren't good choices for the hot and humid Southeast. 'Blue Carpet', with bluish gray-green foliage, is 8 to 12 inches tall and spreads to about 5 feet. 'Blue Star', featuring silver-blue

Mahonia nervosa

foliage, is 16 inches tall and spreads to 3 feet. Zones 4 to 7 or 8.

J. virginiana. Eastern red cedar. Another native from eastern and central North America, this species reaches 40 feet but offers some ground covers with low, spreading habits. Cultivars to look for include 'Kosteri', which is 3 to 4 feet tall and spreads to 30 feet. 'Blue Cloud', with gray-green foliage is 4 feet tall and spreads to 6 feet. 'Silver Spreader' is 2 to 3 feet tall and spreads from 4 to 6 feet. This species has been classified as invasive in Oregon. Zones 3 to 9.

Mahonia spp.
Mahonias, grape hollies

EXPOSURE: Full sun to full shade
HEIGHT: 1 to 3 feet
SPREAD: 3 to 5 feet

These handsome evergreen shrubs spread by suckers to form colonies. All of the species listed here bear spiny, pinnate leaves (with leaflets arranged in a featherlike fashion) and racemes of yellow flowers followed by blue-black berries. Although the plants will grow in a range of soils, they prefer a spot with rich, moist, well-drained acid soil. They need a site protected from drying winds. Plants tolerate some drought, but they're happiest with steady moisture and do not withstand heat well. In the South, a spot with afternoon shade is best. The plants prefer partial to full shade but tolerate full sun provided the soil remains moist. Use them as edgings for walkways and sitting areas, or plant them in drifts along the shady edge of a wooded area. The species listed here are all native to western North America.

M. aquifolium. Oregon grape holly. This species from northwestern North America bears 1-foot-long compound leaves. Its yellow spring blooms are carried in dense, 3-inch-long racemes and are followed by clusters of handsome blue-black berries. While the species ranges from 3 feet to as tall as 9 feet, there are fine low-growing cultivars. 'Compactum' is 2 to 3 feet tall and spreads from 3 to 4 feet wide. 'Apollo' is 2 feet tall, spreading to 3 feet or more, and bears golden orange flowers. 'Mayhan Strain' is about 3 to 4 feet tall and spreads to 5 feet. Zones 4 or 5 to 8.

M. nervosa. Cascades mahonia. This compact suckering shrub native from British Columbia to Idaho and south to California is 1 to 1½ feet tall and spreads to 4 or 5 feet. Its compound leaves reach 2 feet in length and turn red-purple in fall and winter. Dense, 8-inch-long racemes of yellow flowers appear from late spring into early summer followed by showy clusters of blue-black berries. Zones 6 to 8.

M. repens. Creeping mahonia. A 1- to 1½-foot-tall species that spreads from 4 to 5 feet, creeping mahonia is native from British Columbia to California and Colorado. Plants bear pinnate, 10-inch-long leaves that turn purple in winter. They produce small clusters of dark yellow flowers in mid- to late spring. Zones 5 to 9.

Microbiota decussata
Siberian cypress

EXPOSURE: Full sun to light shade
HEIGHT: 1 to 2 feet
SPREAD: 8 to 12 feet or more

A native of Siberia, as its common name suggests, this low, spreading conifer looks like a juniper. Plants usually are only 1 foot tall and have scalelike leaves that turn bronzy purple in winter. They make excellent ground covers for medium to large areas and also can be used as foundation plants or for covering slopes. Plant need rich, moist, well-drained soil and do not survive for long in damp conditions or heavy soil. They also are not particularly heat resistant, so a spot with afternoon shade is best in warm climates. An established planting tolerates drought but is best when watered deeply during dry weather. To propagate, take cuttings in summer. Zones 2 to 8.

Conifer Cultivars for Covering

Dwarf conifers that feature spreading habits make stellar ground covers, whether used alone or when combined together for contrast.

Use dwarf conifers to cover ground, edge walkways, or face down a hedge or shrub border and thus link it to the lawn and other landscape features. All require a site in full sun (unless otherwise indicated) and well-drained soil that is evenly moist. Hundreds of cultivars are available, and this is just a short list to get you started. Prune out any growth that reverts, meaning it no longer resembles the cultivar in terms of growth habit or color.

Chamaecyparis spp. False cypresses.

C. pisifera. Japanese false cypress. 'Nana' (2 feet tall, spreading to 4 feet); 'Filifera Nana' (2 to 3 feet tall, 3 to 4 feet wide); 'Golden Mop', also sold as 'Mops' (5 feet tall, spreading to 7 feet); 'Plumosa Compressa' (3 feet tall, spreading to 3 or 4 feet). Zones 4 to 8.

Picea spp. Spruces.

P. abies. Norway spruce. 'Nidiformis' (2 to 4 feet tall, 4 to 5 feet wide); 'Pygmaea' (1 foot tall, 2 feet wide); 'Reflexa' (6 inches, unless grafted higher, and spreading indefinitely); 'Repens' (3 to 5 feet, spreading to 5 or 6 feet or more). Zones 3 to 8.

P. pungens. Colorado spruce. Native to the Rocky Mountains. 'Glauca Pendula' (blue needles, 1 to 2 feet tall, 5 to 6 feet or wider). Zones 3 to 7.

Pinus spp. Pines.

P. densiflora. Japanese red pine. 'Prostrata' (1 to 2 feet tall, spreading to 8 feet); 'Umbraculifera Compacta' (4 to 6 feet tall, spreading to 8 feet or more). Zones 4 to 7.

P. flexilis. Limber pine. Native to the Rocky Mountains. 'Glauca Pendula' (prostrate, 1 to 2 feet tall unless grafted, spreading 5 to 10 feet). Zones 3 to 7.

P. mugo. Mugo pine. The species is 15 to 20 feet or taller, spreading to 25 feet or more. *P. mugo* var. *mugo* is 8 feet tall by 15 feet wide, but can be variable. For compact plants, stick with cultivars, including 'Gnom' (15 inches tall, 3 feet wide), 'Slavinii' (3 feet tall, 5 feet wide), and *P. mugo* var. *prostrata* (3 to 5 feet tall, spreading to 10 feet). Zones 3 to 7.

P. nigra. Austrian pine. 'Hornbrookiana' (2 feet tall, spreading to 6 feet). Zones 5 to 8.

P. parviflora. Japanese white pine. 'Bergman' (16 inches tall, 3 feet wide). Zones 6 to 9.

P. strobus. Eastern white pine. Native to eastern North America. 'Haird's Broom' (1 foot tall, spreading to 3 feet); 'Merrimack' (2 to 3 feet tall, spreading to 4 feet or more). Zones 4 to 9.

P. sylvestris. Scots pine. 'Albyn's Prostrate' (1 to 1½ feet tall, spreading 3 to 6 feet); 'Hillside Creeper' (2 feet tall, spreading 6 to 8 feet). Zones 3 to 7.

Tsuga spp. Hemlocks.

T. canadensis. Canada hemlock. Native to eastern North America. 'Cole's Prostrate' (1 foot tall, spreading to 3 feet); 'Pendula' (2 to 12 feet tall, spreading to 20 to 25 feet). Partial shade to full shade. Zones 4 to 8.

Picea abies 'Little Gem'

Pyracantha koidzumii 'Santa Cruz'

Taxus baccata 'Repandens Aurea'

Pyracantha spp.
Pyracanthas, firethorns

EXPOSURE: Full sun to light shade
HEIGHT: 1½ to 3 feet
SPREAD: 3 to 9 feet

While pyracanthas are generally large shrubs, there are a few cultivars with low, spreading habits that make fine ground covers. They feature evergreen leaves, clusters of white flowers in late spring or early summer, and showy orange-red berries from fall into winter. Grow the plants in well-drained neutral to acid soil. They are fairly drought tolerant and can be used to cover slopes or fill terraced beds, either alone or combined with other low ground covers. Good air circulation helps reduce disease problems. Propagate by taking cuttings in summer.

P. coccinea. ▼ Scarlet firethorn. While this species grows 12 feet high and wide, the cultivar 'Lowboy' only reaches 2 to 3 feet tall and spreads to 6 or 8 feet. Like the species, it is susceptible to scab and is hardy in Zones 5 to 9.

P. hybrids. 'Rutgers' is a disease-resistant cultivar that grows to 3 feet tall and spreads to 9 feet. Zones 6 (5 with protection) to 8. 'Red Elf' is 2 or 3 feet tall and spreads to 4 feet, while 'Ruby Mound' is 1½ feet tall and spreads to 3 feet; both are hardy in Zones 7 to 9.

P. koidzumii 'Santa Cruz'. Resistant to disease, this selection grows 2½ to 3 feet tall and spreads to 5 or 6 feet. Zones 7 to 10.

Taxus spp.
Yews

EXPOSURE: Full sun to full shade
HEIGHT: 2 to 5 feet
SPREAD: 8 to 15 feet or more

Cultivars of several different species of yew can be used as ground covers. All bear dark green needles, and female plants produce seeds covered by fleshy berrylike arils. All parts of the plants, except the red arils, are toxic if ingested. Use dwarf yews as ground covers for large sites. Give them average to rich soil that is well drained. Established plants are fairly drought tolerant. Propagate by taking cuttings in late summer or fall.

T. baccata. English yew. This species is a tree that reaches 40 feet or taller, but 'Repandens' is 2- to 4-foot-tall cultivar that spreads to 12 or 15 feet or more. Plants are hardier than the straight species and can be grown in Zones 5 to 7.

T. canadensis. Canada yew. An underused native from central and eastern North America, this species makes a fine ground cover. Plants grow from 3 to 5 feet tall and spread to 8 feet. The needles turn red-brown in winter. This species does not tolerate heat or drought, needs a cool, shady site, and also needs shade in winter, so a north-facing site is best. Use it under large deciduous trees, to hold soil on shady slopes, or as a specimen in a shade garden. Unlike other yews, plants of this species tolerate soil that is periodically wet. Zones 3 to 6.

T. cuspidata. ▼ Japanese yew. Dwarf cultivars of this 40-foot-tall tree make good ground covers. 'Cross Spreading' is 3 to 4 feet tall and spreads to 8 feet. 'Densa' is 3 to 4 feet tall and spreads to 7 or 8 feet. 'Monloo', sold as Emerald Spreader , is 2½ feet tall and spreads to 8 or 10 feet. Zones 4 to 7.

T. × media. Anglo-Japanese yew. Dwarf cultivars include 'Chadwickii', 2 to 4 feet tall, and 'Densiformis', 3 to 4 feet tall. Both spread to 4 to 6 feet. Zones 4 to 7.

Selections for Shade

A site in partial to full shade may seem like an intimidating planting challenge, but there are plenty of great perennial ground covers that will thrive there.

Species with low, spreading habits are an excellent alternative to lawn grass for shady sites. A mix of shade-loving ground covers won't need all the care that a lawn requires — including mowing and trimming — although they will need weeding, watering, and other basic care at least until they are established. In addition, since lawn grass grows best in full sun (it survives but does not thrive in shade), shade-loving ground covers simply are a better choice for covering the ground in partial to full shade.

Use the ground covers listed here to fill sites under trees, on the north side of buildings, and any other spot that does not receive full sun. Many also will grow happily in sites that receive sun in the morning but are shaded in the afternoon. All of these shade-loving plants can be used to edge walkways or fill in around and under shrubs and trees. For a very informal planting with lots less work than a traditional garden, consider covering an area with drifts of several different selections from this list. When choosing plants for this sort of planting, pay particular attention to foliage in order to create combinations with long-lasting appeal. Select plants with different leaf sizes and shapes as well as contrasting patterns and colors. Certainly many of these plants also produce flowers, but by paying attention to foliage you will ensure a planting that is attractive all season.

This list includes many native species as well as nonnative ones. See Native Plants for a Woodland Floor on page 165 as well as Flowering Ground Covers for Shade on page 159 for more plants to consider.

1. *Hosta* 'Abba Dabba Do'
   Hosta

2. *Geranium macrorrhizum* 'Ingwersen's Variety'
   Bigroot geranium

3. *Hosta* 'Halcyon'
   Hosta

4. *Hakonechloa macra* 'Aureola'
   Japanese hakone grass

5. *Athyrium niponicum* var. *pictum*
   Japanese painted fern

6. *Lamium maculatum* 'Beacon Silver'
   Spotted deadnettle

7. *Asarum europaeum*
   European ginger

8. *Epimedium* × *perralchicum* 'Fröhnleiten'
   Epimedium

9. *Asarum shuttleworthii*
   Mottled wild ginger

10. *Helleborus* × *hybridus*
    Lenten rose

11. *Persicaria virginiana* 'Variegata'
    Persicaria

12. *Pulmonaria saccharata* 'Roy Davidson'
    Pulmonaria

Ajuga spp.
Ajugas, bugleweeds

EXPOSURE: Partial shade
HEIGHT: 6 to 16 inches
SPREAD: 1 to 2 feet

The two species covered here spread by rhizomes, but both lack stolons and thus spread more slowly than their lightning-fast relative, creeping bugleweed (*A. reptans;* see page 90 for more on that species). Ajugas generally prefer a site in partial shade, although they can tolerate more sun in northern zones, where temperatures are cooler, and also do fine on sites with morning sun and afternoon shade. They need average to rich soil that is evenly moist but well drained. Propagate by dividing clumps in spring or potting up rooted plantlets in spring or early summer.

A. genevensis. Geneva bugleweed. This species produces 8- to 16-inch-tall rosettes of rounded evergreen leaves on plants that spread to about 1½ feet. Spikelike clusters of dark blue-purple, two-lipped flowers appear in late spring and early summer. 'Pink Beauty' bears pink flowers, 'Alba' has white ones. Zones 3 to 8.

A. pyramidalis. Pyramid bugleweed. This 6- to 10-inch-tall evergreen or semi-evergreen species spreads 1 to 2 feet. 'Metallica Crispa' features rosettes of bronze-purple leaves that have a heavily crinkled texture. Zones 3 to 8.

Asarum spp.
Wild gingers

EXPOSURE: Partial to full shade
HEIGHT: 3 to 8 inches
SPREAD: 1 to 2 feet

Although gingers bloom, they're grown primarily for their heart-shaped foliage, since their bell-shaped flowers are borne under the leaves, next to the soil. (This is to attract the ground-dwelling insects that pollinate them.) Give wild gingers a site with average to rich soil that is evenly moist but well drained. Propagate by dividing clumps in spring.

A. canadense. Canadian wild ginger. Native to eastern North America, this perennial produces broad drifts of deciduous 2- to 4-inch-wide leaves. Plants grow 6 inches tall and spread to 2 feet or more. Zones 2 to 8.

A. europaeum. European ginger. A popular evergreen perennial, this species produces handsome clumps of glossy dark green leaves that are 2 to 3 inches wide. Plants are about 3 inches tall and spread fairly slowly to form 1- to 1½-foot-wide mounds. Zones 4 to 8. Other species of ginger are less hardy but quite handsome and worth the trouble to get them started. Sierra wild ginger or cyclamen-leaved ginger (*A. hartwegii*), native to California and Oregon, and mottled wild ginger (*A. shuttleworthii*), native to the southeastern United States, have evergreen leaves marked with silver or cream. Both are hardy in Zones 6 to 8.

Aspidistra elatior
Cast iron plant

EXPOSURE: Partial to full shade
HEIGHT: 2 feet
SPREAD: 3 feet

Although most often thought of as a houseplant, this is a tough rhizomatous species that makes a fine ground cover in mild climates. The flowers are insignificant, but the large evergreen leaves are attractive, and the plants form handsome clumps. The dark green leaves range from 12 to 20 inches long. Cultivars with variegated leaves are available, including 'Variegata' with leaves striped in creamy white. Plant variegated forms in full shade, since the variegated portions of the leaves turn brown in sun. Rich, moist, well-drained, somewhat sandy soil is ideal. Zones 7 or 8 to 10.

Asarum europaeum

Athyrium niponicum var. pictum
Japanese painted fern

EXPOSURE: Partial to full shade
HEIGHT: 8 to 12 inches
SPREAD: 2 to 3 feet or more

Despite its delicate, lacy appearance, this is a fairly tough fern that spreads to form a good-size mound and can hold its own against a wide range of perennials. Plants spread slowly by rhizomes and bear dark green fronds marked with silver and purple-red. Give them a site in rich, moist, well-drained soil. This fern doesn't tolerate drought, but if the foliage dies back in dry summer weather, new fronds will appear once the soil is moist again. Foliage color is best in partial shade or a site with morning sun and afternoon shade. Propagate by dividing clumps in spring. Zones 4 to 9.

Carex spp.
Sedges

EXPOSURE: Partial to full shade
HEIGHT: 1 to 2 feet
SPREAD: 1½ to 2 feet or more

With their narrow, grasslike leaves and plain, understated flowers, sedges often are overlooked as garden plants, and certainly as ground covers. Yet several can do a fine job of covering ground if given the chance, and they're especially effective because of the grassy texture they bring to shade gardens. Arrange plants in drifts — most spread slowly and must be massed to cover the ground — and combine them with other perennials such as broad-leaved ground covers or ferns, or both, in order to highlight the textural contrasts. A few can be used to replace lawn grass and can even be mowed if necessary. Unless otherwise stated below, give these plants aver-

Athyrium niponicum var. *pictum*

Carex morrowii 'Gold Band'

age to rich soil that is moist but well drained. Propagate by dividing clumps in late spring or early summer.

C. elata. 'Aurea'. This deciduous, chartreuse-leaved selection, commonly known as Bowles' golden sedge, is much more often grown than the species. Give plants moist or wet soil and a site in sun or light to partial shade. Provide more shade if the soil is not reliably moist, although the foliage color will suffer. Plants are 2 feet tall in bloom and spread to 1½ feet. Zones 5 to 9.

C. morrowii. Another sedge that's mostly represented in gardens by cultivars, this species is evergreen except toward the northern edges of its hardiness range. Plants are about 1 foot tall and spread to about 2 feet. 'Gilt' has creamy white leaf edges; 'Gold Band' has creamy yellow ones. Zones 5 to 9.

C. muskingumensis. Palm sedge. A North American native, this species is deciduous and spreads by rhizomes. Plants are 2 feet tall and spread to 2 feet or more. They grow in moist, well-drained soil in shade, although in constantly moist soil, plants can grow in full sun. 'Oehme' has yellow-edged leaves. Zones 3 to 8.

C. nigra. Black-flowering sedge. This evergreen species grows naturally in bogs and other areas with moist soil. Plants are 6 to 9 inches tall and spread slowly by rhizomes to 1 foot or more. Zones 4 to 8.

C. oshimensis 'Evergold' (formerly *C. hachijoensis* 'Evergold'). This evergreen cultivar produces 1-foot-tall clumps of linear green leaves, each with a central creamy yellow stripe. Plants spread slowly by rhizomes to 14 or 15 inches. Zones 6 to 9.

C. pensylvanica. Native to woods and thickets in the eastern United States, this semievergreen species makes a good lawn grass substitute. Individual plants are 8 inches tall and spread to 1 foot or more, but a planting can be mowed to a height of 2 or 3 inches. The species tolerates a wide range of conditions, including dry soil in sun or shade, and even sandy soil in shade. Plants are tough enough to be used in parking lot islands. Zones 4 to 8.

C. plantaginea. Plantain-leaved sedge. Native to rich, moist woods in North America, this is a clump-forming evergreen that can be massed to cover ground. Plants are 1 to 2 feet tall and spread to 2½ or 3 feet. For the best results, give them partial shade and evenly moist soil. Zones 5 to 9.

C. siderosticha 'Variegata'. This 8- to 12-inch-tall selection spreads slowly by rhizomes to 1½ or 2 feet, provided it is planted in rich, moist soil. Plants have strap-shaped, deciduous green leaves edged and striped with white. Zones 6 to 9.

Carex siderosticha 'Variegata'

Epimedium spp.
Epimediums, barrenworts

EXPOSURE: Partial to full shade
HEIGHT: 6 to 16 inches
SPREAD: 1 to 3 feet or more

These tough, tolerant perennials are prized for both their flowers — borne in mid- to late spring — and their pinnate leaves that have from three to nine or more leaflets. The flowers appear before the foliage does. Although the individual blooms are small, they're borne in loose racemes or panicles, and established clumps give quite a springtime show. Epimediums spread by rhizomes, and the species listed here are the best spreaders for use as ground covers.

Give the plants rich, evenly moist, well-drained soil. They'll tolerate full sun provided the soil is always moist. Established plants also tolerate dry shade. Some species are evergreen or semievergreen; to highlight the flowers, cut the foliage back to the ground in late winter before the bloom stalks appear. Propagate epimediums by dividing the clumps in early summer, after flowering, or in fall. Another option is to take cuttings of rhizomes and root them in winter in a cool room or greenhouse.

E. alpinum. Alpine epimedium. A deciduous, 6- to 9-inch-tall species, alpine epimedium spreads to 1 foot. Plants bear spiny-margined leaflets and small brownish red and yellow flowers that have very small spurs. Zones 3 to 8.

E. grandiflorum. Long-spurred epimedium. Reaching 8 to 12 inches tall and spreading to 1½ feet, this deciduous species bears loose clusters of 1- to 1½-inch flowers in white, yellow, pink, or purple. Its leaflets are heart shaped and have spiny margins. 'Rose Queen' produces bronzy new leaves and rose-pink flowers. 'White Queen' bears white flowers. Zones 4 to 8.

E. × perralchicum. This hybrid is 12 to 16 inches tall and spreads to 2 feet or more. It bears evergreen or semievergreen leaves and bright yellow ¾-inch flowers. 'Fröhnleiten' has yellow 1-inch-wide blooms. Zones 5 to 8.

E. perralderianum. Evergreen in warmer climates, this species is semievergreen in the northern part of its range. Plants grow 10 to 12 inches tall and spread to 2 feet or more. Their leaves are bronzy when young and have three-toothed leaflets. The plants bear yellow ¾-inch flowers with brown spurs. Zones 5 to 8.

Epimedium × perralchicum 'Fröhnleiten'

E. warleyense. This species has evergreen or semievergreen leaves flushed with red in spring and fall. Plants produce showy, loose clusters of orange-and-yellow flowers. They are 1½ feet tall and spread 2 to 3 feet. Zones 4 to 8.

Euphorbia amygdaloides var. *robbiae*
Wood spurge

EXPOSURE: Partial to full shade
HEIGHT: 1 to 2 feet
SPREAD: 1 to 2 feet or more

Unlike many euphorbias, this species thrives in shade. It bears evergreen leaves that are shiny dark green and clusters of greenish yellow flowers from midspring to summer. Established plants spread vigorously by rhizomes, and in some situations this species can become invasive. Select a site with rich, evenly moist soil, although established clumps also tolerate dry shade. Propagate either by dividing clumps in early spring or by taking cuttings from shoots at the base of the plant in spring or early summer. Dip the cuttings in warm water to prevent the flow of milky white sap. Zones 6 to 9.

Geranium macrorrhizum
Bigroot geranium

EXPOSURE: Full sun to partial shade
HEIGHT: 1½ feet
SPREAD: 2 feet or more

This vigorous species produces lobed semievergreen leaves that are aromatic and turn a good red-purple in fall. The clumps are topped by loose clusters of pink to purplish pink flowers in spring to early summer. Bigroot geraniums bloom best in bright or dappled shade, but they flower in shade as well. Select a site with rich, well-drained soil. The plants have thick, fleshy roots and spread by rhizomes to form nice-size clumps that are more drought tolerant than many geraniums. 'Ingwersen's Variety' has pale pink flowers. 'Czakor' is a foot tall and bears magenta flowers and leaves that turn purple in fall. Propagate by dividing clumps or by taking cuttings of stems with rosettes of foliage in spring. Zones 3 to 8.

Hakonechloa macra
Japanese hakone grass

EXPOSURE: Light to full shade
HEIGHT: 12 to 14 inches
SPREAD: 2 to 3 feet

This ornamental grass forms a clump of arching, linear leaves. It's hard to beat an established planting for ornamental quality. Plants spread slowly by rhizomes and have insignificant flowers. The species bears green leaves, but variegated forms are even more popular: yellow-striped 'Aureola', white-striped 'Albo Variegata', and chartreuse 'All Gold' are available. All need rich, moist soil to thrive, although established plants survive short dry spells. In areas with cool summers, a site in full sun is fine, but plants need cool, moist conditions to grow well elsewhere. Use hakone grass in masses since it's a slow spreader, and plant under trees, along woods edges, or in combination with broad-leaved ground covers to add contrast. Propagate by dividing clumps in spring. Zones 4 to 9.

Helleborus × hybridus
Lenten roses, hellebores

EXPOSURE: Light to full shade
HEIGHT: 1 to 1½ feet tall
SPREAD: 2 feet

Also sold as *H. orientalis,* Lenten roses are not rhizomatous, but they make very good ground covers because they form dense clumps, have handsome evergreen leaves, and also self-sow. Plants bear leathery palmate leaves with toothed leaflets. Clusters of showy, saucer-shaped flowers in creamy white, greenish, pink, maroon, or purple appear from late winter to midspring. Give the plants rich, moist, well-drained soil — neutral to slightly alkaline is ideal, although they tolerate acid soil too. A spot protected from winter wind helps preserve the foliage. Cut the old foliage to the ground in late winter to better display the flowers. Stinking hellebore (*H. foetidus*), hardy from Zones 6 to 9, also self-sows and makes a good ground cover. It bears chartreuse flowers in winter and deeply cut evergreen leaves. Its stems are biennial, and they produce foliage the first year and flowers the second. Cut off stems once the flowers fade. Propagate by sowing seeds in late summer or by moving self-sown seedlings any time. Zones 5 to 9.

Helleborus × hybridus

Hosta hybrids
Hostas

EXPOSURE: Partial to full shade
HEIGHT: 2 inches to 3 feet
SPREAD: 6 inches to 4 feet or more

These handsome perennials, grown more for their foliage than their flowers, form broad clumps and are excellent ground covers when massed. They produce ovate, lance-shaped, rounded, or heart-shaped leaves and racemes of flowers that usually are bell to funnel shaped. Leaves come in many colors, including solid green, blue-gray, or chartreuse, and the foliage of many cultivars is handsomely variegated with combinations of any of those colors as well as cream or white. Hostas grow in any well-drained soil, although they are happiest and grow most vigorously in rich, moist conditions. They are not very drought tolerant but do withstand constantly moist soil provided their crowns are set higher than the water line. Plants grow in full sun in cool climates, but leaves scorch in hot, dry weather. Propagate hostas by dividing their clumps in spring or fall.

Hosta cultivars grow at different rates, and the best choices for use as ground covers are vigorous growers that produce plenty of offsets. (When buying, look at plants from the side of the clump and buy specimens that have many offsets. You can divide these at planting time to help them spread more quickly.) Here are some of the many popular cultivars that can be used as ground cover. Heights given are for the main mound of foliage. All are hardy in Zones 3 to 8.

'Abba Dabba Do'. Dark green leaves edged with yellow; 2 feet tall, spreading to 4 feet or more.

'Birchwood Parky's Gold'. Chartreuse leaves; 14 to 16 inches tall, spreading to 2½ feet.

'Francee'. Dark green leaves edged with white; 22 inches tall, spreading to 3 feet.

'Golden Tiara'. Green leaves with yellow margins; 1 foot tall, spreading to 2 feet or more.

'Ground Master'. Green leaves edged with white; 10 inches tall, spreading to 2 feet.

'Halcyon'. Blue-gray leaves; 14 to 16 inches tall, spreading to 2½ feet.

'Honeybells'. Green leaves, fragrant flowers; 2½ feet tall, spreading to 4 feet.

'Kabitan'. Lance-shaped chartreuse leaves edged with green; 8 inches tall, spreading to 1 foot.

'Mountain Fog'. Creamy white, lance-shaped leaves with dark green edges; 8 inches tall, spreading to 1½ feet.

'Patriot'. Puckered green leaves with wide white margins; 22 inches tall, spreading to 3 feet.

'Piedmont Gold'. Chartreuse leaves; 20 inches tall, spreading to 3 feet.

'Ryan's Big One'. Blue-gray leaves; 3 feet tall, spreading to 5 feet.

'Saishu Jima'. Green, lance-shaped leaves; 8 inches tall, spreading to 16 inches.

'Vera Verde'. Narrow dark green leaves edged with cream; 6 inches tall, spreading to 16 inches.

A collection of various hosta cultivars covers the ground well.

Lamium maculatum ▼
Spotted deadnettle
EXPOSURE: Partial to full shade
HEIGHT: 6 to 8 inches
SPREAD: 1 to 3 feet

Also simply called lamium — perhaps by gardeners who dislike the moniker "deadnettle" — this perennial spreads by both rhizomes and stolons. Plants form low mounds of rounded to somewhat triangular leaves that are often marked with silver or white. Whorls of small, two-lipped, pinkish purple flowers appear in summer. Cultivars of this species generally are well-behaved ground covers that will mix well with other perennials in small areas. 'Beacon Silver' has silver leaves edged in green with pale pink flowers. 'White Nancy' has similar leaves with white flowers. 'Beedham's White' has chartreuse leaves with white flowers. Give spotted deadnettles a spot with rich, well-drained, moist soil. Plants don't tolerate heat, drought, or high humidity. They can be grown in full sun in northern climates. In warm climates, give them partial to full shade or a spot that is in sun in the morning and shade in the afternoon to help them cope with heat, which causes taller, sprawling growth. Cut back plants that become leggy. To propagate, divide plants in spring or fall or take cuttings of shoot tips in early summer. Zones 3 to 8.

Luzula spp.
Wood rushes
EXPOSURE: Light to full shade
HEIGHT: 1½ to 2 feet
SPREAD: 2 to 3 feet

These are rhizomatous, grasslike plants, often with evergreen or semievergreen foliage. They form loose clumps of linear leaves and spread fairly slowly; mass them to create large drifts. The plants tolerate light foot traffic and are adaptable when it comes to soil: they'll grow in poor to average soil but are especially happy in rich, moist, well-drained conditions. Propagate by dividing clumps in spring or fall.

L. nivea. Snowy wood rush. Evergreen in mild climates, this species produces clumps of linear leaves and clusters of tiny white flowers from early to midsummer. Clumps are about a foot tall and from 1½ to 2 feet in bloom. Plants spread slowly by rhizomes to 1½ or 2 feet. They grow in moist to slightly dry soil and can tolerate full sun with consistent soil moisture, especially at the northern end of their range. Zones 5 to 9.

L. sylvatica. Greater wood rush. This species, also evergreen in mild climates, is a good ground cover for shade. Plants spread by rhizomes to form clumps 2 to 3 feet wide or wider. With time, plants form a thick cover that resists weeds. They grow in most soils, including heavy clay, and although they are happiest with evenly moist conditions, they also tolerate drought well. 'Aurea' has yellow-green leaves. 'Marginata' features dark green leaves with cream edges. Zones 5 to 9.

COVERING WHEN THERE'S NO SOIL

SITES LOCATED UNDER shallow-rooted trees like maples (*Acer* spp.) are a headache for gardeners, whether they're trying to grow ground covers or lawn grass. Tree roots that crowd the surface make it nearly impossible to plant, and even if you can find a pocket of soil to tuck in a ground cover, it's likely the tree's roots will crowd out that plant as soon as it finds the improved, moist soil. Plopping soil on top of the roots leads to a similar problem. Besides being bad for the tree, the tree's roots will inevitably grow upward and infiltrate, again crowding out ground covers.

In such cases, vines may be the best choice for covering the ground. To further keep down weeds, first cover the site with layers of newspaper (four to eight sheets) topped with several inches of mulch, then plant your vines away from the crowded soil under the tree, outside the drip line. Train the stems back over the mulched area. The vines will naturally grow toward the sun, so if you can plant on the north side, so much the better. Wood vamp (*Decumaria barbara*), climbing hydrangea (*Hydrangea anomala* subsp. *petiolaris*), Virginia creeper or woodbine (*Parthenocissus quinquefolia*), and English ivy (*Hedera helix*) all grow in shade. See page 125 for more on the first two plants, page 126 for more on Virginia creeper, and page 54 for more on English ivy.

Setting large tubs under the tree is another option. Fill them with shade-loving perennials, annuals, or vines that will spill out to cover the soil. Another alternative is simply to mulch the area. Spreading layers of newspaper, as described above, and then topping it with mulch will keep weeds down. Be sure to feather out the thickness of the mulch layer around the trunk of the tree; the mulch should not touch the trunk.

▼ May be considered invasive in some regions.

Omphalodes verna
Blue-eyed Mary

EXPOSURE: Partial shade
HEIGHT: 8 inches
SPREAD: 1 foot

Also called creeping forget-me-not, this species spreads by stolons or short rhizomes and produces oval leaves that are evergreen in southern areas, semievergreen farther north. Clusters of blue flowers with white eyes appear in spring. Give creeping forget-me-nots a site in partial shade, or morning sun and afternoon shade (full sun causes stunted growth), and moist, well-drained soil. Dependable soil moisture is essential in hot summer weather. Propagate by dividing clumps in spring. Zones 6 to 9.

Oxalis spp.
Shamrocks, sorrels, oxalis

EXPOSURE: Partial to full shade
HEIGHT: 1 to 12 inches
SPREAD: 1 foot to indefinite

This genus contains charming wildflowers native to the Pacific Northwest as well as potential weeds. All bear palmate leaves with three to many leaflets. Oregon oxalis or redwood sorrel (*O. oregana*) is a rhizomatous 8- to 10-inch-tall species with heart-shaped leaflets that spreads indefinitely. Plants bear 1-inch-wide, cup-shaped flowers from spring to fall. A nonnative to consider is *O. regnellii,* an 8-inch-tall species from South America that produces white flowers from spring to summer and leaves with many triangular leaflets. *O. regnellii* var. *triangularis* features purple foliage and pale pink flowers; unlike the species, it goes dormant in winter when exposed to drought or low light levels. Give oxalis rich, moist, well-drained soil. Zones 7 to 10.

Persicaria virginiana 'Variegata'

Persicaria virginiana
Persicaria

EXPOSURE: Light to full shade
HEIGHT: 2 to 4 feet
SPREAD: 5 to 6 feet

This species, native to eastern North America as well as Japan and the Himalayas, was formerly listed as *Persicaria filiformis, Polygonum filiforme,* and *Tovara virginiana.* Plants bear green leaves, but variegated forms are most commonly seen in cultivation. 'Variegata' bears leaves marked with green and white; 'Painter's Palette' has leaves marked with green, white, yellow, and red-brown. Plants produce 3- to 10-inch-long leaves and are accented by clusters of tiny pink flowers in late summer and fall. The plants spread fairly aggressively by rhizomes. Give them a site with rich, moist soil, and keep them away from less vigorous perennials. They self-sow, and variegated cultivars come true from seeds: Rogue out all-green seedlings. Propagate by dividing clumps in spring or fall. Zones 4 to 8.

Polygonatum spp.
Solomon's seals

EXPOSURE: Partial to full shade
HEIGHT: 1 to 5 feet tall
SPREAD: 2 to 3 feet or more

The upright habit of Solomon's seals adds handsome contrast to shade gardens. These plants spread by rhizomes to form broad clumps. Their erect stems bear paired leaves, with small, bell-shaped or tubular flowers that are white or creamy white in the leaf axils. The blooms are followed by berrylike fruit. Give plants a site with moist, rich soil that is well drained. Propagate by dividing the clumps in spring or fall.

P. biflorum. Small Solomon's seal. A wildflower native from Ontario and roughly the eastern half of the United States, this species bears lance-shaped to rounded leaves and tubular, greenish white flowers from late spring to midsummer. Plants grow 1 to 3 feet tall. Giant Solomon's seal (*P. biflorum* var. *commutatum,* formerly listed as *P. commutatum*) ranges from 3 to 5 feet

Polygonatum odoratum var. *thunbergii* 'Variegata'

tall. The flowers of both are followed by round black fruit. Zones 3 to 9.

P. odoratum. Fragrant Solomon's seal. This species, which grows 2½ to 3 feet tall, bears lance-shaped to ovate green leaves. *P. odoratum* var. *thunbergii* 'Variegata', with green leaves edged in white, is more common in cultivation than the species. It bears tubular white flowers tipped in green; the blooms are followed by black fruit. Zones 3 to 8.

Pulmonaria spp.
Pulmonarias, lungworts

EXPOSURE: Light to full shade
HEIGHT: 9 to 12 inches
SPREAD: 2 to 3 feet

Extra-early spring flowers coupled with handsome foliage make members of this genus excellent additions to any shade garden. The plants produce low clumps of large leaves often marked with white or silver, and they spread slowly by rhizomes. Clusters of funnel-shaped flowers appear early in the season — in fact, these are among the earliest perennials to bloom. The foliage usually remains attractive all season long. Give plants rich, well-drained soil that is evenly moist. Propagate by dividing the clumps in spring or fall.

P. longifolia. Long-leaved lungwort. This species produces dense clumps of narrow, lance-shaped, silver-spotted leaves that can reach a length of 1½ feet. Clusters of blue flowers appear from early to late spring. Individual clumps are 1 foot tall and spread to 3 feet; they also travel by rhizomes. 'Cevennensis' has leaves that can reach 2 feet long. Zones 4 to 8.

P. rubra. Red lungwort. Another rhizomatous species, red lungwort bears

MORE GROUND COVERS FOR SHADE

SHADE GARDENERS have plenty of options for covering the ground — more than they might imagine. In addition to the plants listed here, see "Selections for Shade" on page 147, "Flowering Ground Covers for Shade" on page 159, "Native Plants for a Woodland Floor" on page 165, and "Covering Slopes in Shade" on page 119.

Convallaria majalis. Lily-of-the-valley. See page 70.

Dennstaedtia punctiloba. Hayscented fern. See page 74.

Galium odoratum. Sweet woodruff, bedstraw. See page 71.

Lamium galeobdolon. Yellow archangel. See page 72.

Liriope spp. Lilyturfs. See page 83.

Pachysandra terminalis. Japanese pachysandra. See page 73.

Viola spp. Violets. See page 171.

Pulmonaria saccharata 'Roy Davidson'

rounded green leaves that are evergreen in mild climates. Clusters of coral pink flowers appear from late winter to late spring. Plants are 1 to 2 feet tall and spread to 3 feet. Zones 5 to 8.

P. saccharata. Bethlehem sage. A popular perennial garden plant, this species spreads by rhizomes and forms mounds of rounded, silver-spotted leaves. Clusters of pink flower buds that open into blue flowers appear from late winter to late spring. Many cultivars are available, including 'Milky Way', a vigorous blue-flowered selection with leaves heavily spotted with silver, and 'Roy Davidson' with longer, silver-spotted leaves (it is a hybrid with *P. longifolia*) and pale blue flowers. The plants are 1 foot tall and spread to 2 feet. Plants self-sow. Zones 3 to 8.

Azaleas & Rhododendrons

Azaleas and rhododendrons, all of them members of the genus *Rhododendron,* are used as specimens, as foundation plants, in shrub borders, and in all manner of shady plantings.

Low-growing azalea cultivars also make excellent ground cover shrubs, provided they're given a site that suits their cultural needs. Both azaleas and rhododendrons require rich acid soil (pH 4.5 to 6.5) that is cool, evenly moist, well drained, and well aerated. When planning a bed of azaleas to cover the ground, keep in mind that

many moss garden species (see Moss Gardens for Acid Soil on page 182) grow well in similar conditions and make good companions.

These shrubs have fine roots that rot quickly in wet soil and also dry out quickly when the soil is dry. When planting, work plenty of well-rotted compost into the soil

Cercis canadensis with azaleas

Rhododendron 'Coral Bells'

Rhododendron 'Gumpo White'

to increase its moisture-holding capacity and improve drainage. It's also a good idea to check the rootballs of container-grown plants to see if there is a thick buildup of roots on the surface. If so, score the outside of the root ball with a knife before putting the plant in the soil. Water deeply at planting time so both the rootball and the surrounding soil are moist. Although both azaleas and rhododendrons are often planted in full sun, they are far happier in partial shade south of Zone 5. Plants growing in too much sun are likely to have problems with lace bugs as well as other pests and diseases.

The genus *Rhododendron* contains from 500 to 900 species and literally thousands of cultivars. Most bear lance-shaped or elliptic leaves and trusses of tubular, trumpet-, or bell-shaped flowers from spring to early summer. Most rhododendrons are evergreen and bear bell-shaped flowers with ten stamens. Although the ground cover selections listed here are evergreen, azaleas tend to be deciduous and bear funnel-shaped flowers with five stamens.

The list of evergreen azaleas described here is designed to get you started. Consult local experts for advice on which species and cultivars grow best in your area. Many Cooperative Extension Service offices have handouts on these popular plants, as do local public gardens. Also consult respected local nurseries; "big box" stores are more likely to have mass-marketed selections that may or may not be the best choices for your area. For propagation, take cuttings in late summer. Rhododendrons and azaleas also can be grown from seed, but the seedlings will be variable.

R. **Girard hybrids.** While full-size Girard hybrids can reach 5 or 6 feet, compact cultivars make fine ground covers. Look for 'Girard National Beauty' (rose-pink flowers, 2 feet tall); 'Girard Pleasant White' (white flowers, 2 to 2½ feet); 'Girard Renee Michelle' (pink flowers, 4 feet tall); 'Girard's Scarlet' (red flowers, 1½ to 2 feet tall); and 'Girard's Variegated Gem' (rose-pink flowers, 2 to 2½ feet tall). Zones 5 or 6 to 9.

R. **Glenn Dale hybrids.** As with Girard hybrids, most Glenn Dale azaleas are taller than the compact cultivars listed here. Check out 'Guerdon' (lavender flowers, 2 feet tall), 'Illusions' (pink flowers, 3 feet tall), 'Polar Sea' (white flowers, 3 feet tall), 'Sagittarius' (pink flowers, 2 feet tall), and 'Sea Foam' (white flowers, 3 feet tall). Zones 5 or 6 to 9.

R. **Satsuki hybrids.** This compact, heat-tolerant group includes 'Gumpo Red' (red flowers), 'Gumpo Pink' (pink flowers), and 'Gumpo White' (white flowers). Zones 6 or 7 to 9.

R. **Kurume hybrids.** Look for low-growing cultivars such as 'Coral Bells' (pink hose-in-hose flowers, 3 feet tall), 'Hino-Crimson' (red flowers, 2 to 4 feet tall), 'Hinode-giri' (red flowers, 3 feet tall), and 'Sherwood Red' (red flowers, 2 feet tall). Zones 6 to 9.

R. **North Tisbury hybrids.** All of the North Tisbury azaleas are low growing. Prostrate cultivars include 'Alex' (red flowers), 'Bartlett' (pink flowers), 'Hill's Single Red' (red flowers), 'Pink Pancake' (pink flowers), 'Wintergreen' (deep pink to red flowers), and 'Yuka' (white flowers sometime striped with pink). Zones 5 or 6 to 9.

Flowering
Ground Covers for Shade

Foliage may be the backbone of shade gardens, but the perennials listed here allow you to add color from flowers as you cover ground.

All are less vigorous spreaders than most typical ground covers, but they will form mounds that are one to several feet across with time. For maximum impact, plant them en masse — with drifts consisting of several plants of the same species. Space them fairly closely together to blanket the site more quickly. Another option is to combine them with other ground covers that spread a bit more widely to get good coverage. All thrive in rich, well-drained soil that is evenly moist. For the best bloom, give all of these species a spot in partial or dappled shade — a site with high shade under trees such as oaks is ideal. They'll also bloom, albeit quite a bit less, if planted in full shade under deciduous trees. Be aware that few plants can compete with very shallow-rooted trees, such as many maples, which have densely branching roots that are very close to the surface. These trees leave little room for ground cover roots and also monopolize any rainwater that reaches the soil surface. Preparing soil for planting ground covers on top of shallow tree roots simply encourages the tree to fill the new space with roots, and creating raised beds or piling soil over tree roots can also smother and kill the tree. In these cases, a thick layer of mulch — perhaps with large containers sitting on top of it — is the best choice. Also keep in mind that although the plants listed here grow in shade, they require good light to grow. None will survive for long under evergreens or in other sites that receive no direct sunlight whatsoever. Propagate any of these plants by dividing the clumps in spring.

1. *Geranium maculatum*
   Wild geranium

2. *Primula vulgaris*
   Common primrose

3. *Hosta* 'Grand Tiara'
   Hosta

4. *Dicentra* 'Luxuriant'
   Bleeding heart

5. *Tradescantia* 'Sweet Kate'
   Spiderwort

6. *Astilbe chinensis* var. *pumila*
   Dwarf chinese astilbe

7. *Alchemilla mollis*
   Lady's mantle

8. *Primula veris*
   Cowslip primrose

9. *Astilbe* 'Fanal'
   Astilbe

10. *Phlox stolonifera*
    Creeping phlox

159

Flowering Ground Covers for Shade

Dicentra 'Luxuriant'

Alchemilla mollis
Lady's mantle

EXPOSURE: Partial shade
HEIGHT: 1½ to 2 feet
SPREAD: 3 feet

This perennial produces a clump of pleated, lobed leaves topped by frothy clusters of tiny chartreuse flowers in summer. Plants form handsome drifts in the right site and also self-sow. Give plantings partial shade; they can take full sun as long as the soil moisture is adequate. Zones 4 to 7.

Astilbe spp. and hybrids
Astilbes

EXPOSURE: Partial shade
HEIGHT: 8 inches to 2 feet or more
SPREAD: 2 feet or more

Popular hybrid astilbes such as white 'Deutschland', pink 'Peach Blossom', and red 'Fanal', which bloom from late spring to summer, can be massed and used to cover the ground. These are clumping plants ranging from 2 to 2½ feet tall and spreading from 1½ to 2 feet, forming broad mounds where happy. They can be planted in full sun where summers are cool, provided they are sited in rich, cool, moist, well-drained soil. Dwarf Chinese astilbe (*A. chinensis* var. *pumila*) is another suitable ground cover that grows 8 to 12 inches tall and spreads to 1 or 2 feet or more where happy. Plants bear purplish pink flowers in late summer. Hybrids of *A. simplicifolia*, sometimes called star astilbe, include 'Sprite'; it grows 1½ feet tall, can spread to 3 feet, and produces pale pink flowers in summer. All astilbes are shallow rooted and not very drought tolerant, but dwarf Chinese astilbe tolerates more drought than most. All are hardy in Zones 4 to 8.

Dicentra spp.
Bleeding hearts

EXPOSURE: Light to full shade
HEIGHT: 1 to 2 feet
SPREAD: 1½ to 2 feet or more

Two native species and their hybrids make an excellent show in shade gardens. Fringed bleeding heart (*D. eximia*), from the eastern United States, and western bleeding heart (*D. formosa*), from British Columbia south to central California, both produce handsome mounds of fernlike leaves with racemes or panicles of dainty, dangling, heart-shaped flowers in shades of pink or white. Provided the soil remains evenly moist, plants bloom all summer long. They do not tolerate drought well. Cultivars include pink-flowered 'Bountiful' and 'Luxuriant' and white-flowered 'Langtrees'. Zones 3 to 9.

Disporum sessile
Japanese fairy bells

EXPOSURE: Partial shade
HEIGHT: 1 to 2 feet
SPREAD: 2 to 3 feet

This rhizomatous perennial spreads widely and forms loose drifts. For this reason, it's best combined with other shade-loving perennials. Plants bear rounded leaves that clasp the main stem. In late spring and early summer they produce clusters of one to three tubular white flowers with green tips. 'Variegata' has white-splashed foliage. Zones 4 to 9.

Geranium maculatum
Wild geranium, spotted geranium

EXPOSURE: Light to partial shade
HEIGHT: 1 to 2 feet
SPREAD: 2 to 3 feet

This species, native to eastern North America, bears deeply cut leaves with narrow, toothed lobes and loose clusters of pink flowers from late spring to midsummer. Plants are shallow rooted and don't have much tolerance for drought: Select a moist spot, ideally in a wild or informal garden, since plants have a loose habit and a tendency to self-sow. Zones 3 to 8.

Astilbe chinensis var. *pumila*

Hosta spp. and hybrids
Hostas

EXPOSURE: Full sun to full shade
HEIGHT: 2 inches to 3 feet
SPREAD: 6 inches to 4 feet or more

While grown primarily for their foliage (and heights given here are for the foliage mound, not the flowers), many hostas produce racemes of flowers that are very attractive. One of the top selections with fragrant flowers is August lily (*H. plantaginea*), with 2-foot-tall foliage and spreading to 3 feet or more. It bears racemes of fragrant white flowers in summer and usually blooms better in very light shade or full sun. Other vigorous hostas with fragrant flowers that need similar conditions include 'Fragrant Bouquet' (1½ feet tall, spreading to 3 feet or more), 'Honeybells' (2 feet tall, spreading to 4 feet), and 'Invincible' (1 foot tall, spreading to 3 feet or more). Hostas with showy flowers that are not fragrant include purple-flowered *H. ventricosa* and its cultivar 'Variegata' (2 feet tall, spreading to 3 feet), 'Love Pat' (1½ feet tall, spreading to 3 feet), and the Tiara series cultivars — including 'Golden Tiara', 'Diamond Tiara', and 'Grand Tiara' (all with lavender flowers, 1 foot tall, spreading to 2 feet).

Jeffersonia diphylla
Twinleaf

EXPOSURE: Partial to full shade
HEIGHT: 10 to 12 inches
SPREAD: 16 inches

Native from Ontario to New York south to Alabama, this clump-forming perennial bears deeply cleft, kidney-shaped leaves and solitary cup-shaped white flowers in spring or early summer. Established plants tolerate drought but grow best in evenly moist soil. Zones 5 to 7.

FLOWERING SHRUBS FOR SHADE

WHAT SHADE GARDEN WOULD BE COMPLETE WITHOUT SHRUBS?

Not only do shrubs add colorful flowers and lush foliage, but they also contribute fall color as well as winter texture and structure. Use these ground-covering shrubs either alone or with herbaceous shade lovers.

Abelia × grandiflora **'Prostrata'. Glossy abelia.** Grows 1½ to 2 feet tall, spreading to 2 feet or more. Evergreen or semievergreen. Clusters of small white flowers from midsummer to fall. Full sun to partial shade. Zones 6 to 9.

Aesculus parviflora. **Bottlebrush buckeye.** See page 132.

Clethra alnifolia. **Summersweet.** See page 136.

Cornus stolonifera **(formerly *C. sericea*) 'Kelseyi', also listed as 'Kelsey's Dwarf' and 'Nana'.** Native to eastern North America. Grows 1½ to 2½ feet tall, spreading 2 to 5 feet. Deciduous. Clusters of small white flowers in late spring or early summer. Full sun. Can grow in wet soil. Zones 3 to 8.

Daphne cneorum. **Rose daphne, garland daphne.** Grows 6 to 12 inches tall, spreading to 3 feet. Evergreen. Clusters of small, fragrant, rose-pink flowers in late spring. Part shade; needs acid soil. Zones 5 to 8.

Euonymus obovatus. **Running euonymus, running strawberry bush.** Native from Ontario to Tennessee and Missouri. Grows 6 to 24 inches tall, spreading to 4 feet. Deciduous. Insignificant reddish green flowers in early summer and red fruit. Partial to full shade. Zones 4 to 7 or 8.

Gardenia augusta **'Radicans'. Cape jasmine.** Grows 2 to 3 feet tall, spreading to 4 feet. Evergreen. Fragrant white flowers from summer to fall. Partial shade. Zones 8 to 10.

Leucothoe axillaris. **Fetterbush, coast leucothoe.** A southeastern native growing 2 to 4 feet tall, spreading 4 to 6 feet; more compact cultivars are available. Evergreen. Clusters of small white flowers from spring to early summer. Light to full shade; well-drained, acid soil. Zones 5 or 6 to 9.

Mahonia **spp. Mahonias, grape hollies.** See page 143.

Prunus laurocerasus. **Common cherry laurel.** At 25 feet, the species is too large to use to cover ground. Look to dwarf cultivars, including 'Grünerteppich', also sold as 'Green Carpet', which grows 3 feet tall and 10 feet wide. 'Otto Luyken' is 3 feet and spreads to 5 feet. Both are evergreen and bear clusters of small, fragrant, white flowers in spring. Full sun to full shade. Zones 6 to 8.

Rhododendron **spp. Azaleas and rhododendrons.** See page 156.

Sarcococca humilis. **Dwarf Himalayan sweet box.** Grows 1 to 2 feet tall, spreading slowly to 6 feet. Evergreen. Clusters of tiny, fragrant, white flowers in spring. Partial to full shade; needs acid soil. Zones 6 to 8 or 9.

Tsuga canadensis **'Cole's Prostrate' and 'Pendula'. Canada hemlock.** See page 144.

Viburnum acerifolium. **Mapleleaf viburnum.** See page 137.

Xanthorhiza simplicissima. **Yellowroot.** See page 135.

Lush Cover for Shade

ROCKY GROUND CAN BE A PARTICULARLY DIFFICULT SITUATION to deal with, but this combination does it brilliantly. *Hosta* 'Emerald Tiara' combined with epimediums cover the majority of the space, filling in around rocks and smoothing out the site. Drifts of *Primula sieboldii*, a species that thrives in moist soil, add spring color to the planting, and goatsbeard adds a ferny texture to the foreground.

1. *Hosta* 'Emerald Tiara'
   Hosta
2. *Epimedium* spp.
   Epimediums
3. *Primula sieboldii*
   Primrose
4. *Aruncus aethusifolius*
   Goatsbeard

Phlox divaricata

Primula veris

Tradescantia 'Sweet Kate'

Phlox spp.
Phlox

EXPOSURE: Partial to full shade
HEIGHT: 4 to 12 inches
SPREAD: 1 to 3 feet

Two native species of shade-loving phlox add color to spring and early summer gardens. Give these species a spot with evenly moist, well-drained soil that is rich in organic matter. Both produce clusters of flat-faced, five-petaled flowers.

P. divaricata. Wild blue phlox. Native to woodlands from Canada through the eastern United States, this species bears purple, lilac, or white flowers on 8- to 12-inch plants that spread to 2 or 3 feet. Plants also self-sow, and digging up self-sown seedlings is an easy way to propagate this most effective native wildflower. This species is handsome when allowed to fill in around other ground covers. Zones 3 to 9.

P. stolonifera. Creeping phlox. This stoloniferous species, native to woodlands from Pennsylvania and Ohio south to Georgia, has purple-blue, pink, or white flowers on 4- to 6-inch-tall plants that spread to 1 foot or more. Plants are best combined with other woodland wildflowers because the wandering stems don't form a dense mat. Zones 4 to 8.

Primula spp.
Primroses

EXPOSURE: Partial shade
HEIGHT: 4 to 10 inches tall
SPREAD: 1 to 2 feet

Several species of primroses are useful for adding color to shade gardens. All bloom in spring and need a site with cool, moist conditions to perform as perennials. Combine them with other perennials, but keep them away from any vigorous spreaders. They're also nice as edgings. *P. veris* needs constantly moist soil, while the other species listed here require moist, well-drained conditions. All take full sun in cool climates but need partial to full shade in warmer areas.

P. Juliana hybrids. Sturdy, semievergreen hybrids in many colors. 'Wanda', with red-purple flowers, is 4 to 6 inches tall and spreads to 1½ feet. Zones 3 to 8.

P. × *polyantha.* Polyanthus group hybrids. These handsome hybrids produce mounds of leaves topped by flowers in shades of pink, red, yellow, orange, violet, purple, and white. When selecting these primroses, look for cultivars developed for garden use, which are hardy in Zones 3 to 8, since this group also includes florist-type cultivars that are only hardy to about Zone 6.

P. veris. Cowslip primrose. This species grows 10 inches tall and forms 1-foot-wide mounds with yellow flowers. Zones 4 to 8.

P. vulgaris. English or common primrose. The mounded foliage grows 8 inches tall, spreading to 1½ feet. Blooms come in shades of pink, red, yellow, orange, violet, purple, and white. Zones 4 to 8.

Tradescantia hybrids
Spiderworts

EXPOSURE: Light to full shade
HEIGHT: 1 to 2 feet
SPREAD: 3 feet or more

These popular perennials produce clumps of long, lance-shaped leaves and clusters of three-petaled flowers from early summer to early fall. The plants bloom best in partial shade and need a site with rich, moist, well-drained soil. Hybridizers have released new and improved cultivars in recent years: look for 'Sweet Kate', with blue flowers and chartreuse foliage; 'Concord Grape', with rosy purple blooms; and 'Purple Profusion', with violet-blue flowers. Cut plants to the ground in midsummer after the main flush of flowers fade to curtail self-sowing and to encourage fresh new foliage to appear. Zones 4 to 9.

Native Plants
for a Woodland Floor

To create a colorful carpet that thrives in shade, look no further than native wildflowers.

A ground cover planting with species that are all native to North America has special appeal, but for even more authenticity, select species that are native to your own area. Locally native plants are best able to tolerate the heat, humidity, soil, and exposure in your garden. Botanical gardens, native plant groups, and nurseries specializing in native species are all good sources for information about native wildflowers and woody plants. Botanical gardens and native plant groups are also good places to buy natives — many sponsor annual plant sales or operate nurseries. Don't start your ground cover planting by digging plants from the wild or by buying from nurseries that sell wild-collected plants. When shopping, look for plants labeled as "nursery propagated"; those described as "nursery grown" may have been collected in the wild and grown in a nursery for a season or two. As a general rule, native plants require less site modification than nonnative plants and once established need less maintenance. Planting natives also eliminates worries about struggling to control nonnative invasives.

Woodland natives are a great choice for replacing grass under trees, and they also are perfect for other types of shady sites. Look for spots on the north side of the house that receive daylong shade, or grow them on the east side of a house or garage where they'll receive morning sun and afternoon shade. Use drifts of wildflowers under a single shade tree or under clumps of trees and shrubs to create a larger island planting — and to eliminate having to trim grass around tree trunks, too.

1. *Iris cristata* 'Alba'
   Crested Iris

2. *Pachysandra procumbens*
   Allegheny pachysandra

3. *Stylophorum diphyllum*
   Celandine poppy

4. *Mitchella repens*
   Partridgeberry

5. *Gaultheria procumbens*
   Wintergreen

6. *Tiarella cordifolia*
   Allegheny foamflower

7. *Vancouveria hexandra*
   American barrenwort

8. *Tolmiea menziesii*
   Piggyback plant

9. *Chrysogonum virginianum*
   Green-and-gold

10. *Heuchera* 'Autumn Bride'
    Heucheras

Chrysogonum virginianum
Green-and-gold, goldenstar

EXPOSURE: Partial to full shade
HEIGHT: 6 to 8 inches
SPREAD: 2 feet or more

This native of the eastern United States spreads by rhizomes and produces mounds of oval to heart-shaped leaves with scalloped or toothed margins. Starry, five-petaled, golden yellow flowers appear from early spring to early summer. Plants are happiest in partial shade and need rich, evenly moist, well-drained soil. They also grow in full shade and full sun, but the plants require moist soil in order to survive in full sun. Use green-and-gold with other wildflowers, to fill in around shrubs, or for covering medium-size areas. It also can be grown on slopes and tolerates very light foot traffic. Propagate by dividing clumps or potting up runners in spring or fall. Zones 5 to 8.

Chrysogonum virginianum

Gaultheria procumbens
Wintergreen

EXPOSURE: Partial shade
HEIGHT: 3 to 6 inches
SPREAD: 3 feet

Also commonly called winterberry, checkerberry, and teaberry, this native of eastern North America is evergreen and bears leathery dark green leaves that smell of wintergreen when crushed. White or pale pink urn-shaped flowers appear in summer followed by round red berries. Give wintergreen rich, moist, acid, well-drained soil. Plants can grow in sandy soil, provided they receive enough moisture. Use them to edge woodland paths or beds and also to fill in around acid-loving shrubs such as rhododendrons and azaleas (*Rhododendron* spp.). Propagate by taking cuttings in early summer, by dividing the clumps in spring, or by digging and potting up rooted suckers. Zones 3 to 8.

Gaultheria procumbens

Heuchera spp. and hybrids
Heucheras, alumroots

EXPOSURE: Partial to full shade
HEIGHT: 1 to 1½ feet
SPREAD: 1½ feet

While the perennials commonly called coral bells also belong to the genus *Heuchera*, for a shady wildflower garden, look to the popular heuchera hybrids, which are grown for their foliage. These are descendants of two native species: American alumroot (*H. americana*), native to central and eastern North America, and small-flowered alumroot (*H. micrantha*), which is native to British Columbia and the Pacific Northwest. Both produce mounds of handsome ovate to heart-shaped leaves that are topped by loose panicles of tiny flowers that appear in early summer. (Many gardeners cut off the flowers to highlight the leaves.)

Give heucheras a site with rich, evenly moist soil that is well drained. Although these plants will grow in full shade, their leaves are more colorful when the plants are grown in light to partial shade. A site with morning sun and afternoon shade is ideal. The plants must be massed if they are used as ground covers — they are not rhizomatous. Use them to add foliage color and texture to shade plantings, to edge walkways, or to carpet small to medium-size areas. Many cultivars are available, including 'Velvet Night', with black-purple leaves; 'Autumn Bride' with fuzzy leaves and white late-summer flowers; and 'Dale's Strain', a self-sowing seed-grown selection with silver leaf veins. Propagate by dividing clumps in fall or by rooting individual "branches" taken from the crowns in spring or early summer. Zones 4 to 8.

Iris cristata 'Alba'

NATIVE STYLE

NATIVE GROUND COVERS can be set out in traditional informal-style plantings — with drifts of several species arranged in a pleasing pattern. Drifts of five to seven plants are effective, and the drift shape can be free-form or geometric, depending on the style of your garden. Mix different ground covers that feature contrasting foliage colors and textures. For a uniform, lawnlike cover, select plants for each drift that are all about the same height. For a planting that's more like a perennial garden, select ground covers of several different heights and arrange them with the shorter ones toward the front of the planting and the taller ones to the rear.

While you'll probably want to keep very prostrate selections along walk-ways or near the front edge of woodland plantings — otherwise you may never see them — when planting taller selections, mix up the heights a bit. Planting shorter selections next to slightly taller ones creates an interesting rhythm.

An alternative is a natural-style planting, with plants arranged as they might be in the wild. In this case, plant them singly or set them out in small drifts (three or maybe five plants). Let the plants grow together and mix as they will. Consider including some taller native perennials that don't spread — like white wood aster (*Aster divaricatus*) and even black snakeroot (*Cimicifuga racemosa*) — as accents. Native shrubs also are great additions to a planting of shade-loving natives.

Iris cristata
Crested iris

EXPOSURE: Partial to full shade
HEIGHT: 4 to 8 inches
SPREAD: 3 feet or more

This spring-blooming charmer is native to the eastern United States and produces broad clumps of arching, sword-shaped leaves topped by lilac-blue flowers. 'Alba' bears white flowers. Give plants a site with rich, evenly moist soil that is well drained. Slightly acid pH is best. Plant drifts of crested iris among other low-growing ground covers along pathways or to replace lawn under trees. Propagate by digging the clumps in spring. Zones 3 to 9.

Meehania cordata
Meehan's mint

EXPOSURE: Partial to full shade
HEIGHT: 3 to 6 inches
SPREAD: 1½ to 3 feet or more

Also called creeping mint, this unde-rused species is native to rich woods from Pennsylvania to North Carolina and Tennessee. Plants bear long, trailing stems with pairs of leaves that are toothed and somewhat triangular. Clusters of purple flowers, each with two white lips, appear in spring. Plants thrive in rich, moist soil. Use them to cover the ground under trees and shrubs, to cover shaded slopes, and to combine in mixed plantings with other ground-covering perennials. Propagate by digging and potting up layered stems in spring or fall. Zones 4 to 9.

Mitchella repens
Partridgeberry

EXPOSURE: Partial shade
HEIGHT: 1 to 2 inches
SPREAD: 1 to 2 feet

Also called running box, this evergreen native of eastern North American bears rounded white-veined leaves on trailing stems that hug the ground. The stems root at the nodes and plants form very low mats of foliage with time. Pairs of white ½-inch-long flowers appear in early summer, followed by round red berries. Give partridgeberry rich, acid soil that is moist but well drained. Use it as an edging with other low-growing species such as wintergreen (*Gaultheria procumbens*) or in a moss garden. Propagate by potting up rooted sections of stem in spring. Zones 4 to 9.

Ground Covers for Dry Shade

Most shade plants thrive in rich, moist, well-drained soil, and dealing with a site that offers dry shade can be a real challenge.

When selecting ground covers for sites in dry shade — both under trees and under house eaves or other structures that block rainfall — stick with drought-tolerant plants like the ones listed here to minimize the need to water. To increase the amount of moisture available to plants in such sites, be sure to work plenty of well-rotted compost into the soil and keep the soil mulched. You may also want to install soaker hoses to provide water to plants with a minimum of waste: Snake the hoses through the bed once the plants are in place but before the mulch is installed. Soaker hoses can be left in place under the mulch through the winter — just disconnect the hose that runs to them.

Carex pensylvanica. See page 149.

Ceratostigma plumbaginoides. Plumbago. See page 70.

Chasmanthium latifolum (formerly *Uniola latifolia*). Wild oats. See page 86.

Convallaria majalis. Lily-of-the-valley. See page 70.

Deschampsia flexuosa. Crinkled hair grass. Native to the eastern United States, South America, Europe, and Asia. Grows to 2 feet tall, spreading to 1 foot. Clump-former with threadlike evergreen leaves 8 inches long and brown-purple seed heads. Zones 4 to 9.

Dryopteris filix-mas. Male fern. See page 170.

Epimedium spp. Epimediums, barrenworts. See page 150.

Euphorbia amygdaloides var. *robbiae*. Wood spurge. See page 150.

Geranium macrorrhizum. Bigroot geranium. See page 151.

Helleborus × *hybridus*. Lenten rose, hellebore. See page 151.

Hosta spp. and hybrids. Hostas. See pages 71, 152, and 161.

Hystrix patula. Bottlebrush grass. Native from eastern North America, west to North Dakota, and south to Georgia. Grows to 3 feet and spreads to 1 foot. Coarse-textured grass with bristly seed heads that resemble bottlebrushes. Self-sows. Zones 4 to 9.

Lamium galeobdolon. Yellow archangel. See page 72.

Liriope spp. Lilyturfs. See page 83.

Pachysandra terminalis. Japanese pachysandra. See page 73.

Parthenocissus quinquefolia. Virginia creeper. See page 126.

Polygonatum odoratum. Fragrant Solomon's seal. See page 154.

Polystichum acrostichoides. Christmas fern. See page 170.

Pulmonaria saccharata. Bethlehem sage. See page 155.

Rhodotypos scandens. Black jetbead. See page 133.

Sarcococca humilis. Dwarf Himalayan sweet box. See page 161.

Sedum ternatum. Wild stonecrop. See page 169.

Viburnum acerifolium. Mapleleaf viburnum. See page 137.

Waldsteinia ternata. Dry strawberry. See page 95.

Sedum ternatum

Pachysandra procumbens
Allegheny pachysandra

EXPOSURE: Partial to full shade
HEIGHT: 1 foot
SPREAD: 1 to 2 feet or more

This handsome native of the southeastern United States isn't evergreen like Japanese pachysandra (*P. terminalis*), but it is an underused perennial with huge appeal. Plants spread by rhizome-like stems to form broad, dense clumps. They produce white flowers and green leaves in spring. By fall, the semievergreen leaves are handsomely mottled with brown. The foliage is prostrate by winter's end. Zones 5 to 9.

Sedum ternatum
Wild stonecrop

EXPOSURE: Partial shade
HEIGHT: 4 to 8 inches
SPREAD: 1 to 1½ feet

While the best-known sedums are plants for full sun, this hardworking species thrives in partial shade and also prefers moist, well-drained soil. Native from New York to Michigan and south to Georgia, it bears its rounded leaves in whorls of three and produces clusters of small, starry, white flowers from late spring to early summer. This is an underappreciated species and not as widely grown as it should be. If you don't see it at your local nursery, check with native plant specialists or native plant society sales. Plants tolerate drought, heat, and humidity along with competition from tree roots. In the wild, this species is found growing on mossy boulders, on ledges, and in woods. Use it to carpet the ground under trees, edge walkways, cover rocky sites, or replace grass in shade. *S. nevii* is another little-known native that grows in partial shade in

Stylophorum diphyllum

moist, well-drained soil. Native to the Southeast in the Appalachians, it grows about 3 inches tall and spreads slowly to several inches. Propagate both species by cuttings taken in spring or summer. Zones 4 to 9.

Stylophorum diphyllum
Celandine poppy

EXPOSURE: Light to full shade
HEIGHT: 1 to 1½ feet
SPREAD: Indefinite

Not a typical ground cover, this native of the eastern United States is a perennial that spreads indefinitely and aggressively by self-sowing. Nevertheless, it can be used to cover good-size areas in shade, either alone or in combination with larger ground covers. Plants produce rosettes of deeply cut leaves with lobed edges and have orange sap in the stems and leaves. Showy, 1-inch-wide, four-petaled flowers appear in summer. Plant celandine poppies in any moist soil. Plants do not tolerate drought. Use them to fill in around other ground covers, such as large hostas or shrubs. Pull up self-sown seedlings that appear where they are unwanted. Propagate by moving self-sown seedlings in spring or fall. Zones 4 to 8. Note: Do not confuse celandine poppy with lesser celandine (*Ranunculus ficaria*), which also has yellow flowers; the latter is a rampant spreader classified as invasive in a number of states.

Tiarella cordifolia

Tiarella cordifolia
Allegheny foamflower

EXPOSURE: Partial to full shade
HEIGHT: 4 to 12 inches
SPREAD: 1 to 1½ feet

Spreading by both rhizomes and stolons, this species is native from Nova Scotia and south to Georgia and Alabama along the Appalachian Mountains. It produces clumps of somewhat heart-shaped, toothed or lobed leaves that turn bronze in winter. Foliage mounds are topped by wands of tiny white flowers in spring. Many cultivars are available today, including those resulting from crosses with another native from the southeastern United States, Wherry's foamflower (*T. wherryi*), which is clump forming, not rhizomatous. As a result, cultivars may be clump forming rather than spreading. Spreading foamflowers suitable for ground cover include 'Jeepers Creepers', 'Running Tapestry', and 'Slick Rock'. Foamflowers tolerate a wide range of soils but are happiest in rich, moist, well-drained conditions. Combine them with other low-growing ground covers, plant a patchwork quilt of foamflower cultivars (spreading and nonspreading) to replace lawn, arrange them in drifts in woodland gardens, or install them along a pathway. Propagate by dividing clumps in spring or by potting up rooted plantlets that appear at the ends of stolons in spring or early summer. Zones 3 to 8.

Native Ferns for Shade

Ferns make fine ground covers, and there are many native species that can be used to cover the ground in shade.

Unless otherwise noted, all the ferns listed here prefer rich, moist, well-drained soil and partial to full shade. Propagate by dividing the clumps in spring or fall.

Athyrium filix-femina. Lady fern. Grows 2 to 4 feet tall, spreading to 3 feet. Many cultivars with crested and finely dissected fronds. Zones 4 to 9.

Dryopteris filix-mas. Male fern. Grows 2 to 4 feet tall, spreading to 3 feet. Semievergreen to evergreen. Prefers rich, moist woodland conditions; tolerates poor, sandy, and dry soil. Zones 4 to 8.

D. intermedia. Intermediate shield fern, fancy fern. Grows 1½ to 3 feet, spreading to 2 feet. Bears dark green fronds that are semievergreen to evergreen. Zones 3 to 8.

D. marginalis. Leatherleaf wood fern, marginal shield fern. Grows 15 to 18 inches tall, spreading to 2½ feet.

Dryopteris marginalis

Happiest with rich, moist, acid soil; tolerates sandy and poor soils, heat, and drought. Zones 2 to 8.

Matteuccia struthiopteris. Ostrich fern. Grows 3 to 5 feet tall, spreading indefinitely. Tolerates a little bit of drought but best with constant moisture. Zones 2 to 8.

Onoclea sensibilis. Sensitive fern. Grows 1 to 2 feet tall, spreading to 3 feet or more. Has dense, well-branched roots that are good for binding soil. Best in moist soil, where it tolerates full sun, but also grows in wet soil and withstands some drought. Zones 4 to 9.

Osmunda spp. Osmundas. A genus of tall, tough ferns. Cinnamon fern (*O. cinnamomea*) grows 2½ to 5 feet tall, spreading to 2 feet or more; Zones 3 to 9. Interrupted fern (*O. claytoniana*) grows 2 to 4 feet tall, spreading to 2 feet; Zones 4 to 8. Royal fern (*O. regalis*) grows 6 feet tall, spreading to 2 feet; Zones 2 to 10. Cinnamon fern and royal fern thrive in rich, moist to wet, acid soil; both grow in light shade with abundant soil moisture. Interrupted fern prefers drier conditions and is best in moist, but not boggy, soil.

Phegopteris hexagonoptera (formerly *Dryopteris hexagonoptera* and *Thelypteris hexagonoptera*). Broad beech fern. Grows 1½ to 2 feet tall, spreading via creeping rhizomes to 3 feet or more. Requires full shade and rich, evenly moist soil. Zones 3 to 8.

Polystichum acrostichoides. Christmas fern. Evergreen. Grows 1 to 2½ feet tall, spreading to 3 feet or more. Best in rich, moist soil; tolerates some drought. In the Northwest, western sword fern (*P. munitum*), 1½ to 5 feet tall, is a better choice. Both are hardy in Zones 3 to 8.

Thelypteris noveboracensis. New York fern. Grows 1 to 2 feet tall, spreading vigorously and indefinitely by rhizomes. Best in rich, acid soil; tolerates fairly wet soil plus short periods of drought. Zones 2 to 8.

Vancouveria hexandra

Viola labradorica

Viola spp.
Violets

EXPOSURE: Light to full shade
HEIGHT: 6 to 8 inches
SPREAD: Indefinite

Although not commonly thought of as ground covers, some native violets are determined spreaders that can outcompete smaller perennials. Give violets rich, moist, well-drained, acid soil. Plants bloom best in light shade. They don't tolerate drought or heat and need partial shade in the South. Both species listed here spread freely by self-sown seeds. Use them in shade gardens to underplant large perennials and shrubs, in drifts, or in wild gardens. Propagate violets by division in spring or fall or by sowing seeds.

V. sororia, formerly *V. papilionacea.* Common blue violet or woolly blue violet. Frequently found in woodlands, where it forms a dense cover of heart-shaped leaves and produces blue flowers from spring to early summer. Zones 3 to 9.

V. labradorica. Labrador violet. Native to Canada and the northern United States, this species spreads by stolons and produces low mats of heart-shaped, purple-tinged leaves. Pale purple flowers appear from spring to summer. Zones 2 to 8.

Tolmiea menziesii
Piggyback plant

EXPOSURE: Partial to full shade
HEIGHT: 1 to 2 feet tall
SPREAD: 3 to 6 feet

Also called thousand mothers and youth-on-age, this species, often seen as a houseplant, is grown for its handsome, hairy, somewhat maplelike leaves that have an especially interesting feature: they bear new plants on top of the leaves, where the blade and the leaf stem meet. A perennial native to the Pacific Northwest, it spreads quickly by rhizomes and produces racemes of small greenish purple flowers in spring and summer. Combine piggyback plants with other shade-loving perennials such as hostas and heucheras, or plant them under and around shrubs. Give plants a site with moist or even wet soil. Propagate by potting up the plantlets that appear on the leaves in mid- or late summer, or peg them to containers filled with potting medium (use a U-shaped wire) anytime so they can root before they are severed from the parent plant. Zones 7 to 10.

Vancouveria hexandra
American barrenwort

EXPOSURE: Partial to full shade
HEIGHT: 10 to 18 inches
SPREAD: 1 to 2 feet

Also called simply vancouveria, this species is native from Washington state south to California and somewhat resembles epimediums (*Epimedium* spp.). Plants are rhizomatous and bear compound leaves with nine or more bright green leaflets. Loose clusters of small white flowers appear from spring to early summer. Give American barrenworts a site with average to rich, moist, well-drained soil. They spread with moderate speed, so be patient; with time, they will form good-size drifts. This is a handsome species to mix with other low-growing ground covers in a native wildflower garden, in a conventional shade garden to plant around shrubs, or to replace lawn under trees. Unlike epimediums, this species does not tolerate drought and will decline and die in hot, dry summer weather. Propagate by dividing clumps in spring. Zones 5 to 8.

Ground Covers
for Wet Soil

Moisture-loving ground covers make it easy to turn difficult-to-mow wet sites into assets.

Mowing grass is a nightmare on a site with moist to wet soil; not only does the mower bog down, but everything grows faster than it does in drier sites. And when things came down to the competition between weeds and lawn grass, weeds always win. They're simply able to grow far better and faster on such sites than conventional lawn grass does. All the plants listed here will help you transform weedy, out-of-control wet spots into handsome manageable planting beds. All need soil that is constantly moist to wet in order to grow well. In suitable soggy sites, all it takes to get them started is to remove or smother the

grass (see Site Preparation Basics, starting on page 186 for more information on getting rid of grass and other unwanted vegetation), then put in the plants and let them cover. In addition to filling wet sites in the lawn, use the species listed here to plant pond and stream edges, lakeshores, and all kinds of boggy areas. None of the plants listed here are drought tolerant. Be aware, however, that many are very vigorous spreaders and difficult to eradicate once established. Think carefully before planting any of the species that are aggressive to invasive, and watch them carefully to be sure they stay where they're wanted.

1. *Rodgersia pinnata* 'Superba'
   Featherleaf rodgersia

2. *Iris virginica*
   Southern blue flag

3. *Equisetum hyemale*
   Horsetail

4. *Saururus cernuus*
   Lizard's tail

5. *Glyceria maxima* 'Variegata'
   Variegated manna grass

6. *Darmera peltata*
   Umbrella plant

7. *Darmera peltata* (flowers)
   Umbrella plant

8. *Houttuynia cordata* 'Chameleon'
   Houttuynia

9. *Woodwardia areolata*
   Netted chain fern

10. *Acorus gramineus* 'Ogon'
    Japanese sweetflag

11. *Deschampsia cespitosa*
    Tufted hairgrass

Acorus spp.
Sweet flags

EXPOSURE: Full sun to light shade
HEIGHT: 1 to 5 feet
SPREAD: Indefinite

Sweet flags produce clumps of grass- or sword-shaped leaves. The insignificant flowers are borne on a greenish yellow spadix that extends at an angle from the leaves. Plants spread by fleshy rhizomes that are used as herbs and dried for use as a potpourri fixative. Propagate by dividing clumps in spring.

A. calamus. Sweet flag. Native to the eastern United States as well as Asia, this species grows 2 to 5 feet tall with 1-inch-wide leaves that are fragrant when crushed. The leaves were once used as strewing herbs. 'Variegata' has white-edged leaves. Zones 4 to 8.

Acorus gramineus 'Ogon' with *Ranunculus ficaria* 'Brazen Hussy'

A. gramineus. Japanese sweet flag. Growing 1 to 1½ feet tall, this species bears narrow, grasslike leaves. Plants spread more slowly than *A. calamus* and generally form clumps that reach 2 feet or more across. They also tolerate some foot traffic. Cultivars include 'Ogon', with leaves striped with chartreuse and cream, and 3-inch-tall 'Minimus'. Zones 5 to 10.

Darmera peltata
Umbrella plant

EXPOSURE: Full sun to partial shade
HEIGHT: 3 to 4 feet
SPREAD: 6 feet or more

Formerly classified as *Peltiphyllum peltatum,* this species is native to cool, mountainous spots in the Pacific Northwest. Plants produce clusters of pink flowers in spring before the foliage appears. Gigantic umbrella-like leaves follow, and a cool, lightly shaded spot with constantly moist to wet soil encourages the largest leaves to form. Plants grown in full sun need continuous moisture and are generally smaller than those grown in shade. Propagate by dividing clumps in spring. Zones 5 to 9.

Decodon verticillatus
Willow-herb, wild oleander

EXPOSURE: Full sun to partial shade
HEIGHT: 2 to 4 feet
SPREAD: Indefinite

Although related to the invasive exotic loosestrifes (*Lythrum* spp.), this little-known species is native to the eastern United States and useful for filling and holding soil in boggy or swampy areas. It is a woody-based perennial that forms dense thickets. Plants spread by rhizomes and also have arching branches that root wherever they touch the soil.

They bear narrow, willowlike leaves and produce clusters of small tubular pink flowers in summer. Give this species a site with constantly wet soil; it also grows in shallow standing water. Propagate by potting up rooted plantlets or by sticking cuttings in moist soil in spring or summer. Zones 3 to 10.

Deschampsia cespitosa

Deschampsia cespitosa
Tufted hair grass

EXPOSURE: Full sun to partial shade
HEIGHT: 2 to 4 feet
SPREAD: 4 to 5 feet

This ornamental grass produces a broad clump of 2-foot-long evergreen leaves topped by airy, cloudlike flower panicles from early to late summer. Plants thrive in moist soil, including damp woods, and also tolerate heavy clay. They are best in full sun with abundant moisture but also grow in drier soil in shade. Although a clump former, this species is an effective ground cover when massed. Propagate by division in spring or early summer. Zones 5 to 9.

Equisetum spp.
Horsetails

EXPOSURE: Full sun
HEIGHT: 6 inches to 5 feet
SPREAD: Indefinite

Like many ground covers requiring wet soil, horsetails are vigorous to aggressive spreaders and difficult to eradicate once established. Plants produce jointed, rush- or bamboolike green stems and a network of branching rhizomes, which makes them useful for holding banks. Use them anywhere wet soil or standing water makes it difficult to grow other plants — especially in ditches and along ponds, streams, or lakes. Both species described here are evergreen.

E. hyemale. Common horsetail. Native to North America and Eurasia, this species usually grows 2 to 3 feet tall, but sometimes reaches 5 feet. Plants produce clumps of bamboolike dark green stems with prominent brown joints. Zones 3 to 11.

E. scirpoides. Dwarf scouring rush. Smaller than common horsetail, this species grows 6 to 8 inches tall. Plants form a low grassy-looking ground cover. Zones 5 to 11.

Glyceria maxima 'Variegata'
Variegated manna grass

EXPOSURE: Full sun
HEIGHT: 2 to 2½ feet
SPREAD: Indefinite

This variegated form produces broad drifts of green-and-yellow-striped leaves and grows in moist to wet soil as well as in shallow standing water. It is a less aggressive spreader than the all-green species, but it is still strongly rhizomatous and not a plant to be added to a garden without planning. Use it on sites where sidewalks, large areas of mown

Primroses (*Primula* sp.), hostas (*Hosta* sp.), and dwarf scouring rush (*Equisetum scirpoides*)

lawn, or other obstacles will keep it in check. Zones 5 to 9. Blunt manna grass (*G. obtusa*) is native to bogs on the East Coast. It is 2 to 3 feet tall and spreads indefinitely by rhizomes. This species is an important food source for native waterfowl. Zones 6 to 8. Propagate either species by dividing the clumps in spring.

Gunnera magellanica
Gunnera

EXPOSURE: Full sun to partial shade
HEIGHT: 3 to 6 inches
SPREAD: 1 to 2 feet or more

Anyone who has visited gardens in the Pacific Northwest remembers gigantic *G. manicata,* a herbaceous perennial that can reach 8 feet tall and spread to 12 feet or more. *G. magellanica* is a mat-forming relative that bears dark green, kidney-shaped leaves and compact clusters of tiny green summer flowers. Plants spread by rhizomes and only thrive in areas with cool summers. They require very rich, constantly moist soil. Propagate by sowing seed or dividing clumps in spring. Zone 8 to 9.

Houttuynia cordata 'Chameleon'
Houttuynia

EXPOSURE: Full sun to light shade
HEIGHT: 12 to 15 inches
SPREAD: Indefinite

This fast-spreading ground cover bears heart-shaped leaves marked with green, yellow, and red. Four-petaled white flowers appear in summer. Plants often revert to all-green, especially in warm climates, and the crushed leaves are unpleasantly aromatic — they smell something like used cat litter. Plants spread widely and are practically impossible to eradicate once established. Use this species only in an area that has deep boundaries on all sides, or be prepared to let it take over. Plants need constantly moist soil to wet soil and can be planted along ponds or streams and in shallow standing water. Propagate by dividing clumps in spring. Zones 5 to 10.

Houttuynia cordata 'Chameleon'

Iris spp.
Irises

EXPOSURE: Full sun
HEIGHT: 3 to 4 feet
SPREAD: 4 feet or more

Irises suitable for bog and pond margins include the species described here. Propagate by dividing the clumps immediately after flowering.

I. pseudacorus. ▼ Yellow flag. This species has naturalized in North America but isn't native. Plants form 3- to 4-foot-tall clumps of grassy leaves and bear yellow flowers in midsummer. They can be grown in wet soil or shallow standing water. Zones 5 to 9.

I. versicolor. Water flag. A native of eastern North America, this species ranges from 2½ to 3 feet. Plants produce clumps of grassy leaves and bear lavender-blue flowers from early to midsummer. Zones 3 to 9.

I. virginica. Southern blue flag. This species grows 3 to 4 feet tall and is native to the eastern United States. Plants produce clumps of grassy leaves topped by lavender-blue flowers in midsummer. Zones 5 to 9.

Myosotis scorpioides ▼
Water forget-me-not

EXPOSURE: Full sun to partial shade
HEIGHT: 6 to 12 inches
SPREAD: 1 to 1½ feet

A pretty filler for planting around larger ground covers or for carpeting small wet sites, water forget-me-not spreads by creeping rhizomes. Plants bear rounded leaves and bright blue flowers in early summer. They are native to North America, Asia, and Europe and grow best in cool sites with constantly wet soil. Sites in partial shade along streams or ponds are ideal. Propagate by sowing seed where the plants are to grow in fall or by dividing plants in spring. Zones 5 to 9.

Petasites japonicus
Butterbur

EXPOSURE: Light to full shade
HEIGHT: 3 to 4 feet tall
SPREAD: Indefinite

A vigorous rhizomatous perennial, butterbur is not suitable for small properties, because plants are wide spreading and difficult to eradicate once established. Use them along ponds and streams or to hold soil on moist banks. Plants produce huge, toothed, kidney-shaped leaves that are 2½ feet or more across. Clusters of yellowish white flowers appear before the leaves in late winter or early spring. These plants thrive in moist or wet conditions but also grow in ordinary, well-drained garden soil. They wilt dramatically when exposed to even slightly dry conditions. Zones 5 to 9.

Rodgersia spp.
Rodgersias

EXPOSURE: Full sun to partial shade
HEIGHT: 3 to 5 feet
SPREAD: 4 to 6 feet

These handsome perennials produce clumps of large compound leaves and spread by rhizomes. Plumelike clusters of tiny flowers appear in summer, and the foliage turns rich red to red-brown

Rodgersia pinnata 'Superba'

▼ May be considered invasive in some regions.

in fall. All are excellent plants for sites along streams and ponds in moist to wet soil. They need ample moisture if growing in full sun but will tolerate average soil that is moist and well drained, provided they are planted in shade. The heights given here are for plants in leaf; the flower clusters extend about 2 feet above the foliage. Propagate by dividing the clumps in spring.

R. aesculifolia. Fingerleaf rodgersia. This vigorous 3- to 4-foot-tall species spreads to 6 feet. Plants bear palmate leaves (with leaflets arranged like fingers on a hand) and large, 2-foot-long clusters of tiny, star-shaped, white or pink flowers. Zones 5 to 8.

R. pinnata. Featherleaf rodgersia. A 2- to 3-foot-tall species that spreads as far, this rodgersia features pinnate leaves (with leaflets arranged in a featherlike fashion) that can be 3 feet long. The flowers, borne in 1- to 2-foot-long clusters, are starry and yellowish white, pink, or red. 'Superba' has purple-bronze leaves in spring and pink flowers. Zones 5 to 8.

Saururus cernuus
Lizard's tail

EXPOSURE: Full sun to light shade
HEIGHT: 1 to 2 feet
SPREAD: Indefinite

Also called water dragon and swamp lily, this species is native to swampy areas in eastern North America and spreads by rhizomes. Plants grow in moist to wet soil as well as shallow standing water. They bear heart-shaped leaves and curved spikes of tiny white flowers from summer to early fall; both the foliage and the flowers have a citrusy fragrance. Propagate by dividing the clumps in spring. Zones 3 to 8.

MORE GROUND COVERS FOR WET SPOTS

A RANGE of great ground covers thrive in moist to wet soil. Since higher means drier, adjust the amount of moisture plants receive by siting them above the water line.

Carex elata. See page 149.
Coreopsis rosea. Pink coreopsis. See page 79.
Decumaria barbara. Wood vamp, decumaria. See page 125.
Hosta spp. and hybrids. Hostas. See pages 71, 152, and 161.
Ilex verticillata. Winterberry. See page 137.
Itea virginica 'Henry's Garnet'. Virginia sweetspire. See page 133.
Matteuccia struthiopteris. Ostrich fern. See page 170.
Osmunda spp. Osmundas. See page 170.

Gardeners with a boggy site that has very acid soil have a few other options open to them.

Andromeda polifolia. Bog rosemary. Evergreen shrub. Grows 1 to 2 feet tall, spreading to 3 to 4 feet. White or pale pink flowers from spring to early summer. Full sun to light shade. Zones 2 to 6.
Chamaedaphne calyculata. Leatherleaf. Evergreen shrub native to North America as well as northern Europe and Asia. Grows 2 to 4 feet tall, spreading to 4 feet. White flowers in spring. Full sun or dappled shade. Zones 3 to 9.
Vaccinium macrocarpon. American cranberry. Evergreen shrub native to eastern North America. Grows 6 inches tall, spreading indefinitely. Tiny pink flowers and round red fruit. Full sun or partial shade. Zones 2 to 7.

Thelypteris palustris
Marsh fern

EXPOSURE: Full sun to full shade
HEIGHT: 2 feet
SPREAD: 3 feet or more

This is a fairly vigorous fern that spreads by rhizomes and forms handsome clumps when grown alone as a specimen plant. It also can be combined with other moisture-loving perennials. As the common name suggests, plants thrive in moist to very wet soil; and they tolerate full sun in such conditions. They also grow in less damp soil provided they are planted in shade. Propagate by dividing the clumps in spring. Zones 5 to 8.

Woodwardia areolata
Netted chain fern

EXPOSURE: Light to full shade
HEIGHT: 1 to 2 feet
SPREAD: 3 feet or more

This vigorous fern is native to swampy and boggy soils in eastern North America. Plants grow from long, creeping, branched rhizomes and bear fronds that are cut into separate leaflets at the bottom and are deeply lobed at the top. Ideally, give netted chain ferns a site in moist to wet soil. Plants also will grow in ordinary garden soil that is moist but well-drained, provided they are planted in a shady spot. Propagate by dividing the clumps in spring. Zones 2 to 8.

Ground Covers
for Acid Soil

While acid soil is a problem for anyone trying to grow lawn grass, for gardeners it opens up a range of interesting possibilities for covering ground.

A great many ground covers grow in slightly acid soil — a pH of 7 is neutral and anything below that is considered acid — but the plants on these pages require very acid conditions to grow well. Like blueberries (Vaccinium spp.), they prefer a pH of 4.0 to 5.0 or somewhat higher. Although you won't need to spend time spreading lime over the ground to keep these plants happy, all will appreciate additions of organic matter to maintain a loose, friable soil. Ideally, work a few shovels full organic matter into the soil each time you plant — well-rotted, finished compost or purchased, bagged humus are two excellent choices. Also keep the soil mulched with chopped leaves. Mulch not only ensures a steady supply of organic matter, it also helps protect the soil from erosion by wind or rain and protects the soil surface from the impact of raindrops, which causes crusting. Mulch also helps hold moisture in the soil. Pine needles also make excellent mulch, but break down more slowly and add less organic matter to the soil. In addition to the low-growing ground covers on these pages, two other natives are good choices for very acid conditions: wintergreen (*Gaultheria procumbens*), covered on page 166, and partridgeberry (*Mitchella repens*), covered on page 167. All are also fine accents for a moss garden. Do not collect these or any native plants from the wild. Fortunately, as gardeners have become more interested in growing natives, nursery-propagated plants of many of these choice species have become available. Many rhododendrons and azaleas also are excellent ground cover choices for sites with acid soil.

1. *Linnaea borealis*
   Twinflower

2. *Chimaphila umbellata*
   Pipsissewa

3. *Coptis trifolia* subsp. *groenlandica*
   Goldthread

4. *Galax urceolata* (in autumn)
   Galax

5. *Galax urceolata* (in spring)
   Galax

6. *Cornus canadensis*
   Bunchberry

7. *Hedyotis caerulea*
   Bluets

8. *Paxistima canbyi*
   Cliffgreen

9. *Shortia galacifolia*
   Oconee bells

Heaths and Heathers

Gardeners who struggle with poor, sandy, acid soil may have one thing other gardeners envy: a perfect place to grow heaths and heathers.

Heather (*Calluna vulgaris*) is a mounding shrub with scale-like evergreen leaves; it produces tiny white, pink, or red blooms from mid- to late summer. Plants grow 1½ to 3 feet tall and spread to 3 or 4 feet. (Note that *Calluna vulgaris* is classified as invasive in three states on the Eastern Seaboard.) Heath (*Erica carnea*) is 8 to 12 inches tall and spreads to 2 feet or more. Plants bear needlelike evergreen leaves and produce tiny purplish pink flowers from late winter to midspring. Many cultivars of both species are available, and these plants are especially handsome when several cultivars are massed to cover a large area. Both need very acid soil and make great companions for blueberries (*Vaccinium* spp.) and other acid-loving plants.

Heaths and heathers make very satisfying ground covers provided their cultural requirements are met. Give them poor, sandy or gravelly, acid soil. They won't survive in clay soil, and become leggy in soil that is too rich. (If plants become leggy, mow or shear them immediately after flowering.) The soil needs to be well drained but also must retain moisture, so work in plenty of well-rotted compost or humus at planting time. Plants tolerate drought, but deep watering during dry weather keeps them blooming and looking attractive. They also tolerate salt well and are good for seaside gardens. Heaths and heathers bloom best in full sun but also tolerate partial shade. Zones 4 to 7, plus areas of coastal California.

Coral-bark Japanese maple (*Acer palmatum* 'Sango kaku') is dressed up for early spring with an underplanting of heather (*Erica darleyensis* 'Alba').

Chimaphila umbellata

Chimaphila spp.
Chimaphilas

EXPOSURE: Partial shade
HEIGHT: 10 inches
SPREAD: 8 inches or indefinitely

Two species, both bearing evergreen foliage, make fine ground covers. They produce their leaves in a whorl around the stems, which are topped by small clusters of waxy white or pinkish flowers. Although one species is more widespreading than the other, both travel by rhizomes, are native to dry woods, and have fair drought tolerance. Propagate by dividing clumps in spring or by taking cuttings in summer.

C. maculata. Spotted wintergreen. Native to eastern North America, this species bears deeply toothed, lance- to more oval-shaped leaves that are striped with white along the veins. Plants bloom in early summer. They grow 4 to 10 inches tall and spread slowly to 8 inches. Zones 5 to 8.

C. umbellata. Pipsissewa or prince's pine. Native to eastern North America as well as Europe and Asia, this species grows 4 to 12 inches tall. Plants bear shiny dark green leaves and bloom in summer. They spread indefinitely. Zones 4 to 8.

Coptis trifolia
subsp. *groenlandica*
Goldthread

EXPOSURE: Partial to full shade
HEIGHT: 2 to 4 inches
SPREAD: 8 to 12 inches or more

An evergreen species native to Greenland and northeastern North America, goldthread bears three-leaflet leaves and spreads by rhizomes. The leaflets are wedge shaped with scalloped margins. Small, solitary, white flowers appear from spring to summer. Plants needs moist, very acid (pH 5) soil. Propagate by dividing the clumps in spring. Zones 2 to 7 or 8.

Cornus canadensis
Bunchberry

EXPOSURE: Partial shade to full shade
HEIGHT: 4 to 6 inches
SPREAD: Indefinite

This subshrub, also commonly called creeping dogwood or dwarf cornel is native to North America as well as Greenland and northern Asia. Plants spread by rhizomes and with time produce drifts of terminal umbrella-like whorls of leaves on short stems. These are topped by a small cluster of greenish flowers in late spring or early summer. A showy ring of white petal-like bracts is borne beneath each flower cluster. Bright red fruit follow the flowers. Plants need a cool spot with partial shade in spring and fall and dense shade in summer. Propagate by dividing clumps in spring or fall or by sowing fresh seed. Zones 2 to 7.

Galax urceolata

Epigaea repens
Trailing arbutus

HEIGHT: 2 to 4 inches
SPREAD: 1 foot or more

Also called ground laurel and mayflower, this evergreen wildflower native to eastern North America bears small clusters of fragrant, funnel-shaped, white flowers in spring. This subshrub bears rounded, somewhat hairy leaves. Plants require very acid soil (pH 4 to 5) and steady moisture. Propagate by dividing the clumps in early spring, by taking cuttings in late summer, or by sowing fresh seed in early summer. Because the plants grow in conjunction with an essential mycorrhizal fungus, when dividing or moving them, take some soil to replant with new plants. Zones 3 to 9.

Galax urceolata
Galax, beetleweed, colt's foot

EXPOSURE: Partial to full shade
HEIGHT: 6 to 12 inches
SPREAD: 3 feet or more

This species, native to the southeastern United States, bears rounded, evergreen leaves that have toothed edges; the glossy green foliage turns red in fall. Wandlike clusters of tiny white flowers appear above the carpet of foliage in late spring. Plants require evenly moist, acid soil. To propagate, dig up rooted runners and transplant them in fall, or sow seeds in fall. Zones 4 or 5 to 8.

Moss Gardens for Acid Shade

Often dealt with as a lawn weed, for a shady site with moist, acid soil, moss is one of the most handsome ground covers you can grow.

A velvety moss carpet is ideal for areas under trees, along walkways, between stepping-stones, in shady rock gardens, and on shady slopes. Plants tolerate light foot traffic as well.

Give moss a site with partial to deep shade, although it also grows in high or dappled shade. Poor, moist soil with a very acid pH — pH 5 to 5.5, or slightly higher — is ideal. Have the soil tested, and lower the pH by applying sulfur before planting. Unlike most plants, moss prefers soil that is firmly packed. Plants cannot withstand direct sun unless planted on a site that receives it only briefly in the morning. Established plantings tolerate drought by simply going dormant until the weather changes.

If you have patches of moss and weeds or grass in your yard already, one way to establish a moss lawn is to reduce the pH of the soil to favor the moss and eliminate some of its competition. Adjusting pH is bet-ter than digging up the site and replanting, since digging loosens the soil and eliminates the packed soil consistency that moss prefers. If you do need to pull some weeds, be sure to press the moss back down firmly.

To start moss on a new site, collect some from your yard or the yard of a friend or neighbor. (Do not collect moss from the wild.) Crumble it into a blender, then add equal parts buttermilk and water. Blend until you have a concoction that is a little thinner than pancake mix or cream of potato soup. (If in doubt, thicker is better, because the moss plants use the fat and acid of the buttermilk to grow, and a thin, runny mix has less buttermilk and thus fewer nutrients.) Stale beer can also be included in the slurry to provide nutrients for moss. Pour the mix anywhere you want moss, then keep the area moist until the bits of moss begin to grow. Be sure to mist, but not water heavily: a strong stream of water will wash away the bits of moss before they are established.

Moss also can be purchased. Reputable companies grow their own, collect on a sustainable basis from their own property, or work with property developers to collect moss that would otherwise be destroyed. Also stick with suppliers in your region so you receive moss species that will grow well in your garden. You can buy moss plugs or sheets. Plant them by clearing the area, lightly raking the surface, soaking the soil with water, and then firmly pressing them in place. (Be sure to test and adjust the soil pH before planting.)

After planting, mist regularly to keep the site moist until the moss is established — this will probably take several weeks. (Special misting nozzles are available from moss suppliers and watering equipment specialists.) Once the moss is growing, it needs little regular care. Keep leaves and debris from covering and smothering it.

Moss is the ideal ground cover for this shady, moist site.

Hedyotis caerulea
Bluets, Quaker ladies

EXPOSURE: Partial to full shade
HEIGHT: 4 to 6 inches
SPREAD: 2 feet or more

This herbaceous perennial is native from Nova Scotia to Wisconsin and south to Georgia. It bears very small rounded leaves and slender stems topped by a single, ½-inch-wide, pale blue flower. Plants are best combined with ground covers that are not vigorous, and they are an ideal choice for growing up through moss. Select a site with rich, moist, acid soil. Propagate by dividing clumps in spring or fall or by sowing seed in spring. Zones 3 to 8.

Linnaea borealis
Twinflower

EXPOSURE: Partial shade
HEIGHT: 3 inches
SPREAD: 3 feet or more

This tiny, evergreen shrub, native to North America and northern Eurasia, is a prostrate mat former. It bears glossy, oval leaves with scalloped edges and pairs of nodding bell- to funnel-shaped flowers in summer. The plant needs moist, well-drained, very acid soil (pH 4 to 5) for the best growth. Propagate by digging up and potting rooted sections of the stems (they root where they touch the soil) anytime from fall to spring, by taking cuttings in early summer, or by sowing seed outdoors in fall. Zones 2 to 6.

Paxistima canbyi
Cliff green, ratstripper

EXPOSURE: Full sun to partial shade
HEIGHT: 8 to 16 inches
SPREAD: 3 to 4 feet or more

This spreading evergreen shrub is native to the Appalachian mountains. The species has narrow glossy green leaves and spreads by stems that root where they touch the soil. Greenish white flowers are carried in pendent clusters in summer. Plants tolerate some drought and poor soil. Propagate by digging and transplanting rooted sections of stem in spring or fall. Since this species is difficult to maintain in containers, divisions are best moved directly to the garden. Or take cuttings in summer. Zones 3 to 7.

Shortia galacifolia
Oconee bells

EXPOSURE: Partial shade
HEIGHT: 6 to 8 inches
SPREAD: 12 to 16 inches

This herbaceous, evergreen perennial, native to the Appalachian Mountains from Virginia to Georgia, bears rounded, glossy green leaves that turn bronze-red in the fall. Solitary funnel-shaped, 1-inch-wide flowers with toothed petals appear in late spring; they are white and often flushed with pink. Propagate by severing and digging up rooted runners in spring, by taking cuttings from shoots that arise at the base of the plant in early summer, or by sowing fresh seed in summer. Zones 4 to 8.

Linnaea borealis

Paxistima canbyi

Shortia galacifolia

GROUND COVERS CAN BE MIRACLE WORKERS when it comes to reducing upkeep in the garden, but in order to develop into good low-maintenance plants, they need a little TLC at planting time. Giving plants a good start helps them put down roots and gets them growing quickly. It also helps reduce competition from weeds, which are always poised to take over any site, as well as shortening the amount of time it takes for plants to become established and cover the ground.

In this section, you'll find information on all the techniques you need to plant and grow ground covers successfully, including preparing the soil, deciding how many plants to buy, spacing plants, and controlling weeds. In addition to information on planting in tough spots, you'll find a guide to propagating ground covers, a

the site you want to plant before you buy, then select ground covers that will grow in the conditions that exist naturally with as little effort from you as possible. See Knowing Your Site on page 26 and take the advice given there to heart. It will help reduce maintenance and improve your chances of success even before that first plant goes in the ground.

Also, in an effort to cover a site as quickly as possible, don't rush out and buy the fastest-growing ground cover you can find. Admittedly, few gardeners would intentionally plant the champion speedster — kudzu (*Pueraria montana* var. *lobata*) — but other fast-growing ground covers can create maintenance headaches too. A plant like English ivy (*Hedera helix*) covers quickly, but it won't stop spreading when it has reached the edge of its designated bed. Planting it means

Giving plants a good start helps them put down roots and gets them growing quickly.

topic close to the heart of any gardener who is covering a large or difficult site with ground covers on a budget.

Careful plant selection is an essential step in getting a ground cover planting off to a good start. Fight the urge to buy plants whose primary attraction is a cheap price tag. First and foremost, ground covers should be about reducing maintenance, and cheap ground covers are not necessarily the best option. Take time to study

you are committing to a maintenance routine to keep it in its place — and off your house and out of your trees and nearby woodlands. Ground covers that spread more slowly may be somewhat more expensive to plant at the outset (they take longer to produce, and also may have to be spaced more closely together), but they will be easier to control in the long run. Expect to pay more for unusual native ground covers than run-of-the-mill, mass-produced plants.

Planting, Growing & Propagating

3

SITE PREPARATION BASICS

Getting a site ready for ground covers — and doing the job right — takes time and effort, but it's worth the trouble. Ideally, prepare the site as you would to plant perennials, by removing weeds, loosening the soil, and adding plenty of organic matter. Get the soil tested if you're not sure what the pH is or need more information about the soil's fertility. To avoid digging altogether, do some advance planning. See "Smothering and Solarizing" on page 190 for a no-dig weed control and planting option.

Eliminating the Competition

Once you have settled on a place and a shape for your ground cover planting, getting rid of weeds is the first step in preparing the site. You'll need to pull them up, slice them off with a hoe, dig them out, smother them, or kill them with an herbicide. Whatever site preparation method you use, removing or killing weeds thoroughly — roots and all — is important because otherwise they'll quickly resprout and compete with newly planted ground covers. If you are planning to dig or pull weeds — or slice off sod — water the ground thoroughly a day or two before starting work, because moist soil makes the work go easier.

A Weed Wrench is an effective way to get rid of woody weeds.

REMOVING WEEDS BY HAND. A combined approach is often most effective: Hoe out annual weeds and dig perennial ones, for example. Woody weeds, such as poison ivy or poison oak and unwanted scrub trees, are tougher to remove. To eliminate them, use a mattock or spade to dig out the roots. If you have lots of woody weeds to remove — and love practical, well-built tools — consider buying a Weed Wrench (see Resources, page 211). This all-steel tool allows you to use leverage to easily yank out small trees and shrubs and eliminate them. Weed Wrenches come in four sizes, from mini, which pulls up stems up to 1 inch in diameter, to the heaviest-duty model, which extracts stems up to 2½ inches in diameter. Another handy, well-made weeding tool is the Honeysuckle Popper

(see Resources, page 211), which uses leverage to pry shrubs out of the ground — roots and all. Specifically designed to eliminate invasive bush honeysuckles (*Lonicera* spp.), these will work on shrubs with several stems, which may be difficult for a Weed Wrench to grasp.

A simple straightforward way to start a ground cover bed is to dig the soil to a shovel's depth — about 6 inches — and remove any weed roots in the process. For shady sites, it's often best to prepare planting areas rather than entire beds, see Creating Planting Pockets on page 198.

Turf can be dug up in patches and composted, or replanted in other areas.

GETTING RID OF GRASS. If the site is covered by lawn, use a sharp spade to cut it into strips and then roll it up and shave off the grass and roots as you roll, or pry up the sod in small chunks. The best method for removing sod on a large site is to rent a sod cutter. Shake or scrape as much soil off the roots as you can in order to leave as much topsoil as possible on the site. Sod removed in this manner can be placed root side up on the compost pile, but check regularly to make sure it does not resprout. Strips of sod also are useful for patching lawn elsewhere in your yard.

THE HERBICIDE OPTION. Herbicides offer another way to get rid of weeds. Organic herbicides are available but are most effective only on young weeds. Even if you normally follow organic principles, you may consider using nonorganic herbicides to deal with particularly difficult nonnative invasive species. If you select this route, read the label and follow directions carefully. Never spray herbicides during windy weather, because the wind may blow them onto nearby plants that you wanted to keep. One safe method for delivering herbicides directly to plants is to mix weed killer in a bucket and use a mop or toilet brush to coat the leaves. Wear gloves, watch for drips, and keep the bucket and the brush or mop over the area being treated. Before spreading compost and mulch over the site, wait for the recommended period on the label to make sure all the weeds are dead.

POSTWEEDING SOIL PREPARATION. The advantage of digging weeds, removing lawn with a spade or sod cutter, or even using an herbicide is that the site can be prepared and planted right away, or at least soon afterward. Once the weeds are under control or the lawn grass is gone, spread a 1- to 2-inch layer of well-rotted compost over the soil and work it in, if you didn't amend during the digging process. If the site is large, consider using a tiller to loosen the soil and work in compost. (If you're planting around trees and shrubs, though, keep the tiller outside the drip line — the farthest reach of the branches — to avoid damaging the roots.) Also consider spreading a balanced organic fertilizer if the soil fertility is low. Then rake the site smooth and spread another layer of compost or mulch over the soil to prevent it from crusting over. More is almost always better when it comes to compost, so don't skimp on this essential soil conditioner. Compost is a valuable amendment because it improves any soil: It helps sandy soil hold moisture, and it loosens clay soil, letting water drain away and allowing oxygen in to the roots. Even if you just spread compost over the site, in time the earthworms and other soil-dwelling organisms will work it down into the soil for you.

Once you water thoroughly, the site is ready to plant. If you can wait, though, delay planting for about two weeks — especially if you tilled the site. Not only does this let the soil settle a bit, but it also allows any surface weed seeds and root rem-

These individual plants of *Herniaria glabra* will eventually grow in and form a dense, ground-covering mat.

nants to sprout *before* the new ground covers are in place. Most seedling weeds are easy to hoe out; dig up the remains of any perennial weeds that appear. Then rake the site smooth and plant. If you are still not in a hurry to plant, waiting still another week or so to plant will let you do in another batch of weeds.

Keep in mind that while spring and fall are the best times to plant, soil preparation is something you can work on anytime the ground isn't frozen. Fall also is a great time to prepare new beds — long after it's too late to plant in northern zones — because the weather is cool and perfect for digging. Plus there's plenty of time to let the soil settle before spring planting and to ponder which new ground covers could fill the empty bed.

Edges That Stick

Installing edging strips between lawn and ground cover beds — or between drifts of two different ground covers if you want to keep them apart — eliminates the need for repeated trimming and edging.

You'll find edgings made of various types of materials. Plastic edging, sold in rolls at garden centers, is widely available and can be effective for a few years. Over time, however, it tends either to sink down in the soil or to work its way up, making it a less effective barrier for wandering roots. Look for brands that include anchoring stakes to help hold the plastic strips in place. Rubber and fiberglass edgings also are available.

The best choice — and the type commonly used in public gardens — is edging made of steel or aluminum. Although metal edging strips are more expensive to purchase than plastic ones, they are much more durable and long lasting. Since the metal strips are no more difficult to install than plastic, they are well worth considering. If your local garden center doesn't offer them, look for companies that sell commercial-grade landscape tools and equipment, such as A. M. Leonard (see Resources, page 211).

Brick and flagstones are other handsome edging options. Both are long lasting and effective at slowing down many ground covers, but they are also more expensive and more time consuming to install than metal or plastic strips. Ideally, set bricks vertically in a trench to stop most wandering roots. An additional row of bricks set horizontally and abutting the vertical row, makes a wider, more effective edging. Set the bricks with their

In addition to setting bricks vertically (as shown), many gardeners also install an abutting row horizontally for even more effective edging.

Metal edging strips are perhaps the most durable option in edging materials.

HOW TO INSTALL EDGING STRIPS

TO INSTALL EDGING STRIPS — either metal or plastic — start by delineating the edge of the bed: use stakes and string or a garden hose to mark edges.

DIG A TRENCH that is about ½ inch shallower than the height of the edging strips you are installing.

UNCOIL THE EDGING and anchor it in place in the trench with the top ½ inch above the soil surface, then refill the trench with soil. Ideally, you want the strips positioned so that you can run your mower over them, with one wheel in the bed, so mowing and trimming are accomplished in one pass.

tops only ½ inch above the soil surface so you can mow with one wheel on top of them. A brick edging works best if the bricks are set in concrete to keep out grass and weeds. A flagstone edging is also effective; for the best weed, grass, and ground cover control, the flagstones should be set in concrete. See Covering Ground with Hardscape on page 57 for more information on using brick and other materials.

Keep in mind that none of these edgings will slow down invasive ground covers, and they'll only cause really vigorous ones to pause in their wanderings. You will need to monitor grass, ground covers, and edging strips periodically through the growing season. Pull up or dig out any plants that encroach on the barrier, and cut back plants that spread beyond their allotted space. Check regularly to make sure that the edging hasn't moved up or down in the soil.

Smothering and Solarizing

Smothering is another site preparation option that completely eliminates digging while building a terrific planting site with soil rich in organic matter. It also doesn't encourage buried weed seeds to germinate by bringing them to the surface, as digging and tilling do. The downside of smothering is that the bed needs to be prepared a year in advance — in spring for planting the following spring, for example.

THE BASIC SMOTHERING TECHNIQUE. To smother a bed, first scalp all the plants on the site either by mowing or cutting them as close to the soil surface as possible. Then cover the area with a layer of 8 to 10 sheets of newspaper or a layer or two of builder's paper, also called rosin paper. Have a pile or several bags of mulch handy so you can dump some mulch on each set of sheets as you spread them out; otherwise, a gust of wind will blow them all over the yard. Use a layer of corrugated cardboard to deal with woody or other really tough, vigorous weeds. If you are

Newspaper covered with compost or mulch is an effective way to smother weeds.

working alone, it's easiest to spread and cover a site in sections rather than trying to do the whole area at one time.

Whether you're using newspaper, builder's paper, or cardboard, be sure to overlap the layers by several inches. Cover them with a 4- to 6-inch-thick blanket of well-rotted compost or a mixture of topsoil and compost, then top the compost with another couple of inches of mulch. While a single 4- to 6-inch-deep layer of organic mulch over newspaper also works for this method — without the addition of compost and/or topsoil — the thicker the layers of mulch, compost, and topsoil, the easier to plant and more weedfree the site will be. After waiting a year, just plant right into the compost or mulch layer. If you've used mulch alone for smothering, it's a good idea to pull it back at planting time and add a shovel of topsoil to each planting hole.

Smothering also can be used to manage a site that you would like to plant in two or three years. Just cover it in sections, and pull up any weeds that appear until you're ready to plant. Be sure to replenish the mulch cover as needed. Another option is to build a compost pile directly on part of a site that's not going to be used for a couple of years. Keep the rest of the site mulched, and then spread the finished compost over the whole area before planting.

SMOTHERING HARD-TO-CONTROL WEEDS. If the site has woody weeds or hard-to-kill perennials like field bindweed (*Convolvulus arvensis*), tougher measures are in order. Scalp off the vegetation on the site and cover it with a 2- to 3-inch-thick layer of compost or manure, or both. Top that with a thick layer of dry organic matter — at least 6 to 8 inches. Use a mix of materials like grass, dried leaves, hay, and wood chips. Finally, top off the pile with black plastic, corrugated cardboard, or even old carpeting. Wait for a year, then peel back the layers to see if the weeds have been killed. If they haven't, cover the area again for a second year.

Once the roots are dead, remove any plastic or carpet on the top layer and plant into the mulch.

SOLARIZING THE SOIL. Yet another organic method for killing weeds (along with soilborne disease organisms, insect pests, nematodes, and weed seeds) is to solarize the soil. Midsummer is the best time of year to try this technique, since it uses the sun to heat up the soil. Pull up or dig larger weeds, especially perennial and woody ones, and then rake the site smooth and water it thoroughly. Cover the area tightly with a layer of clear plastic (to 4-mil thickness). Seal the edges of the plastic by digging a shallow trench around the site and burying the edges with soil. Leave the site covered for one to two months, and let the sun's heat bake away. Then uncover it and spread a 2- or 3-inch-thick layer of compost over the soil. Plant directly through the remains of the dead weeds. Don't loosen the soil on the site with this method, because digging will bring new weed seeds to the surface.

Using Landscape Fabric

Also called geotextile, landscape fabric is another weed control option that you can install under a layer of mulch. It allows air to infiltrate and water to percolate down to plant roots while serving to some extent as a barrier to sprouting weeds. Spun-bonded landscape fabric is more effective than needle-punched or woven types for controlling weeds, because it has fewer holes that weeds can poke through. Look for thick, feltlike landscape fabric, since weeds easily grow through thinner fabric.

Ideally, landscape fabric should be installed when the site is being prepared, since it is normally laid directly over smooth, prepared, but unplanted, soil. It's more difficult to install around existing plantings because the fabric needs to be fitted tightly around each plant to keep weeds from getting through. For the best results, manually remove weeds or use an herbicide to kill weeds on the site before installing the fabric, because weed shoots will find their way between the seams

Use a layer of clear plastic to solarize the soil and kill weeds, weed seeds, insect pests, and soilborne disease organisms.

and up around the edges of the fabric. Overlap adjoining sheets of fabric by 6 to 8 inches, and use U-shaped landscape pins (biodegradable ones are available) to secure the edges of the sheets. Cut and fit fabric tightly around existing trees or other plants. Once the fabric is in place, make holes just big enough for planting the ground covers down through the fabric. Cover the landscape fabric with a 2- to 4-inch-layer of organic mulch to make it more attractive and to protect the fabric from the sun's ultraviolet rays, which will cause it to degrade.

Landscape fabric does have disadvantages, and a great many gardeners avoid using it completely. First, it doesn't eliminate weeds: existing weeds in the soil can eventually sprout up through the fabric, and weed seeds that land on top of the fabric can send roots down through it. Either way, landscape fabric doesn't eliminate the need to weed routinely, and the weeds are difficult to remove because the roots become entangled in the fabric. In addition, once landscape fabric is in place, improving the soil beneath it is impossible, and routine maintenance including dividing or moving plants becomes very difficult.

BUYING & INSTALLING GROUND COVERS

After considering your site characteristics and going through the plant lists to select the perfect ground covers for a particular bed, figuring out how many plants you'll need should be a simple process. However, the number of plants required to cover a particular site depends on several factors. The size of the site is an obvious variable, but the size of the plants you've purchased — from tiny cuttings to established perennials or shrubs — and how far apart they should be spaced are other factors.

Buying Options

Ground covers are sold in various sizes, from bare-root plants to gallon-size or larger, and a single species may be sold in any number of sizes. Whatever size you buy, keep in mind that there are options for saving money regardless of where you shop. Look for quantity discounts from your local garden center or buy from a wholesale source, for instance.

BARE-ROOT PLANTS. These are dormant plants that are sold for spring planting. They do not have soil on the roots, which usually are wrapped in damp newspaper or wood shavings. Bare-root plants are less expensive than plants sold in larger pots, and they cost less to ship. They need more care to become established, though. Since they're smaller, they're generally spaced closer together, so you'll need to buy more of them than you would if you were installing larger plants.

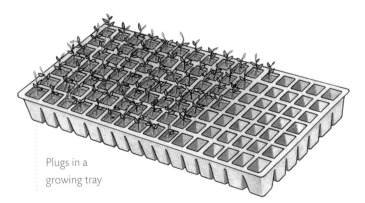

Plugs in a
growing tray

Keep bare-root plants packed in the material they arrived in — moisten it if necessary — and plant as soon as possible. (If you can't plant right away, "heel in" the plants by burying the roots in loose, moist soil or compost.) Before planting, soak the roots in a bucket of water for an hour, and carry them to the garden still in the bucket so the roots stay hydrated. If the seller hasn't already cut the plants back, it's best to trim the tops by about half before planting. This reduces moisture loss and helps the plants get established.

Unless directions that came with the plants indicate differently, form a cone of soil in the bottom of each planting hole. Spread the roots out over the cone, making sure the crown of the plant (where the roots meet the top growth) sits at the soil surface. Refill the hole halfway with soil, firm it in place, and flood the hole with water. Once the water has drained away, fill up the rest of the hole with soil, firm it again, and flood with water once more. As a general guideline, space bare-root plants 4 to 8 inches apart.

PLUGS. These are small plants grown in specially designed flats with individual openings filled with potting medium. They're usually sold to wholesalers, who pot them up and grow them on to sell in larger containers, but ground covers also are sometimes sold in retail outlets as plugs. If you can't plant right away, set them in a shady, cool, protected spot and be very careful to keep them well watered: plugs do not have much extra soil and dry out very quickly. Watch each species closely: plugs of tough, drought-tolerant species will need less shade and perhaps more air circulation than shade- and moisture-loving ground covers while they're being held for planting.

Soak plugs thoroughly before planting, and also moisten the soil before planting them, since dry soil can quickly suck moisture out of the plug. To plant, push the plug out of the flat from below and set the plant in the soil. Be sure the planted plugs are at the same depth they were in the flats — usually with the crown right at the soil surface. Like bare-root plants, plugs are less expensive than larger container-grown plants, but they need more care (especially in the form of regular watering) to become established. They should also be spaced more closely than larger plants. As a general rule, space plugs 4 to 6 inches apart.

MARKET PACKS AND 2¼-INCH POTS. Plants growing in small pots, whether they're market packs with four or six plants or individual 2¼-inch pots, are more established and more expensive than bare-root plants or plugs. They are easier to care for after planting, though, and begin growing more quickly. Water the plants and moisten the soil before planting to prevent dry soil from sucking the moisture away from the roots. Push plants growing in market packs out from the bottom. Take plants out of 2¼-inch pots by placing two fingers on each side of the plant, across the top of the pot, and then turning the pot upside down. If the plant doesn't slip right out, press gently on the corners of the pot to loosen it. Before planting, look closely at the sides of the rootball. If they are crowded with roots, score the sides with a knife before planting. Set the plants at the same depth they were growing in the pot, firm the soil gently, and water. As a general rule, space plants from market packs and 2¼-inch pots 8 to 12 inches apart.

FLATS AND TRAYS. Some ground covers are sold with many plants growing in an undivided container — either a flat or a smaller tray. In this case, use a sharp knife to block out the plants by cutting between them to create equal-size sections. Don't worry if the size of the blocks you cut varies; as you cut around the plants, just make sure to leave a good supply of roots for each plant. Ideally, block plants a few days before you plan to transplant, water thoroughly, and set them in a shady protected spot to recover. After a few days, plant as you would for market packs or 2¼-inch pots.

2¼-inch pot

Gallon pot

Flat

PINT, GALLON, AND LARGER POTS. Plants from larger pot sizes establish most quickly and also are most expensive. Especially for a small site, one or two of these larger plants may be all you need. Remove container-grown ground covers from their pots the same way you would a smaller plant — by sliding one hand over the top of the plant and turning the pot over with the other hand. If the plant doesn't slip out easily, lay the container on its side and press down on the sides to loosen the plant. Score the sides of the rootball if they are crowded with roots, and also trim away any roots that are spiraling around the bottom of the pot. This encourages roots to grow out into the soil. Moisten the soil and set the plants so they are growing at the same depth they were in the container. If in doubt, set them slightly higher, since plants often will settle somewhat in a new bed.

As a general rule, space perennials grown in these sizes of containers from 1 to 2 feet apart. Space shrubs farther apart. You will find spacing recommendations on labels for both perennials and shrubs, but closer-than-recommended spacing — somewhat less than the plant's spread at maturity — is generally best for ground covers.

PUTTING THEM TO THE TEST

CAN'T DECIDE WHICH GROUND COVERS TO USE for a particular bed? Why not buy one plant of each of the selections on your short list for the site, then conduct your own performance trial? Prepare the site, plant, mulch, and watch to see how each of your test subjects performs. Or use a corner of an existing perennial garden — one that offers similar growing conditions to the site you are planning. Ideally, watch the plants for at least a year, especially if you're planning a large ground cover planting in the future, because you can see how plants perform in all sorts of weather. Jot down notes on bloom times, foliage appearance, speed of spread, and other characteristics. Watch for plants that grow at similar rates and will make a handsome combination. Also look for aggressive spreaders and less aggressive species that will be engulfed if left to fend for themselves.

This approach does involve the initial cost of buying all the different plants to trial, but it can save frustration in the long run. Once you've selected the winners, move the others to another part of your garden or share them with friends. You may also want to hold the successful candidates in a nursery bed and propagate them while getting the entire site ready for planting.

How Many Plants?

To create a thick, weed-smothering cover as quickly as possible, space ground covers close together. While you don't want plants growing on top of one another, you also don't want vast stretches of mulched soil in between them either, since large areas of mulch invite weeds. The best spacing depends on several factors, and you'll have to decide for yourself what works in your garden — both in terms of your budget and your time. Saving money by spacing plants farther apart means more work getting them established. For example, take a species that spreads to 2 feet. Set plants on 18-inch centers and they'll grow together in a season or two, depending on growth rate. You'll need more plants if you set them on 12-inch centers, but they'll knit together more quickly. The farther-apart spacing will save you some money on plants but will increase the amount of time and effort required to get the plants established, since you'll have to mulch and weed for a longer period of time. Although plants set closer together can become crowded, they usually do just fine. Also consider how fast the ground covers you are planting will spread: fast spreaders can be spaced farther apart than slow-spreading ones.

To determine how many plants you'll need, first calculate the size of the bed you are planting in square feet.

- **For a rectangular bed,** measure length times width: L × W.

- **For a triangular bed,** the formula is half the base times the height: B × H ÷ 2.

- **For round beds,** multiply pi (3.14) times the radius (the distance from the edge to the center) squared: $3.14 \times r^2$.

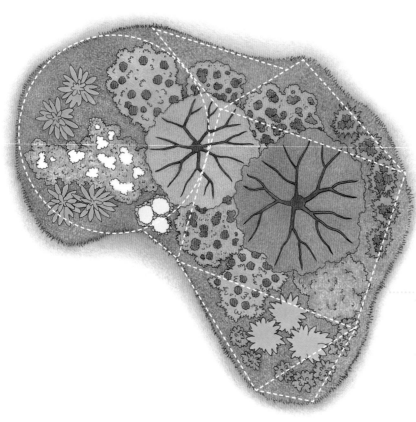

To estimate the square footage of unusual-size beds, divide the space into a combination of rectangles, triangles, and circles, then calculate the area of each and add them together.

Once you have the square footage calculated and know how far apart plants will be spaced, use the chart at right to determine how many plants you'll need to cover the site. The basic formula: spacing multiplier times the square footage of the bed equals the number of plants needed. For example, to fill a 50-square-foot bed with ground covers that will be spaced 4 inches apart, you need 450 plants (50 × 9 = 450). To cover the same bed with plants that should be set on 18-inch centers, you need 22 plants (50 × 0.44 = 22). Or to plant the area with shrubs spaced 36 inches apart and underplanted with ground covers that are set on 6-inch centers, you need 5 or 6 shrubs (50 × 0.11 = 5.5) and 200 smaller ground cover plants (50 × 4 = 200).

Good ground cover plantings will save hours of work and provide untold pleasure, but it's easy to see that buying enough plants to cover an area can quickly become expensive. Instead of falling into the trap of spacing fewer, cheaper plants farther apart, see Planting over Time on page 198 for ideas on how to spread out the cost of installing a ground cover planting.

Planting Basics

Although container-grown ground covers can be planted anytime during the growing season, the best times of year to install them are early spring and fall when cooler temperatures make it easier for plants to recover from the shock of transplanting and become established. If possible, try to plant on a cool and cloudy or even rainy day to minimize disturbance to the plants.

Whether you're growing bare-root plants or container-grown ones, handle them with care from the start. Set them in a protected spot and keep them watered and cool until you're ready to plant. It's best to avoid production-line planting strategies — spreading plants out across the site and planting them in turn. This exposes them to the sun while they're waiting for their turn to be planted, and the plants may dry out and become damaged. Instead, set plants in the ground one at a time, and keep unplanted ones in a protected spot until it's their turn to go into the ground. This minimizes stress and — especially with bare-root plants and plugs, which dry out quickly — can mean the difference between success and failure.

Whenever you set the plants in the ground, gently firm the soil around each one to settle it into the soil. While roots need some air, large pockets of it cause the roots to dry out and can prevent the plants from getting established or kill them outright. Water after setting each plant in the ground.

Transplant stress can be a killer. If you can't plant during a spell of cool and rainy or overcast weather and the new bed is in full sun, the plants may wilt. In this case, protect new transplants by shading them with spun-bonded row covers (such as Reemay, a product normally used in the vegetable garden), sheets of lath, or screening for the first few days until they've overcome transplant stress. Spun-bonded row covers can rest directly on the plants, but prop up other screens so they're slightly above the foliage.

INCHES BETWEEN PLANTS	SPACING MULTIPLIER
4 inches	9.00
5 inches	5.76
6 inches	4.00
7 inches	2.94
8 inches	2.25
9 inches	1.78
10 inches	1.45
11 inches	1.19
12 inches	1.00
15 inches	0.64
18 inches	0.44
24 inches	0.25
30 inches	0.16
36 inches	0.11

PREPLANTING PLANNING

IT'S A GOOD IDEA TO PLAN how the plants are going to be watered before you plant, because once the soil is prepared and the ground covers are in the ground, the less foot traffic the site receives the better — especially while plants are becoming established. To minimize the need to walk on the site, set up sprinklers with hoses leading off the site so that you don't have to walk on the soil to move the sprinklers. Soaker hoses are an especially efficient way to water. Keep in mind that water from a soaker hose trickles down and does not spread out much over the soil surface. As a result, you'll need hoses arranged throughout the bed so they fall near every plant or between rows of closely spaced plants. Soaker hoses can be installed under mulch. They also can be set up with regular hoses that lead off the site, so you can connect a series of them to the water supply without trampling the site after planting.

PLANTING ON SLOPES

Getting ground covers established on sloping sites can be a challenge. Sticking plants in the ground is simply awkward and physically more difficult on a slope, but a sloping site also makes it more difficult for all kinds of ground covers to get established. A major reason is that water tends to run off the surface rather than soak down into the soil; thus, sloping sites are apt to be dry and soil erosion can be a problem. For this reason, any technique that slows the speed at which water flows off a slope — thus giving it time to percolate into the soil — helps ground covers become established. Water also carries soil with it as it rushes over the ground, so slowing water flow also helps prevent soil erosion.

To cover a slope successfully, start by selecting ground covers that can tolerate the tougher conditions. See Ground Covers for a Sunny Slope on page 113 and Covering Slopes in Shade on 119 for lists of plants to consider. A mix of plants is often more effective than planting a monoculture — covering the slope with just one kind of ground cover. That's because different plants have different kinds of root systems, and planting a diverse selection takes advantage of the fact that they hold the soil in different ways.

Whether you cover a slope with one species or several, use the techniques described here to help you get the plants established. Once the plants are in place, the slower you can apply the water the better. A blast of water from an overhead sprinkler will largely run right off, so for the best results spread soaker hoses along the slope, ideally under the mulch. Then run them very slowly so the water drips out and seeps down into the soil where roots can use it.

SPACING PATTERNS

GROUND COVERS can be arranged randomly, without measuring or aligning plants in a row, but setting them out in a pattern helps ensure even coverage of the site. The plants can be set in a grid of equidistant rows, but a diamond pattern — or staggered rows — is best, since it discourages the formation of small gullies, which can form when water runs off even small slopes.

Use a yardstick to line up and space the plants, or take a tip from vegetable gardeners and make a planting stick; use an old broom handle or a 5- or 6-foot-long piece of 1×2-inch lumber. Ideally, mark several different spacing patterns along the length so you can use it for different planting areas. Use a permanent marker or paint, or cut notches in the stick. When planting, lay the planting stick along the row and space the plants according to the marks. Yet another option that works for close spacing is to use a trowel or other tool, or to measure the width of your hand — perhaps with fingers extended — and use that to determine spacing.

If you are planting a bed with drifts of more than one ground cover, and the plants are similar in size, spacing isn't a problem: just use the same spacing for all of them. You can alternate plants, arrange them in drifts, or plant in another pattern. If the bed is being planted with two different sizes of plants — shrubs underplanted with ground covers, for example — set out the larger plants first and then adjust the smaller plants so they are spaced evenly around them.

Plan on mulching between plants — and regularly pulling up any weeds that appear — until the new ground covers have become established and are covering the site. See Caring for New Plants on page 199 for more on looking after new plantings.

CREATING TEMPORARY TERRACES. Carving out flat planting spaces across the face of a slope is an effective way to slow the flow of water as it runs down. One option is to create small individual terraces for each plant. This works best on gentle slopes: Carve out a site for each plant that is slightly angled *into* the slope. Make a low rim of soil on the outer edge of each planting area to help hold water near the plant.

For small plants on gentle slopes, another option is to dig a series of narrow planting trenches across the slope. The objective is to create a trench that's slightly angled into the slope with a slight depression for each plant. Mound soil in a rim around each plant to hold water. With either method, stagger the spacing of the plants in the rows.

Since a heavy rain can wash out unreinforced terraces, creating somewhat longer-lasting ones may be a better option. To do this, build a series of small level terraces, each reinforced with lumber. Either install short pieces of lumber below each plant, or install longer pieces across the slope to create flat rows in which to plant ground covers. (If termites are a severe problem in your area, consider using plastic edging strips instead of wood to hold terraces in place.) Recycled or warped boards are ideal for this purpose; don't choose pressure-treated lumber, though. Use pine — 2 × 6-inches is a good size, but many other sizes will work fine. Pound wooden pegs along the boards to hold them in place across the slope, and fill in soil along the base of each board; otherwise, the water will find holes and wash down the slope instead of percolating into the soil. Simply leave the lumber in place to rot. By the time pine boards rot, the ground covers should be established and able to hold the slope. Mulch the slope to further protect the soil. Pegging burlap, which is biodegradable, over the rows or over the entire site also helps prevent erosion.

BUILDING PERMANENT TERRACES. Another way to transform slopes is to simply turn them into level gardening space with a series of terraces.

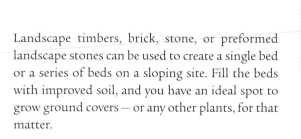

Temporary terraces (with or without wooden reinforcements) help plants get established on steep planting sites.

Landscape timbers, brick, stone, or preformed landscape stones can be used to create a single bed or a series of beds on a sloping site. Fill the beds with improved soil, and you have an ideal spot to grow ground covers — or any other plants, for that matter.

PLANTING THROUGH GRASS. If the site is covered with lawn grass, another option is to use an herbicide to kill the grass, then plant ground covers directly into the dead sod. This way, the roots of the lawn grass will hold the slope while the ground covers become established.

SPACING CLOSE TOGETHER. Quick cover is especially important on a sloping site, so buy enough plants to position them close enough together that they fill in quickly. If expense is a problem, see Planting over Time on page 198 for ideas about spreading out the cost and labor of the installation.

PLANTING OVER TIME

Planting a ground cover bed over the course of several months — or years — makes sense for a variety of reasons. It not only spreads out the cost of buying ground covers, but it also spreads out the site preparation effort. Instead of preparing soil and planting a huge bed in a single weekend — not to mention weeding and caring for all the plants while they are becoming established — keep the project manageable by developing a long-range plan that gets the job done over several weeks or seasons. Here are some tactics to consider.

PREPARING SOIL IN BLOCKS OR DRIFTS. Once you have selected a site, improve the soil in sections. The easiest way is to start at one end of the area, then dig, amend, and mulch in sections over several seasons. The sections can be rectangles or free-form drifts, but since you may be living with the evolving shapes for several seasons, try to create beds that are fairly easy to work and mow around. Clearly mark the edges of prepared sections, so you'll know where to start each time you begin work on a new one. You can prepare a bed over time whether you're digging the soil or using one of the techniques covered in Smothering and Solarizing on page 190. Consider building compost piles on-site so you'll have plenty of finished compost to work into the soil at planting time.

CREATING PLANTING POCKETS

ROOTS CAN MAKE IT TOUGH to prepare planting sites for ground covers that are to grow under trees. While it's next-to-impossible to plant under shallow-rooted species like maples (see Covering When There's No Soil on page 153 for suggestions), there's plenty of soil space under oaks and other deep-rooted species. Whether you're preparing an entire bed at once or installing it gradually over time, to minimize damage to the tree, avoid cutting as many roots as possible. Instead, look for spaces between larger roots, where it's possible to loosen and improve pockets of soil in which to plant ground covers. To find planting pockets, dig with a trowel or digging knife to locate areas of loose soil between big roots.

CONNECTING THE DOTS. Another option that's effective for gradually developing ground cover plantings under a shrub border or under trees is to plant the shrubs and trees first. Prepare individual planting sites in the lawn, mulch the shrubs or trees after they're installed, and mow around them. Then gradually dig or smother ever-expanding beds around each plant as time permits, and plant them with ground covers. Obviously, this is also a good technique for reducing maintenance in a yard where trees and shrubs are dotted all over the place and are separated by lawn. Keep mowing around individual areas until all the lawn grass has been dug up or smothered.

PLANTING IN STAGES. Even if you can manage to prepare the soil over a huge site — or can pay someone to do the work for you — spreading the planting out over a couple of seasons may still make sense from a maintenance aspect. To get a good start, newly planted ground covers need regular watering and weeding. On a sloping site, you also will have to watch for and correct any gullies that form and begin to wash away soil. It may be easier to keep a small bed in top-notch shape until the plants are established, and then plant a new section. Keep in mind that the best times to plant are spring and fall.

Hiring help to look after a new planting also makes sense. For example, if you have a ground cover bed that was planted in spring and you are going to be on vacation for a month in summer, consider hiring someone to keep the bed watered and weeded while you are away. A dry spell in August can severely stress or damage a new planting, and a wet spell can mean you'll return home to a bed that has been taken over by weeds.

GROWING YOUR OWN. Planting over time has another benefit: it allows plenty of time to propagate your own plants. Start with a few purchased plants and gradually produce the rest of the ground covers you'll need. For details on propagation techniques, see page 203.

CARING FOR NEW PLANTS

While established ground covers are low-maintenance plants, newly installed plantings require ongoing basic upkeep, at least initially. Here's a basic rundown on the care they'll need.

WATERING AND MULCHING. After planting, water the bed and cover the soil with a protective blanket of organic mulch. Mulch helps the soil retain moisture and also keeps it cool. It also helps prevent erosion as well as pounding and compaction caused by rain hitting the soil.

Shredded bark is commonly available, but well-rotted compost makes an excellent mulch as well. Another mulch option is shredded leaves — just pick them up in a bagging lawn mower. Leaves are such good mulch that they're well worth collecting and stockpiling. While these and other organic mulches are normally best, stone or gravel may be a better choice in arid climates. Stone or gravel also is a good option if you're planting alpines or species subject to root rot that do not tolerate moisture around the crowns. Another alternative for plants that may develop root rot is to use an organic mulch, but keep it several inches away from the crown of the plant.

The optimal thickness of the mulch layer varies by material. Spread about 1 inch of compost, and if you don't have enough to mulch the entire bed, spread it around each plant and fill in the rest of the space with shredded bark or chopped leaves. Spread shredded leaves about 3 inches thick, and shredded bark or bark chips in a 1- to 2-inch layer. Even if you didn't use one of the smothering techniques described in Smothering and Solarizing on page 190, a blanket of newspaper can still help control weeds; spread a layer of six to eight sheets around plants before covering it with mulch.

Whether you're planting herbaceous plants or shrubs, gradually feather down the mulch layer so that it doesn't actually touch plant stems; mulch piled up around stems can kill plants.

MONITORING CLOSELY. For the first couple of weeks after planting ground covers, check the new bed daily to see what it needs. Pull back the mulch and stick a finger into the soil to assess how damp it is, and water whenever the soil begins to dry out. For most plants, soil that is evenly moist but not wet is best, but the ideal amount of soil moisture varies depending on what you've planted. Drought-tolerant species like sedums prefer somewhat drier conditions than moisture-loving ground covers, such as many ferns.

Check to see how far the water has penetrated before shutting off the hose, and water deeply each time — 6 to 8 inches of soil should be wet after every watering. Deep watering encourages plants to grow deep roots. If you're using an overhead sprinkler, measure how much water is being delivered by setting out an empty cat food or tuna can and watching it fill. In general, hand sprinkling with a hose isn't effective, because not enough water is delivered to really get the soil wet.

PULLING WEEDS REGULARLY. Another task to tackle on daily inspections is to pull up or hoe out any weeds that appear. They're far easier to remove the minute they're spotted than weeks later after they have put down roots and become established.

Proper mulching helps suppress weeds without smothering plants; be sure not to pile up mulch around the stems of newly planted ground covers.

WATCHING FOR SIGNS OF STRESS. Keep an eye out for signs your new ground covers are under stress. Yellow or curled leaves can indicate that plants need water, but it can also indicate that the soil is too wet or that pests such as aphids or spider mites are attacking the new plants. If plants show any abnormal symptoms, figure out what the problem is and take steps to correct it.

RELAXING YOUR VIGIL. After the first couple of weeks, you'll have a good idea of how much monitoring the bed needs and you can relax a bit. Begin checking every few days, then after a month begin checking weekly, although the more frequently you check, the sooner you'll be able correct problems. Again, test soil moisture regularly, and water as necessary. Soil that dries out too much will damage plant roots and curb the growth of the plants. Also keep on top of any weeds that appear. Pulling a few a day is the best way to keep them under control and eliminate the need for a weeding session that lasts for hours. Also reset and firm the soil around any plants that have been uprooted by wildlife. Squirrels and chipmunks appreciate loosened soil almost as much as newly planted ground covers do, and birds also may uproot plants. A layer of spun-bonded row cover or screen will discourage wildlife.

While your new ground cover bed will gradually need less attention, don't stop monitoring it regularly — perhaps every other week — for the first full year. Throughout the winter check for plants that have been pushed out of the soil by frost heaving and reset them.

FEEDING. If you want to give plants an extra boost and speed growth, feed new plantings with quarter-strength fertilizer once a month for the first season. Stop two months before your first fall frost date to give the plants a chance to harden off before winter.

Ongoing Care

Once established, good ground covers need far less care than most other garden plants, but they do need occasional attention. Ideally, they'll need little in the way of watering. If the plants you've selected can tolerate any amount of drought, you have little to worry about once they're established. Otherwise, leave soaker hoses in place to make watering easy and efficient whenever it's needed.

Replenish the mulch on the bed annually, at least until the plants have grown so close together that soil is no longer visible. An annual topdressing of compost helps keep the soil in top-notch form and also eliminates the need to fertilize.

As a rule, ground covers need minimal pruning, but keep an eye out for and remove dead branches when they appear. Pull up any all-green growth that appears on variegated plants; it will be more vigorous and will outcompete the variegated growth. Also trim off growth that is headed in an undesirable direction. If the bed is planted with aggressive spreaders, check regularly to make sure they're staying put. Prune them back hard as necessary. If excessive spreading is a problem consider digging a 6- to 8-inch-deep trench around it. Bear in mind that this is not a low-maintenance solution, because without a permanent barrier in the trench, you'll have to redig it every year or so to keep the plants from wandering.

Many ground covers benefit from an annual trim to keep them neat and to remove last year's foliage. Mow perennials in late winter while the plants are still dormant. Either set your mower on its highest setting or use a string trimmer. Use a blade attachment on the trimmer for tough-stemmed herbaceous species or woody ground covers. After cutting off the tops of the plants, rake up the excess. This technique works particularly well for ground covers such as lilyturfs (*Liriope* spp.), epimediums (*Epimedium* spp.), and sweet woodruff (*Galium odoratum*). Reapply mulch just after cutting back plants.

RENOVATING GROUND COVERS

Existing beds of ground covers occasionally need a complete overhaul. Perhaps none of the plants in the bed are thriving, or one is overwhelming all of its bedmates. There are different ways to renovate an existing bed. If it's not a bed you planted, start by identifying all the plants growing there. See Knowing Your Site on page 26 and use the information there to familiarize yourself with the conditions that exist, since a bad choice of ground cover may be at the root of the problem. Get a soil test done to see if pH or poor fertility is part of the problem. Also look for soil compaction or poor drainage, two other common problems. Amending the soil, adjusting the pH, or taking care of other soil problems are fairly simple fixes and may be all you need to do.

If soil conditions don't seem to be causing the problem, and the remaining plants are sickly or old and no longer vigorous, the best approach may be to dig everything up, enrich the soil with compost or other organic matter, and replant with another species. Don't replace sickly ground covers with new plants of the same species, because they will be prone to the same pests, diseases, or other problems that may have built up in the soil. Sites planted with ground covers that aren't growing well because the soil is crowded with tree roots — a common problem under shallow-rooted trees such as maple — are tough to renovate. Adding soil on top of the roots doesn't work, because the tree's roots will simply grow up into the new soil. See Covering When There's No Soil on page 153 for ideas on dealing with such sites.

Here are some other problems and solutions to consider.

DIGGING AND DIVIDING. If the bed is planted with herbaceous ground covers that have died or thinned out in the center of the clumps, leaving rings of healthy growth around scraggly looking centers, division may be a good option. Dig the clumps, discard the old woody growth at the center of the clumps, and replant the healthy, vigorous portions of the plants from the outside of the clumps. For large plantings, a schedule helps: renovate part of the bed each year. This approach works well with many plants including yarrows (*Achillea* spp.), artemisias (*Artemisia* spp.), astilbes (*Astilbe* spp.), bergenias (*Bergenia* spp.), and heucheras (*Heuchera* spp.).

RENEWAL PRUNING. Many shrubs used as ground covers can be cut back hard — to the ground or nearly so — using a technique called renewal pruning, which encourages vigorous, healthy new growth. For species that aren't too woody, a lawn mower may suffice as a tool; otherwise use pruning shears or a trimmer with a blade attachment. The sheared-back plants will be unattractive after a harsh haircut but will recover quickly. If in doubt about whether this approach is appropriate for the ground covers in your bed, cut back a single plant and see how it recovers. Plants that routinely produce new shoots from the base are excellent candidates.

Another option for shrubby ground covers is to remove one or two of the older branches from all of the plants each year to make room for the younger growth. This approach takes more time but will keep the bed in good shape, and you can avoid the dramatically sheared look that results from using a lawn mower or blade trimmer.

An overgrown ground cover planting (left) can be trimmed back with a string trimmer (right).

ADDING COMPANIONS. If the plants are healthy looking but are not providing dense enough cover, consider adding another species to the mix instead of starting over. Increasing diversity often improves coverage. Look for compatible ground covers that grow well in the existing conditions and spread at about the same rate as the plants already in the bed. Look for possible candidates in the lists in part 2, as well as in neighborhood gardens, at public gardens, or at nearby nurseries that have demonstration gardens. To plant, loosen the soil in the bare patches, amend it, then add the new ground covers. If possible, mulch the entire planting with compost to improve all of the soil.

This is also a good approach if you have healthy plantings that are simply a bit boring. Remove some of the plants (and share them with fellow gardeners) to make room for additional ground covers that will bloom at a different time or add foliage contrast.

BALANCING COMPETITION. This approach ranges from correcting combinations that need slight editing to taking care of plantings that need wholesale eradication. If the problem is one ground cover that's outcompeting another in the bed, there are two options. The first is to dig up all the slower-spreading plants that are in danger of being smothered and move them to another spot, leaving the remaining ground cover to take over the entire bed. Cover the spaces where plants were removed with a layer of compost or remulch the entire bed to speed it along.

The other option is to remove the more aggressive plants and encourage the remaining plants to fill the space. If the aggressive species is an invasive spreader — especially if it is nonnative — herbicide may be the best option for removal. See Eliminating the Competition on page 186 for a way to deliver herbicide directly to specific plants in a garden bed.

PINCH PENNIES PROPAGATING

CRUNCH SOME NUMBERS and it quickly becomes clear that buying enough ground covers to cover even a medium-size site can be an expensive undertaking. By far the cheapest way to add them to your garden is over the garden gate — by planting ground covers provided by a neighbor who is renovating a bed. Before you accept such donations, make sure the plants offered are well behaved. Graciously accept those that have performed well in a neighbor's garden, and decline plants that are being ripped out because they're taking over. Another great way to start propagating is to ask your neighbors if you can take cuttings from their plants, or even help them

divide overgrown clumps in exchange for some excess plants.

Finally, there's the local nursery. Buying a few starter plants and using them for propagation doesn't require a big investment, although it does take time to grow new plants. Install a nursery bed (see Growing Your Own on page 203) or plant part of the ground cover bed with the starter plants and systematically propagate from them. Despite the cost of a single plant, or even a few plants, there are still substantial savings to be had.

Bare-root plants are the least expensive, but to plant a 50-square-foot bed at a spacing of 4 inches, you'll need 450 plants.

Use 2¼-inch plants, also on 4-inch centers, at about $3.60 each and the cost becomes $1,620 for 450 plants.

Plant quart-size perennials (in 4-inch-wide, 4-inch-tall pots) and space them on 8-inch centers, and you'll need fewer plants — about 113. But the savings are still substantial, since quarts cost about $6 each, so 113 plants will cost $678.

Shrubs in gallon-size containers start at about $10, and when spaced on 18-inch centers, they'll cover the same 50-square-foot bed for $220.

When you consider how much it costs to purchase plants, it's easy to see that propagating your own ground covers is a great way to fill your garden without going broke.

Growing Your Own

One of the best ways to minimize the cost of installing a bed of ground covers is to propagate your own plants. Although you'll need a little bit of patience, the basic techniques aren't all that difficult, and the savings can be substantial. The plant descriptions in this book list recommended propagation methods and the best seasons to attempt them. You'll find step-by-step directions in the pages that follow.

Keep in mind that all of the plants you propagate will need some extra care to grow into strong, vigorous ground covers. One of the best ways to provide that care, without having the propagation effort take over all your gardening time, is to install a nursery bed. This is a special growing area for seedlings, new divisions, rooted cuttings, and other plants that are too small to move out into the garden. Keeping newly propagated ground covers in a nursery bed makes it easy to water and weed them regularly. It also ensures they won't be overtaken by more robust bedfellows or succumb to less than perfect care out in the garden.

To make a nursery bed, select a protected site that is within easy reach of a hose. Depending on your garden and the plants you're propagating, you may need a spot in sun or shade — or both. A site with rich, well-drained soil is best. Loosen the top 1 foot of soil and add plenty of well-rotted organic matter to ensure optimal conditions for plant roots. Building a raised bed is a good idea, especially if soil drainage is a problem. Set the cuttings or new divisions in rows or blocks so weeding and caring for the new plants will be easy. You can also direct-sow seeds in a nursery bed. Mulch to keep the soil cool and moist. As plants become large enough to move to the garden, dig them up in either spring or fall and transplant them out into the garden.

Starting ground covers from seed is often more economical than buying plants. These seedlings of *Cyclamen coum* are ready to be pricked out and transplanted.

Ground Covers from Cuttings

A wide range of ground covers are easy to root from cuttings. Most species can be propagated from more than one type of cutting, and the type of cutting you choose depends on the maturity of the wood at the time you harvest it. The plant entries in part 2 recommend the best season to collect cuttings — the time of year when that particular species is most likely to have growth on it that will produce roots. Use the information below to determine the best type of cutting to try. The easiest kinds of cuttings to root are softwood, basal, and semi-ripe cuttings, all of which can be used to propagate a wide range of herbaceous and woody ground covers. Hardwood cuttings are a little more difficult but are well worth the effort.

SOFTWOOD CUTTINGS. These are stem cuttings taken in summer from new, nonwoody growth at or near the tip of a leafy stem. (It's also possible to take softwood cuttings at other times of year from tender plants overwintered indoors, or from lush new growth produced in fall, for example.) To determine if a shoot is at the best stage for making a softwood cutting, try firmly bending one of the plant's stems. Growth that snaps off cleanly is ideal, while stems that simply bend over are too soft. Ones that crush or partially break are old and may be slow to root.

Softwood cuttings have leaves and lose moisture and wilt rapidly; thus, minimizing moisture loss before new roots form is essential to success. Ideally, fill pots with a premoistened rooting medium before you collect the cuttings, so you can plant them immediately. If that isn't possible, put the stems in wet paper towels or a jar of water as soon as you collect them, and wrap the upper parts of the cuttings in damp paper towels. Either way, collect softwood cuttings in a plastic bag, and keep them out of direct sun to minimize moisture loss. Also, gather them early in the day while the stems are full of water, since cuttings from water-stressed plants do not root well. Water the plants the day before gathering cuttings if the weather has been dry, and take cuttings from healthy, vig-orous growth with fully expanded leaves. Avoid spindly shoots or very fast-growing stems.

Take shoots that are 2 to 6 inches long and have at least two leaf nodes (nodes are the joints where leaves attach to the main stem). Use pruning shears or a sharp knife to make clean cuts. To prepare cuttings for planting, trim each stem to a length of 2 to 4 inches. Try to leave at least two nodes on each cutting, and make the bottom cut just *below* a leaf node. Remove the leaves from the bottom half of the cutting as well as any flowers or flower buds.

Dip the base of the stem in a rooting hormone such as Rootone to speed root formation. Then stick a finger or a pencil into a pot filled with premoistened medium to make a hole for the cutting. (Inserting the cutting into the medium without poking a hole first removes the rooting hormone.) Stick the cutting about halfway in, to just below the lowest leaves. Gently press the medium down to support the cutting. Stick the remaining cuttings (several will fit in a single pot), spacing them 1 to 4 inches apart. The cuttings shouldn't touch, so if the leaves are large, either space the cuttings farther apart or trim the leaves slightly (by no more than one-half). Use a separate pot for each type of plant, since roots form at different rates. Label each pot with the name of the plant and the date, and water thoroughly.

Place the cuttings in a warm (65° to 75°F) spot, and set up a tent using a cleaner's bag or large clear plastic bag to provide high humidity. Make a frame to keep the plastic from touching the plants — a couple of stretched-out wire clothes hangers make a fine frame. Cuttings root fastest when the medium is a little warmer than the air temperature (70° to 75°F); a heated propagating mat makes providing this bottom heat very easy.

Give cuttings good light, but not direct sun. Indoors, set them under fluorescent lights such as those used to start seed; outdoors, set them at the base of a north-facing wall or in a spot that's lightly shaded all day. Keep the medium evenly moist, but never soggy, and immediately remove

① To prepare a softwood cutting, remove leaves from the bottom half of the cutting, and trim to 2 to 4 inches.

② Stick the cutting in a pot of premoistened potting medium.

any dead leaves or dead cuttings to prevent disease. Open the plastic or other enclosure for an hour or so about three times a week to allow some air circulation.

Most softwood cuttings start rooting in two to five weeks. When you see new growth, tug lightly on a stem; cuttings that feel firmly anchored are ready for transplanting to individual pots. Gradually remove or open the enclosure over a period of a few days to increase ventilation and to decrease humidity. This will help the new growth harden off and reduce the chance of wilting. Then transplant the rooted cuttings to a nursery bed until the plants are large enough to fend for themselves in the garden.

BASAL CUTTINGS. Also called basal stem cuttings, these are cuttings taken from shoots that arise at the base of a plant, typically in spring. They're usually produced by herbaceous plants and are an excellent way to propagate many kinds of ground covers. Nonflowering shoots work best. Some of these shoots may already have roots forming at the base (look closely, since they may be very small), making them even easier to propagate. Collect and root basal cuttings as you would softwood cuttings. (If the cuttings you collect do have baby roots already forming, don't dip them in rooting hormone before planting.)

SEMI-RIPE CUTTINGS. These are cuttings taken in summer from partially matured growth on a woody plant. The base of a semi-ripe cutting is woody, while the tip is still soft. Sometimes called semi-hardwood cuttings, this type of cutting is used to propagate a wide range of shrubs, vines, and trees. While deciduous plants generally root best from softwood cuttings, they also root from semi-ripe cuttings. Semi-ripe cuttings are especially effective for rooting evergreens, both needled and broad-leaved, including rhododendrons and azaleas (*Rhododendron* spp.) and hollies (*Ilex* spp.).

Collect and treat semi-ripe cuttings just as you would softwood cuttings. Many propagators

CUTTING MIX

SEED-STARTING MEDIA generally hold too much moisture for cuttings, causing them to rot before roots form. To get cuttings off to a good start, mix equal parts perlite and vermiculite in a bucket or other container. Wear a mask to avoid inhaling the dust as you mix, and moisten the mixture thoroughly with water before filling containers. Firm the medium in the containers, and let the excess water drip away before sticking any cuttings.

remove the shoot tip just *above* a node. Dip the cut base of each cutting into rooting hormone. On large-leaved or broad-leaved evergreen plants, to reduce transpiration, or water loss through the leaves, cut the leaves in half before sticking the cuttings into pots of premoistened rooting medium. Set cuttings to be rooted indoors on a heated propagation mat to encourage root formation.

HARDWOOD CUTTINGS. These are cuttings taken from fully mature, hardened growth on a deciduous, woody-stemmed shrub, vine, or tree. Gather hardwood cuttings from fall to midwinter, at least two weeks after the plants have dropped their leaves. Vigorous, pencil-thick shoots from wood of the current year's growth (first-year shoots) usually root best, but second-year or older growth may root as well. Cut stems at least 8 inches long (one long stem can yield several smaller cuttings). Trim 1 to 2 inches off the tip of the shoot.

Cut hardwood cuttings into 4- to 8-inch lengths, with at least two buds on each piece. Make a straight cut about ½ inch *above* a bud at the top end of each piece (the end that was closest to the shoot tip) and a sloping cut about ½ inch *below* the bud at the base. Cuttings planted upside down won't root, and this system keeps track of which end is which.

In areas with mild winters (roughly Zone 6 southward), dip the base of each cutting in rooting hormone and plant immediately, either by sticking the cuttings directly in a nursery bed or into pots. Stick hardwood cuttings vertically into moistened, loose soil, leaving only one or two buds aboveground, and lightly firm the soil around the cuttings. Mulch the soil around the cuttings after the ground freezes to prevent rapid thawing and refreezing, which can damage the new roots.

In northern climates, store hardwood cuttings for early spring planting. Storing protects them from extreme cold and promotes the formation of callus tissue at the base of each cutting, which increases the chance the cuttings will root. To store the cuttings, treat the base of each with rooting hormone, gather them into bundles with the top ends all facing in one direction, and secure them with rubber bands. To keep them cool and moist over the winter, bury them outdoors in a well-drained spot filled with sandy soil, sand, or sawdust. Place the bundles horizontally, 6 to 8 inches deep. Or place them vertically but *upside down*, with the bases 3 to 4 inches from the soil surface. (The latter, seemingly unlikely, position keeps the bases slightly warmer to encourage callus forma-tion and the tips cooler, encouraging the buds to remain dormant.) Or store them in boxes of moist sand, sawdust, or peat moss in an unheated room or garage or in the refrigerator.

In early spring, stick the stored cuttings outdoors in moist, well-prepared soil, setting them deep enough to cover all but the top one or two buds. Space them roughly 4 to 6 inches apart. Hardwood cuttings may take several months to a year to root. Once they have rooted, set them in a sheltered spot or in a cold frame for the winter instead of transplanting them right away. Feed them after you see new growth start in spring, then move them to individual pots about two to four weeks later. In mid- to late summer, transplant them to a nursery bed, then move them to the garden the following spring or fall.

Ground Covers from Rhizomes

Many ground covers spread by rhizomes that travel along the soil surface or underground. True rhizomes are actually horizontal stems — not roots — that have nodes and internodes just like vertical stems do. Rhizomes produce roots at the nodes (visible joints or swollen areas) and are an excellent way to propagate some ground covers, including crested iris (*Iris cristata*) and sweet woodruff (*Galium odoratum*). The same techniques used to propagate them can work well for ground covers with sprawling or trailing stems, such as partridgeberry (*Mitchella repens*).

To improve coverage in a bed filled with rhizomatous or trailing plants, one option is to direct aboveground rhizomes or trailing stems into thinner patches and pin them in place with bent pieces of wire. Or use rhizomes or trailing stems somewhat like conventional softwood cuttings: Cut them into pieces that are two or three nodes long and root them in plastic boxes filled with moistened cutting mix. Lay them horizontally on the mix. Many root readily enough that they can be cut into sections and planted directly in a nursery bed; in this case, well-drained sandy soil is best.

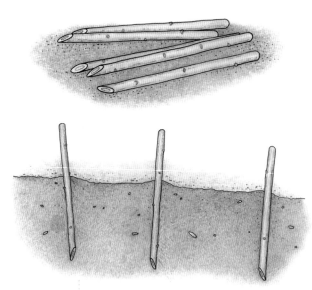

An easy way to remember the polarity (which way is up) of hardwood cuttings is to trim the bottom of the cutting at an angle. Stick cuttings outdoors in spring, in moist, well-prepared soil.

Potting Up Plantlets

Houseleeks (*Sempervivum* spp.), strawberries (*Fragaria* spp.), and other ground covers that produce plantlets do much of the work for you. These small plants typically appear on runners, stolons, or rhizomes. To propagate a ground cover that produces plantlets, first check to see if the plantlet has grown any roots. If so, sever it from the parent and either pot it up or move it to a nursery bed. Watch plantlets closely until they are well established — keep them shaded and in evenly moist (but not wet) soil until they have recovered. If they wilt dramatically, try treating them like cuttings and cover them loosely with plastic. Another option is to sever the new plant but leave it right where it is growing for a few weeks to give it time to grow more roots and get over the shock of being severed from its parent.

Multiplying by Division

Gardeners use division in several different ways — to chop off a piece of a favorite perennial to share with a friend, to rejuvenate a clump that's died out in the center, or to reduce the size of a clump that's spread beyond its allotted space. Division also is a very productive way to propagate ground covers, especially if applied systematically. If you are starting with purchased plants, select overcrowded pots in need of division. Offering to help divide plants at a friend's or neighbor's garden and dividing clumps in your own garden are other great ways to get propagating stock.

Spring and fall are the ideal times to divide most plants. For the best results, divide during a spell of cool and rainy or overcast weather to reduce stress on the new plants, which have limited root systems that can have trouble supplying top growth with water.

To divide a plant, dig around it with a spade several inches away from the base of the stems, then lift the clump out of the hole. Very large, heavy clumps often are easiest to divide while still in the hole: Dig around the entire clump, then cut it into manageable pieces before lifting them out.

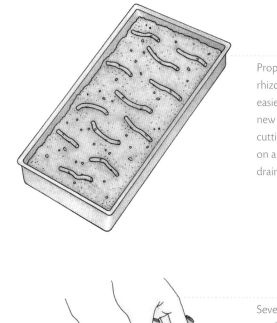

Propagating from rhizomes is one of the easiest ways to start new plants; simply lay cuttings horizontally on a moist but well-drained medium.

Several new plants can be created from dividing just one.

The exact division technique depends on the species. Pull plants that have fibrous roots, such as sedums (*Sedum* spp.) and wild gingers (*Asarum* spp.), into pieces with your fingers. Use a sharp knife to divide bergenias (*Bergenia* spp.), plumbago (*Ceratostigma plumbaginoides*), and other plants with tough or woody crowns or dense clumps of rhizomes. Cut large clumps apart with a sharp spade or force them apart with two garden forks placed back to back, or chop really dense, woody clumps apart with a mattock or an ax. Candidates for these heavy-duty division techniques include daylilies (*Hemerocallis* spp.), large hostas (*Hosta* spp.), and rodgersias (*Rodgersia* spp.).

If you have difficulty deciding where to separate a clump, trimming the top growth back by about half will give you a better view. (Cutting off some top growth also reduces water loss, so the plants recover faster.) You may also make the job easier if you wash the soil off the roots with a stiff stream of water from the hose before dividing.

However you divide the clumps, each piece needs to have its own roots and shoots or dormant buds, but the pieces can be any size, from not much bigger than cuttings to good-size plants, depending on how many you need. (Small divisions will need more care than larger ones, and planting them in a nursery bed while they get established is an excellent option.)

Keep the roots moist while the plants are out of the ground by covering them with mulch or a piece of plastic. Discard old, woody growth. It's not as vigorous as the younger portions of the clump and not worth using for propagation. Be sure to loosen the soil on the site and add organic matter before replanting. Water the new divisions deeply. If the weather is sunny, shade them with propped-up bushel baskets, spun-bonded row covers, or burlap for a few days, until they recover from the stress.

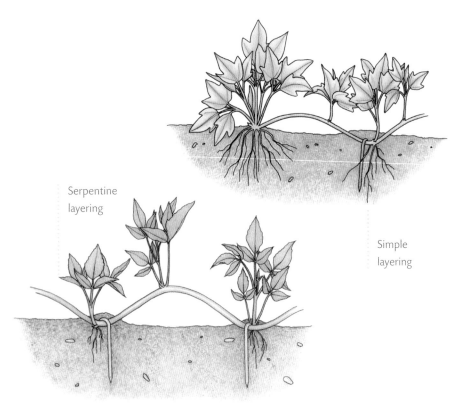

Serpentine layering

Simple layering

Increasing by Layering

Both shrubs and vines can be propagated by layering, a technique that causes a stem to form roots at a leaf node by covering it with soil while it is still attached to the parent plant. Once it is rooted, the resulting plant is severed from the parent plant and grown on.

Simple layering, the most common layering technique, can be used to propagate many shrubs and vines, and some perennials too. In late winter or early spring, select a long, low, flexible stem that is easy to bend to the ground. One-year-old shoots are best; older growth is less likely to produce roots. Loosen the soil to a depth of 4 or 5 inches, and work in compost or other organic matter in the area where the stem will touch.

Pick off all the leaves from the stem to be layered except those at the tip. Then use a sharp knife to wound the stem at a leaf node (leaves indicate where these are located); slice into it to form a thin 1- to 2-inch-long flap or tongue of bark on the bottom of the section that will be buried. Take care not to cut too deep. Place a toothpick or thin sliver of wood in the wound to keep it open. Then bury the wounded section about 3 inches deep in the area where you improved the soil. Pin it down with a U-shaped wire pin if necessary (it's easy to make one from a cut section of coat hanger). Stake the tip, which remains aboveground. Keep the soil moist all summer. The following fall or spring, sever the rooted layer from the parent plant and pot it up or move it. Keep the new plant evenly moist and partially shaded until it is well established.

Vines and shrubs that have particularly long, flexible stems — such as clematis and forsythia — can be propagated using a similar technique called serpentine layering. In this case, the stems are snaked above and below the soil to induce production of roots and shoots at selected leaf nodes. In late winter or early spring, select a stem, then loosen and improve the soil along the area where it will touch the ground as for a simple layer. Roots form at buried leaf nodes and shoots form at the ones left aboveground, so you need to have at least one bud above the soil for each one that's buried.

Determine which buds will be buried, then prepare the stems at each spot as you would for a simple layer. Bury each wounded section and pin it in place, then keep the soil moist all summer. The following spring, check for roots at each buried section then cut apart and pot up the new plants.

Growing from Seed

One of the most economical ways to propagate ground covers is to start from seed, and you can plant a bed for the cost of a seed packet or two. Seed is best for species, though, since many improved cultivars do not come true, meaning the seedlings may or may not exhibit the plant habit, foliage color, or other characteristics for which the cultivar is grown. Some of the many candidates for growing from seed include Roman chamomile (*Chamaemelum nobile*) and wall rock cress (*Arabis caucasica*), as well as blue fescue (*Festuca glauca*), tufted hair grass (*Deschampsia cespitosa*), and a number of other ornamental grasses.

Seed can be started indoors, like annuals or vegetables, but one of the easiest ways to sow perennials and shrubs is in pots that you set outdoors in a protected location. Start by filling containers with premoistened seed-starting mix (buy a commercial seed mix or combine 2 parts commercial potting mix with 1 part perlite or vermiculite). Press the mix down gently so it is about ½ inch below the rim of the container.

Spread the seed evenly over the soil surface. Don't sow too thickly or the seedlings will be crowded and hard to untangle for transplanting. Cover larger seeds lightly, but just press tiny seeds onto the surface of the medium, then mulch the pots with very small washed pea gravel (the kind sold in pet stores for aquariums). The gravel prevents the formation of moss, which can outcompete seedlings. Be sure to label each pot with the name of the plant and the date sown.

Set the containers in a protected spot outdoors, such as next to a shrub or on the north side of the house for germinating. Either group the pots in a flat or sink them to within an inch

MOUND LAYERING

ALSO CALLED STOOLING, this is a useful technique for propagating plants with stiff or short shoots that are difficult to bend to the ground. It's commonly used on shrubby herbs such as thymes (*Thymus* spp.), lavenders (*Lavandula* spp.), lavender cottons (*Santolina* spp.), and artemisias (*Artemisia* spp.). Mound layering also can be used to renew these plants, which tend to get woody, less attractive, and less productive as they age.

In spring, pile 3 to 5 inches of loose, sandy soil or mulch mixed with compost over the top of the plant. Leave 3 or 4 inches of each shoot tip exposed. Be sure to sift the soil carefully around the base of the stems; roots won't form if air pockets are present. Water gently to moisten and settle the soil, but avoid washing it away. Keep the mound evenly moist and replenish the sandy soil or mulch as necessary.

In late summer or early fall, gently brush the mound away to see if roots have formed. If they have, sever the stems, taking as many roots as possible with each piece. Pot up the individual plants or move them to a nursery bed or another spot in the garden. If roots haven't formed, re-cover the plant and check again the following spring or early summer.

of the rim in the soil. Water as necessary (rainfall often is sufficient).

Schedule sowing times based on the requirements of the seeds. This is an especially easy way to handle plants that need a cold treatment to germinate, such as candytuft (*Iberis sempervirens*) and daylilies (*Hemerocallis* spp.); sow them in winter and set the pots in a protected location outdoors immediately. For plants that germinate best from fresh seeds, such as hellebores (*Helleborus* spp.), twinleaf (*Jeffersonia diphylla*), and wild gingers (*Asarum* spp.), sow in midsummer as soon as seeds are ripe for germination the following spring. Bunchberry (*Cornus canadensis*), coralberry (*Symphoricarpos* spp.), cotoneasters (*Cotoneaster* spp.), and other seeds with complex dormancy requirements are easy to handle in containers too, because they can be left outdoors for several seasons.

USDA Hardiness Zone Map

The United States Department of Agriculture (USDA) created this map to give gardeners a helpful tool for selecting and cultivating plants. The map divides North America into 11 zones based on each area's average minimum winter temperature. Zone 1 is the coldest and Zone 11 the warmest. Recently, the zones were further divided into "a" and "b", with "a" being the colder portion. To locate your zone, refer to the map here, or use the Zone Finder on the National Gardening Association's website (http://garden.org/zipzone/index.php), which identifies zones by zip code.

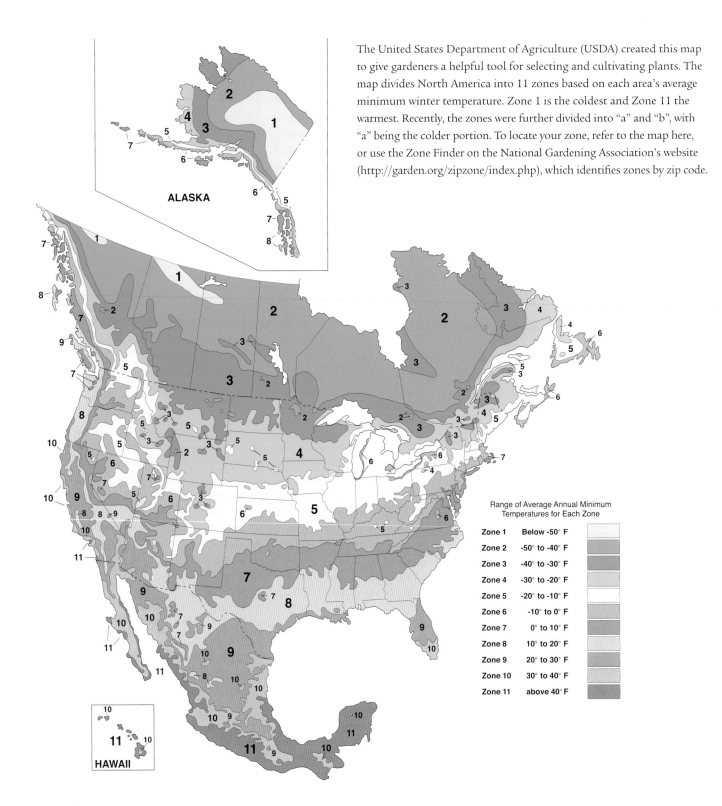

Range of Average Annual Minimum Temperatures for Each Zone

Zone 1	Below -50° F
Zone 2	-50° to -40° F
Zone 3	-40° to -30° F
Zone 4	-30° to -20° F
Zone 5	-20° to -10° F
Zone 6	-10° to 0° F
Zone 7	0° to 10° F
Zone 8	10° to 20° F
Zone 9	20° to 30° F
Zone 10	30° to 40° F
Zone 11	above 40° F

ALASKA

HAWAII

CREDITS

Interior Photography

© **Rob Cardillo:** 2, 16, 25 bottom left, 33, 38, 42, 49, 70 top, 127 right, 132, 156, 162, 275

© **Jerry Pavia:** 4-5, 7, background 8-9 etc., 12, 14, 30, 39, 41, 43, 44, 52 top, 53, 54, 55, 56, 62, 63 right, 66, 67, 68 all except 9, 70, 71 bottom, 72, 73, 75, 76 all, 78, 79, 81, 82, 83, 84, 85, 88 all except 2 and 6, 90, 92, 96 all except 3, 8, and 9, 99, 101, 103, 104 all except 1, 106 left, 107, 109, 110, 112 all except 1, 3 and 4, 114, 115 top, 116, 118, 122 all except 9, 124, 125, 126, 127 left, 128 all, 130, 131, 133, 134, 135, 136, 137, 138, 140, 143, 145 right, 146 all, 149, 150, 151, 154, 155, 157, 158 all except 10, 160, 163, 164 all, 166, 167, 169, 170, 171 left, 172 all except 2, 4, and 6, 174 right, 176, 178 all except 2, 6, and 7, 181, 182, 183

© **Saxon Holt/PhotoBotanic:** 6 left, 17, 18, 20, 27, 36, 50, 80, 86, 96 3 and 9, 100, 139, 148

© **Marion Brenner:** 6 right, 11, 88 2, 93, 94, 95

© **R. Todd Davis Photography:** 10, 48

© **Charles Mann:** 13, 21, 23, 24, 25 top left and right, bottom right, 57, 112 3, 117

© **Mark Turner/Turner Photographics:** 15, 26, 28, 29, 45 right, 60, 96 8, 98, 144, 180

© **Karen Bussolini:** 35, 37, 45 left, 58, 59, 61, 63 left, 64, 65, 87, 102, 104 1, 106 right, 108, 111, 121, 141, 158 10, 174 left

© **Barbara Ellis:** 46

© **Derek Fell:** 52 bottom, 91 right

© **Country, Farm and Garden Photo Library:** 68 9

© **Alan and Linda Detrick:** 88 6, 91 left

MACORE, Inc.: 112 1 and 4, 122 9, 145 left, 172 4 and 6, 178 2 and 7

© **New England Wild Flower Society/William Cullina:** 115 bottom. NEWFS is America's oldest plant conservation institution and promotes the conservation of North American native plants. Located at Garden in the Woods, Framingham, MA. (www.newfs.org or 508-877-7630)

© **Rosemary Kautzky:** 120, 152, 168

© **Paul Tukey:** 171 right

© **Painet, Inc./Patrick Lynch:** 172 2

© **iStockphoto:** 178 6

Garden Design

Washington Park Arboretum: 180

Martin Gritschle and Richard Brinckmann: 29

John and Betty McClendon: 28

Cynthia Rice: 59

Robin Zitter: 88 (center)

Chanticleer, A Pleasure Garden: 162, 175

Longwood Gardens: 2

Eve Thyrum: 16

Piedmont Designs: 25

Appleford Estate: 33

Andrew Bunting: 127

Farmingdale State University: 15, 132

Roger Warner: 11

Bob Clark: 93

Juanita Flagg: 65

Tim Callis: 108

Valley Brook Gardens: 87

Mary Ellen Keskimaki: 21

South Coast Botanic Garden: 13

Robert Howard: 23

Inta Krombolz, Fox Hollow Design: 42

Stephanie Cohen: 49

Eleanor McKinney and Scott Thurmon: 58

Howard Smith: 64

Nancy Goodwin: 79

Denver Botanic Gardens: 120

Frankie Holt: 14

Mary Reid: 17, 86

Suzanne Porter: 18

Jeff Rosendale: 20

Andrew Yeoman: 36

Sally Cooke: 67

RESOURCES

TOOL SUPPLIERS

A.M. Leonard
www.amleo.com
800-543-8955

Weed Wrench
www.weedwrench.com

Honeysuckle Popper
www.honeysucklepopper.com

PLANT SUPPLIERS

Stepables
www.stepables.com

Jeepers Creepers
www.jeeperscreepers.info

WEB SITES

Global Invasive Species Database
www.invasives.org

USDA Plants Database
www.plants.usda.gov

National Invasive Species Information Center
www.invasivespeciesinfo.gov

New England Wild Flower Society
www.newfs.org

Canadian Botanical Conservation Network
www.rbg.ca/cbcn/en/index

Index

Page numbers in **bold** indicate main discussions; those in *italic* indicate photographs or illustrations.

money plant. See *Lunaria annua*

moneywort. See *Lysimachia nummularia*

monitoring beds, 200

monocultures, 20, 43

morning sun or shade, afternoon sun or shade, 33, 34

moss campion. See *Silene acaulis*

moss gardens, 16, 25, *25*, 26, *26*, 156, *182*, **182**

moss phlox, moss pink. See *Phlox subulata*

moss sandwort. See *Arenaria verna*

mother-of-thyme. See *Thymus serpyllum*

mottled wild ginger. See *Asarum shuttleworthii*

mountain laurel. See *Kalmia latifolia*

mountain mint. See *Pycnanthemum muticum*

mountain rockcress. See *Arabis* × *sturii*

mountain spinach. See *Atriplex hortensis*

Muehlenbeckia spp. (wire vines), **116**

   axillaries (creeping wire vine), 111

   complexa (complex wire vine, maidenhair vine), 111, **116**

mugo pine. See *Pinus mugo*

mulch

   caring for plants, 199, *199*, 200

   hardscaping, 64

   plants, mulching with, 32, *45*, 45–46

mullein. See *Verbascum thapsus*

Muscari spp. (grape hyacinths), **102**

Myosotis scorpiodes (water forget-me-not), **176**

Myrica pensylvanica (bayberry), 111, **137**

myrtle. See *Vinca minor*

myrtle euphorbia. See *Euphorbia myrsinites*

N

Nandina domestica (nandina, heavenly bamboo), **137**

Narcissus spp. (daffodils, narcissus), 46, **102**

   bulbocodium subsp. *conspicuus* (hoop-petticoat daffodil), **102**

natal plum. See *Carissa macrocarpa*

native (wild) plants, 47–49, *48–49*

   ground covers and, 9

   shady sites, *164–71*, 165–71

   site knowing your, 30

   vigorous natives, 74

Nepeta spp. (catmints), 48, 78, 111, *111*, 133

   × *faassenii*, 36, *84*, **84**, 108, *108*, 111, *111*,121

netted chain fern. See *Woopdwardia areolata*

new spaces, creating, 22, 23, *23*

New York fern. See *Thelypteris noveboracensis*

Nierembergia repens (white cup flower), **100**

ninebark. See *Physocarpus opulifolius*

Norway spruce. See *Picea abies*

number of plants needed, determining, *194*, 194–95

nursery bed, 203, 205, 206

Nyssa sylvatica (tupelo), 28

O

oakleaf hydrangea. See *Hydrangea quercifolia*

oaks. See *Quercus* spp.

Ocimum basilicum (basil) 'Spicy Globe', 16

oconee bells. See *Shortia galacifolia*

Oenothera spp. (evening primroses, sundrops), **118–19**, 121

   fruticosa (common sundrops), **119**

      subsp. *glauca*, *118*, **119**

   macrocarpa, *O. missouriensis* (Missouri primrose, Ozark sundrops), *112–13*, 113, **119**

   speciosa (showy evening primrose), 62, *62*, 112, *113*, **119**

   'Rosea' (*O. berlandieri*, Mexican evening primrose), **119**

old-fashioned weigela. See *Weigela florida*

Olympic St. John's wort. See *Hypericum olympicum*

Omphalodes verna (blue-eyed Mary), 121, *154*, **154**

One Wild Landscape (Design Idea), 49, *49*

Onoclea sensibilis (sensitive fern), **170**

Ophiopogon spp. (mondo grass, lilyturf), 46, **84**, 110, 121

   Ophiopogon japonicus, 16, **84**

   Ophiopogon planiscapus, *45*, *45*, **84**

orange Asiatic lily. See *Lilium asiaticum*

orange coneflower. See *Rudbeckia fulgida*

orange daylily. See *Hemerocallis fulva*

ordering materials, hardscaping, 59

oregano. See *Origanum vulgare*

Oregon grape holly. See *Mahonia aquifolium*

Oregon oxalis. See *Oxalis oregana*

Oriental bittersweet. See *Celastrus orbiculatus*

Origanum vulgare (oregano), 36, **80**, 121

ornamental sweet potato. See *Ipomoea batatas*

Osmunda spp. (osmundas), **170**, 177

   cinnamomea (cinnamon fern), **170**

   claytoniana (interrupted fern), **170**

   regalis (royal fern), **170**

ostrich fern. See *Matteuccia struthiopteris*

Outdoor Carpets (Design Idea), 23, *23*

over time, planting, 197, 198

Oxalis spp. (shamrocks, sorrels, oxalis), **154**

   oregona (Oregon oxalis, redwood sorrel), **154**

   regnellii, **154**

      var. *triangularis*, **154**

Ozark sundrops. See *Oenothera macrocarpa*

P

Pachysandra

   procumbens (Allegheny pachysandra), 9, 38, *164*, **165**, 169

   terminalis (Japanese pachysandra), 20, **73**, 110, 119, 155, 168, 169

Paeonia spp. (peonies), 34, 46, **109**, 110

   suffruticosa, *104–5*, *105*, *109*

pale-leaved barberry. See *Berberis candidula*

pale St. John's wort. See *Hypericum ellipticum*

palm sedge. See *Carex muskingumensis*

panic grass. See *Panicum* sp.

Panicum sp. (panic grass), 86, *86*

   virgatum 'North Wind', 49, *49*

parsley, 16

Parthenocissus

   quinquefolia (Virginia creeper, woodbine), 48, 111, 121, *122*, 123, **126**, *126–27*, 168

   tricuspidata (Virginia creeper), 119

partridgeberry. See *Mitchella repens*

pasture rose. See *Rosa carolina*

paths & stepping-stones ground covers, *88–95*, 89–95

pathways, 21. See *also* hardscaping

patterned garden, sun lovers for a, *76–85*, 77–85

pavers for hardscaping, 59, *59*, 61, 63, *63–64*, 64, 65

Paxistima canbyi (cliff green, ratstripper), *178*, 179, *183*, **183**

Pennisetum alopecuroides (fountain grass), **86**

pennyroyal. See *Mentha pulegium*

peonies. See *Paeonia* spp.

perennial pea. See *Lathyrus latifolius*

perennials

   alkaline (chalky) soil, 120–21, *121*

   bold cover in sun, *104–9*, 105–9

   seaside sites, 110, *110*

   sunny slopes, *117–18*, 117–19

periwinkles. See *Vinca* spp.

permeable or grid pavers, 65

Perovskia atriplicifolia (Russian sage), 119

Persian violet. See *Exacum affine*

Persicaria

   affinis, (Himalayan fleeceflower), 92, *96*, 97,*100*, **100**, 121

   virginiana, 146, 147, 154

Peruvian verbena. See *Verbena peruviana*

Petasites japonicus (butterbur), **176**

Petrorhagia saxifraga, **92**

pH (acidity and alkalinity) of soil, 32

Phalaris arundinacea var. *picta* (variegated ribbon grass), *55*, **55**

Phegopteris hexagonoptera (broad beech fern), **170**

Phlox spp. (phlox), 163

   divaricata (wild blue phlox), 40, *163*, **163**

   × *procumbens* (hybrid or trailing phlox), **101**

   stolonifera (creeping phlox), 15, **101**, *158–59*, *159*, **163**

   subulata (moss phlox, moss pink), 43, *96*, 97, **100–101**, 110, 121

Phormium tenax 'Atropurpureum', *106*

Physocarpus opulifolius (ninebark), **137**

Picea spp. (spruces), **144**

   abies (Norway spruce), **144**

   pungens (Colorado spruce), **144**